—— ISLAMISM IN THE SHADOW OF AL-QAEDA ——

ISLAMISM IN THE SHADOW OF AL-QAEDA

François Burgat

TRANSLATED BY PATRICK HUTCHINSON

UNIVERSITY OF TEXAS PRESS
Austin

Requests for permission to reproduce material from
this work should be sent to:
Permissions
University of Texas Press
P.O. Box 7819
Austin, TX 78713-7819
www.utexas.edu/utpress/about/bpermission.html

∞ The paper used in this book meets the minimum requirements of
ANSI/NISO Z39.48-1992 (R1997) (Permanence of Paper).

Library of Congress Cataloging-in-Publication Data

Burgat, François.
[Islamisme à l'heure d'Al-Qaida. English]
Islamism in the shadow of al-Qaeda / François Burgat ; translated by
Patrick Hutchinson. — 1st ed.
p. cm.
Includes bibliographical references and index.
ISBN 978-0-292-71760-2
ISBN 0-292-71760-1
1. Arab nationalism. 2. Group identity—Islamic countries—History—
20th century. 3. Terrorism. I. Title.
DS63.6.B8713 2008
320.5'57—dc22
2008018323

Originally published as *L'Islamisme à l'heure d'Al-Qaida:
réislamisation, modernisation, radicalisations,* © Éditions La
Découverte, 2005

CONTENTS

TRANSLATOR'S NOTE AND ACKNOWLEDGMENTS vii

ACKNOWLEDGMENTS xiii

INTRODUCTION 1

1. THE IDENTITY MATRIX OF "MUSLIM-SPEAK" 7

2. FROM NATIONAL STRUGGLE TO THE DISILLUSIONMENTS
OF "RECOLONIZATION" 31
The Triple Temporality of Islamism

3. THE ISLAMIST FIELD BETWEEN NATIONAL SPECIFICITY
AND TRANSNATIONALIZATION 55

4. RED SEA SECRETS OR ISLAMISM WITHOUT
COLONIZATION 65

5. THE BROTHERS AND THE SALAFIS 77
*Between Modernization and Literalism,
with or without Radicalization*

6. ISLAMIC RADICALIZATION 89
Between Religious Sectarianism and Political Counterviolence

7. FROM SAYYID QUTB TO MOHAMMED ATTA 101
Sectarianism or Political Counterviolence?

8. FROM FEARS INHERITED TO FEARS EXPLOITED 121
The War of Representations

9. HARD POWER AND IMPOSED REFORM 139
The Illusions of the Western Response to Islamism

CONCLUSION 149
Against Terrorism—the Absolute Weapon?

APPENDIX 153
The Islamists as Seen by the West in 1992

NOTES 157

INDEX 179

TRANSLATOR'S NOTE AND ACKNOWLEDGMENTS

Patrick Hutchinson

*Toute "bonne" traduction doit abuser . . . (Any "good" translation
must abuse . . .)*

—JACQUES DERRIDA

There are major, necessary works of corrosive irony and human indignation which use the tools of analysis and insider intelligence to go to the
dark heart of their time, in this case the crisis of our own time: I believe
that *Islamism in the Shadow of al-Qaeda* is one of them. This translation
has involved more than simply translating the text from French to English as neutrally as possible (as in the case of a scientific textbook, for example). It has also been a quasi-literary task (the author is a writer) and
quasi-political act of militancy and participative commitment (in the
widest, nonpartisan sense of these terms). This has required not merely
producing a diluted version of the author's thought but manifesting
something of his stylistic temperament and moral tone, in order to carry
over from the source to the target the operative power of the original: its
intellectual efficacy.

Translating Burgat has thus necessarily entailed leapfrogging several
reassuring dichotomies: first and foremost, the gap (already much less
prevalent in the social sciences in France) between the "two cultures" (see
Immanuel Wallerstein, *European Universalism: The Rhetoric of Power*):
the literary and the scientific. Authors of French political science more
often tend also to be real writers in the strong literary or philosophical
sense of the term. Translating them requires a considerable, sometimes
acrobatic, stylistic makeover, with the ever-present danger of "falling
between the two stools" (the politically, or at least ethically, committed and the scientific). The book at hand is indeed an act of exceptional
scientific and political courage. It not only convincingly establishes and
scientifically supports a number of little-known and still less widely ac-

cepted facts and analyses but succeeds in holding up to our contemporaries an unwelcome political and ethical mirror, revealing what many of us would prefer not to know. It is thus characterized by an unusual combination of analytical lucidity and a capacity for contained ethical indignation whose stylistic equivalent must emerge somewhere between the impersonally objective and the playfully complicit. The author uses a very savvy combination of rigorously formal scientific protocol and direct, at times almost familiar irony: as a committed writer, he likes to play in the political forecourt and employs a lot of lift and spin.

All this naturally leads me to a very brief sally into discussion of the theoretical options of translation itself. I believe that translation is a secondary form of authorship—any writer is a "translator," any translator is a "writer"—but only in the sense and to the degree that a highly creative author in the source language requires an almost equal degree of creativity and authorship on the part of the translator in order to bring the work into the target language with any chance of success (or degree of truth).

This also explains the particular difficulty of translating the social sciences, as so often observed. In addition to being generally proficient and articulate in both the source and the target languages, the translator must be something of a sociologist, anthropologist, and political scientist himself. He must be deeply conversant with the concepts, style of reasoning, and general intellectual approach of the author and be capable not only of "transporting" them across the linguistic divide but also of "re-creating" them in accordance with the materials and corresponding academic and intellectual context in the source language. This context will never be entirely homothetic temporally or culturally and (perhaps more particularly in the case of books on politics and sociology) will necessarily have shifted with the change of place and time. Thus the criterion of success cannot be only some impossible word-for-word "faithfulness" to the original, while merely avoiding the most obvious traps of literalism. In order to bring over the work's "truth," the translator must sometimes also be a creator, thinking and feeling with the author. It may be necessary to accentuate certain stylistic traits that remained latent in the original source language but may need to be manifested otherwise in the target language, at times even coining new and perhaps somewhat startling terms, verbal combinations, and concepts.

The twin concepts of accentuation and manifestation, well known to literary scholars and originally developed to address the theoretical problems of literary translation in authors such as Friedrich Hölderlin (see Antoine Berman, *Hölderlin: la traduction comme accentuation et manifestation*, special issue of *Détours d'écriture*), must also apply to the translation of major works in the social sciences. This does not mean spurious orthopedic rectification or abusive substitution to "naturalize" the original, in the well-known French tradition of *les belles infidèles* (fair deceivers: misleading stylistic equivalents), considering the original susceptible to improvement because it is not in French (or in this case English) and hence deemed to be lacking in "universality." But a translation really only kick-starts with the first "fecund transgression" of the strict letter of the original by the translator, who thus becomes more than any translating machine could ever be: an "author" who is welcoming another writer into a different language. The translator will necessarily alter to some degree or accentuate somewhat differently the expressive potential of the original, in the best of cases more powerfully manifesting some aspects or stylistic traits that remained more subdued or implicit in the source.

In other words, an act of translation is always a squaring of the circle, a series of asymmetrical compromises and arbitrations; the expression in the two languages is never chronologically or contextually simultaneous, making pure or perfect bilingualism impossible. The translator is also constantly confronted with an exorbitant choice between being faithful to form or being faithful to meaning, accentuating one aspect or another. Although the translator must always attempt to sacrifice as little as possible of either, some degree of loss in one or the other is inevitable. A translation is thus always a re-creation, more or less expressive according to the translator's success in realizing the expressive potential of the original in the idiomatic and contextual virtualities of another language.

In translating Burgat, I have thus tried to be sensitive to the English language's capacity to welcome his unique combination of passionate eloquence and shrewd analytical clarity. Perhaps I have even tended (two years later and after the growing revelations of a deepening crisis) to accentuate the original's ring of moral indignation. Of course, a small part of this accentuated indignation may also be my own. I hope that this translation does in this way at least to some degree manifest an extra dimension to the book.

It is not only a doughty academic work of historical research and political and sociological analysis but a critical masterpiece, one of the great works of political and ethical surgery. While translating, I have thus grown increasingly aware of its capacity to confront and denounce the monstrous outgrowths of our world-system, its unflinching propensity to take a scalpel to the heart of darkness of contemporary Western policy-making, particularly in the case of the so-called Greater Middle East. We may or may not venture to disagree with some aspect of its macroscopic historical framework. The "three temporalities" of Islamism, however convincingly argued, may seem too universally applied a set of categories or perhaps somewhat overdetermined by the author's North African and Yemeni experiences, not sufficiently taking into account the global crisis of liberalism and the disruption of Western-powered modernity at the end of the Cold War. But we cannot contest its impassioned lucidity, its political and moral courage, its unique capacity to mobilize strong realism without lapsing at any point into cynicism. It is bitter but indispensable medicine that ought to be read again and again not only by the decision-makers but by you and me, if only to realize to what degree "man's inhumanity to man" is at the basis of so many of the contemporary world's worst bifurcations.

From time to time such works see the light of day: recognizable by their enduring youthfulness, high mental energy, and indefatigable will to engage with the complexities of human reality, however hostile or perverse, through the rigors of real knowledge, analysis, and painstaking erudition. They reflect an impassioned belief that this reality can somehow still be confronted (or should be ethically and politically transformed) through the sole weapons of reason. Such works (whether in the realm of symbolic, artistic production or political thought and the social sciences) pay us the compliment of treating us as adults and pulling no punches; they are almost immediately recognizable by their directness of diction and by the implacable, committed style of their arguments. Neither a monument of narcissistic erudition nor an alluringly commodified invitation to the virtual worlds of paranoia, Burgat's book has nothing to peddle, no conspiracy theory. It lays bare the direst distortions of modern history itself, the discomforts of (an often ugly) reality of which we all partake and from which it proposes no easy escape.

This patiently constructed refusal to give way to the generalized "flight from reality" is of course by no means a symptom that its author has espoused some particularly virulent strain of nihilism but, on the contrary, the sign that he has not relinquished all hope in the human. His book, for all its specialized knowledge, transgresses the limits of its allotted academic constituency to speak directly to people (citizens) and proves that there is no absolutely watertight frontier between scientific analysis and ethical or political commitment, only the firewall of argumentative rigor. My chief hope here is that something of this hidden but very definitely present ethical dimension—its somber, at times Dantean or at least Swiftian undertone—comes out from time to time in my own commitment to the urgent task of welcoming this important book into English.

ACKNOWLEDGMENTS

My special gratitude and lasting recognition are first and foremost due to Alix Philippon, without whose constant inspirational energy, advice, ready hand, and vivifying companionship—albeit thousands of miles distant—the completion of this translation would almost certainly never have been feasible under the prevailing circumstances. My heartfelt thanks are also due to Ciaràn Carey for his prompt, selfless generosity as reader and corrector and for having at times set his own shoulder to the wheel. It would be unjust not to thank Pascal Ménoret for his timely aid in referential research, Jim Burr for his patient, friendly stewardship of the editorial process, and Kathy Lewis and Victoria Davis for their extraordinary blend of minute professionalism and literary sensitivity in copyediting.

ACKNOWLEDGMENTS

François Burgat

Islamism in the Shadow of al-Qaeda saw the light of day in Aix-en-Provence. It therefore owes a lot to the scholarship, experience, and critical acuity of my fellow researchers at the Centre National de la Recherche Scientifique (CNRS) but also to the students of the "Arab World" option in the master of comparative political science at the Institute of Political Science at Aix-en-Provence. It is just as indebted to the patience or the impatience of my close allies. From Alix to Sylvie, including Samy and all the others, from Camille, who is currently discovering the "bearded men of her father's memory," to Marie, who has spent a long furlough construing them, they all know my debt to them. I would also like to thank James, Yahya, and my colleagues from the Oxford Centre for Islamic Studies for making the impossible come true: the warming of a rainy Oxford spring.

Finally, and perhaps "over and above all," it was on the high plateaus of Yemen, at the French Center for Archaeology and the Social Sciences in Sanaa and on the dusty roads of the Peninsula, that this book came to maturity over six long years.

For the better, the inhabitants and the visitors to this region who have played so intimate a part in this work are numerous: Pascal Ménoret, who nurtured it with his fruitful Saudi extrapolations; Éric Vallet, who often helped push it out of ruts, and not only those related to style; Laurent Bonnefoy, for his ever resourceful pathfinding; Stéphane L., Marie and Ségolène, Laure, Houda Ayoub, and her enlivening students from the École Normale Supérieure (ENS); Ibtissam and her poetical impertinence; Mohamed Sbitli also, as well as so many Yemeni friends, from the *qadhi* Ismail al-Akwa to Mohamed Qahtan, including Nassir Yahya and a host of others.

Finally, François Gèze has long been much more than a publisher for me. And all and sundry who must know that . . . no, they are not forgotten. Again for the best, I owe a lot to those "who are deeply concerned by the double entendres of Tariq Ramadan" and have the privilege of repeating it to us morning, evening, and night here in France in prime time on state-funded TV channels and radio stations or on the front pages of all the magazines which echo them. Without them, I confess, I would probably have got far less of a kick out of writing this book, if only to be in a position to convey, at the foot of this page, my affectionate compassion to them.

Ensues-La-Redonne, September 2005

ISLAMISM IN THE SHADOW OF AL-QAEDA

INTRODUCTION

No, when all is said, I would far rather see the Muslim Brothers co-opted by the Egyptian military, with the latter retaining the lion's share of power, than contemplate their winning free elections, then setting up someone like Tariq Ramadan as Minister of Culture. . . . Therefore I support maintaining the most enlightened—or even not enlightened at all—dictatorships possible in Egypt and in Saudi Arabia rather than the implementation, in these regions of the world, of democratic principles which, for the time being, would only entail chaos and violence.

—ALEXANDRE ADLER, FRENCH ESSAYIST, *LE FIGARO*,
SEPTEMBER 6, 2004

We all remember the man who saw the man who saw the man . . . who saw the bear who ate the postman and who was not scared. A small portion of the glory of the last is inherited by the first. In this case, it is the toxic fragrance which hangs round anyone who knows a person whose friend sometimes says nice things about someone who one day inadvertently shook the hand of one of Tariq Ramadan's close friends. It has become like a byword for anyone who wants to denounce any political initiative, stance on some issue, network or periodical, trend, or even slogan . . . ramadanism, ramadanian, ramadanizing. It is useless to add anything. . . . And it is not only for those who have engaged in criticizing his work that the mere name of the intellectual from Geneva thus bears the semblance of an insult or a provocation. No. It is among the ranks of those who take ignorance for a virtue—or for the necessary consequence of militant contempt.

—LAURENT LÉVY, FRENCH ANTIRACIST ACTIVIST, *SOCIALISME INTERNATIONAL* (SPRING 2005)

Bin Laden has been precise in telling America the reasons he is waging war on us. None of the reasons have anything to do with our freedom, liberty, and democracy, but have everything to do with U.S. policies and actions in the Muslim world.

—MICHAEL SCHEUER (FORMER CIA AGENT), *IMPERIAL HUBRIS: WHY THE WEST IS LOSING THE WAR ON TERROR* (2004)

At the core of the tragic misunderstanding which is fueling the ongoing tensions between Europe, the United States, and the Muslim world resides a difficulty shared by the West as a whole: that of undertaking a rational and well thought out assessment first of the political and second of the intellectual and ethical roles of the various trends of "political Islam," "Islamism," or "radical Islamism," too frequently considered to be just so many stumbling-blocks on the road to consensual modernity and the peaceful coexistence of all the world's tribes.

Since the epoch-making antiterrorist summit at Sharm el-Sheikh in March 1996, the United States, Europe, and Israel, but also Arab authoritarian regimes and a fraction of Arab intellectual elites, have adopted a language and a strategy on the issue which are curiously similar. Less than ten years after the collapse of the Berlin Wall, the specter of "Islamic fundamentalism" has well and truly become the global Public Enemy No. 1.

"If they were not infiltrated by Abu Mus'ab al-Zarqawi's fundamentalists," the rhetoric of today's powerful somehow suggests, "would the Iraqis be refusing the democratic overture which George Bush has so generously come to bestow on them?" "If the militants of Hamas and other Jihadis hadn't corrupted the minds of their fellow citizens, would the Chechens and Palestinians persist in sulkily rejecting the offers of peace made by Vladimir Putin and Ariel Sharon?" If we finally managed to ban Tariq Ramadan from expressing himself in public, would that not put an end not only to those feminine veils which so disfigure the modernist alleys of the French Republic but also to the criminal "gang-bangs" and, why not, to all the insecurity currently reigning in the high-rise stairwells of the suburbs? In short, if Taqi al-Din ibn Taymiyya (in the fourteenth-century Middle East) or Sayyid Qutb (in Egypt in the 1950s) had not "invented" "radical Islamism," would the whole world not be wallowing in that democratic felicity—secular, modern, and consensual—which today seems so far out of reach?

The recent upsurge of the "al-Qaeda generation" has further fraught with passion our interpretations of the phenomenon. There is obviously to be no question here of minimizing the necessary arraignment of its terrorist undertakings. Our goal is to show how the reading which is usually made of its exterior manifestations is too unilateral, simplistic, and overemotional to be rational and hence *effective* in bringing it to an end. And that, by erecting so many walls where we should more than ever be building new bridges, we are accelerating and not winding down the radicalization which currently threatens to engulf us.

THE TRAP OF OUR CATEGORIES

Our knowledge and the rational management of our relationship with the "Islamists" are above all adversely affected by the extreme fragility of the categories we have set up to represent them. The way of thinking of analysts, strategists, and other "experts" is today confined, ever more self-evidently, to the bald assessment (optimistic for some, pessimistic or realistic for others) of the performances and future prospects respectively of the Islamist terrorists and those who, in Washington, Paris, Algiers, or Riyad, devote an equally all-consuming zeal to combating them.

The logic of criminal indictment has irresistibly trampled that of evaluation and analysis. The democracies and other defenders of "freedom" or "tolerance," as we have relentlessly been told since September 11, 2001, are confronted with the terrorist threat of Muslim "fundamentalism." Is this really what it is all about? The following pages are an open invitation to call into question the political and ideological foundations of a worldwide quasi-unanimity concerning the "global war against terror."[1] And to take the full measure of the disastrous consequences which its zealous adepts are busy compounding: the generalization and radicalization of the very revolt which they tell us it is their profession to "eradicate."

Is the violence with which the West is being confronted merely "ideological" and "religious"? Do we always take the time to discern the essential difference between religious sectarianism and political counterviolence, even if they are sometimes inextricably intertwined, without, however, ever completely merging into one? Condemnable though it may be, was the theology of war elaborated by Sayyid Qutb while in the tender care of Nasser's torturers truly the "root cause" of Islamist radicalization or merely the vocabulary of a revolt whose motives are strikingly more down-to-earth?

The Western powers today claim that they are "morally assaulted" by the "hatred of democracy and freedom" which they allege increasingly grips their aggressors as they "teeter on the edge of radical Islam." But this anti-Western revolt might be much better understood as highlighting a relatively predictable reaction to the unilateralism, selfishness, and iniquity of policies implemented, directly or indirectly through the intermediary of pet dictators, in a whole region of the world. In the vanguard of the "Imperial West"—a role in which it first caught up with then overtook colonial Europe and Russia—the United States is today harvesting the bitter fruits of utterly irresponsible policies which it has been implementing for several decades in the Third World in general and in the Muslim world in particular: in these countries, the thousands of victims of such policies, just as innocent as those of the World Trade Center, and the West's decades-long unswerving support for tyrannical dictatorships have fostered in their populations a sentiment of deep despair, favorable to the most extreme forms of revolt.

Beyond the question of an "Islamist" form of violence, it is easy to see that what is at stake is the difficulty of conceding the very banal resurgence of an Islamic political lexicon in societies of Muslim culture and the fact that a non-Western culture should dare aspire to erode the age-old Western monopoly on the expression of the universal. Caught in the crossfire between the "negative intellectuals" of late denounced in France by Pierre Bourdieu for their involvement in the dirty work of the Algerian junta[2] and today's "façade intellectuals" of the South, who dissemble from the Western public—whom they wish to woo or manipulate—the real condition of societies whose sole ambassadors they nevertheless purport to be, does the social science-based mediation of the world of the Other still have any chance to play its role?

Since the beginning of the 2000s, the international community— under the *de facto* hegemony of the U.S. superpower—has aspired to promote within the Arab world a set of "cultural" and "educative" reforms, concerning which it may legitimately be wondered whether they do not serve more to criminalize the forms of resistance to that world's own malfunctions than to find any realistic and equitable solution to them. In the face of the growing imbalances of the world order, is giving in to the temptation to criminalize all forms of critical introspection really the best option to prevent future confrontation?

BREAKING THE DEADLOCK OF THE
"GLOBAL WAR ON TERROR"

The purpose of this book is to find ways to break out of this deadlock. Almost twenty years after proposing the first blueprint for an intellectual and political "instruction manual" for the "Islamist" bogeyman in my *The Islamic Movement in North Africa,* at the end of a long spell of fieldwork in the Maghreb and ten years after widening the underpinnings for my initial analysis and sharpening the focus of its terms in *Face to Face with Political Islam*[3] after a five-year stay in the Mashreq, I am here reverting to this strife-torn issue, which has been eating away at the very tissue of the relationship between the West and a Muslim world which has now become part and parcel of itself. Empowered by a six-year stay in Yemen, my approach henceforth integrates some of the lessons imparted by the Arabian Peninsula, where the imprint of colonialism has been less direct than elsewhere in the Arab world but which nonetheless represents—as the events of September 11 have shown—an essential field of study for an overview of Islamism as an object of research.

The successive re-editions of *Face to Face with Political Islamism* (the latest in 2003) have enabled me to undertake a constant updating of the intellectual or political dynamics sanctioned or accelerated by the September 11 attacks. This third reversion to the object of Islamism intends not only to integrate new factual data but to correlate a double historical perspective: on the one hand, of course, the original statement of my hypotheses elaborated in the mid-1980s; on the other, my ensuing observations on "Islamist" behavior patterns.

These hypotheses set forth in my previous books—to which I refer for their explicit initial formulation—have remained at the core of my present reasoning. In order to confront them both with my later fieldwork and with the test of time, I will attempt to use them as underpinning without, however, repeating anything more than their substance. Even though they have now been brilliantly clarified and substantiated by younger colleagues—to whom this book owes a lot—it may be said that they are still far enough removed from having become commonplace for it to be worthwhile to recall their framework.

In space and time, we will see that it is only the multiplication of such points of observation which will enable us to circumvent the discourse of received wisdom and impassioned conviction which is currently the basis of the Western strategies—purblind and hence dangerously counterproductive—of our terror-fraught "global war against terror."

In this book, I wish first and foremost to recall the necessary distinction between an essential phenomenon of identity, a resurgence of the popularity of something we will here call "Muslim-speak," and the manifold ways in which its supporters have put this "rehabilitated" lexicon to use in political and social life (Chapter 1). In order to reconfigure Islamist mobilization within contexts which, in the space of one century, have vastly evolved, I next propose to distinguish the three main sequences during which (before and after the waves of independence) it became widespread (Chapter 2). We will then explore the tensions between national specificities and the phenomenon of transnationalization; this examination will procure us a better understanding both of the great diversity of the Islamist field and of the forces which have come to shape its dynamics (Chapters 3 to 5). Chapter 6 offers a more precise deconstruction of the mechanics of the radicalization which is at the origin of the emergence of al-Qaeda within this field, whose "sectarian" and "political" dimensions urgently need to be distinguished. Chapter 7 scrutinizes the trajectories of four individuals who are among the most emblematic of this radical configuration, from the ideologue Sayyid Qutb to Mohammed Atta, the pilot who carried out the September 11 attack.

In order to reach an understanding of why emotion often tends to deprive the analysis of its much-vaunted rationality, Chapter 8 recalls that the obstacles which the interpretation of the Islamist phenomenon must overcome are not only linked to fears and misunderstandings inherited from the Western colonial past: they are also deliberately "exploited" today by all those who have a vested interest in discrediting the forms of resistance encapsulated in the Islamist lexicon. Finally, Chapter 9 reviews the contradictions of the unilateralism of the Western "response" following September 11, as well as the counterproductive effects of the security culture which is currently developing to the detriment of what should be a truly effective political response to the threats which "radical Islamism"—along with many other actors on the international scene—holds in store for world peace.

ONE

THE IDENTITY MATRIX OF "MUSLIM-SPEAK"

In economics, someone already having funds at his disposal does not borrow any before assessing whether what he already has is sufficient or not. In the same way, a state does not import before taking stock of its financial resources and of its raw materials. Should not spiritual and intellectual resources as well as the inheritance of the heart be treated like the goods and the money of everyday life? They surely should! But, in this so-called Islamic world, people do not take into account their own spiritual or intellectual inheritance before thinking of importing principles and models, systems and laws, from the other side of the world!

—SAYYID QUTB, *SOCIAL JUSTICE IN ISLAM* (1948)

An Islamist is someone who is not satisfied with society as it is, who wants society to be better. . . . In some cases, for instance, it is someone who wants to be able to say no to America.

—FAHD, TWENTY-TWO YEARS OLD, AN EMPLOYEE IN RIYAD
(2005, QUOTED BY PASCAL MÉNORET)

For want of a terminological convention, words obviously do not have the same meaning, depending on who is using them. At the end of a dangerous emotional slalom, the term "Islamism," which in the nineteenth century had the function of referring to "Islam," has in the course of time taken on a quasi-criminal connotation: for the less vigilant—or the more enterprising—mediators of this segment of the human puzzle, one can today be "suspected of Islamism" or be a "presumed Islamist."

The short-term hegemony of wartime terminology obviously is not of much avail in the task of finding a serene definition for the contours of a complex phenomenon. Let us take up the challenge all the same: neither the demonization of its adepts nor their proclivity for divine reference should prevent us from grasping, thanks to the highly universal instruments of the social sciences, the driving force behind this perfectly human mobilization. Despite all the haziness of the terminology, we shall here assert our right to provide—and the feasibility of providing—an objective picture of what "Islamism" is, to rationalize what we know about it, and to justify, politically and ethically, the answers solicited, if the need arises, by these new required partners of our relationship to the world.

Their agenda is not so obscure or incoherent as all that. They no doubt intend to assert their "right to speak Muslim," and that may well be the cause of part of their difficulty in getting themselves heard. But essentially, behind the veil of religious rhetoric, it is for the recognition of some very universal rights—economic or political, local or global—that they more often than not are staking their claim. Therein perhaps lies the source of the real difficulty experienced by the West in hearing what they have to say. Preceded by an "Islamic" formula, a protest against some military occupation here, against the absolutism of a ruler elsewhere, against the methods of the American superpower everywhere, is so easy to dismiss! In order to avoid having to recognize the legitimacy of any calling into question of their respective hegemony and having to share their power accordingly, the well-heeled of world politics are thus often content to discredit the resistances with which they are confronted merely by using the slur of "exoticism" against the lexicon employed by those who are voicing them.

ISLAMISM OR THE RIGHT TO "(RE-)SPEAK MUSLIM"

Even if it is clear that its roots are to be found deep in the fourteen centuries of Muslim history and the realities or the myths of a long interaction with the West, the explanation of the phenomenon of contemporary Islamism can be circumscribed within the timeline of the last hundred years or so.

It is essential, to reach a better understanding, to distinguish two processes and hence two levels of analysis: on the one hand, the essentially identity-centered reasons for which a generation of political actors originally chose to "speak Muslim," that is, to have recourse in a privileged and at times ostentatious fashion to a lexicon or a vocabulary derived from Muslim culture; on the other hand, the diversified uses that such actors may make of this lexicon, at home or in the North/South arena, contingent on variables which are simultaneously multiple, banal, and profane, which determine their different political claims and mobilizations.

Let us first of all focus on the "identity-centeredness" which characterizes the development of Islamism. The latter is first and foremost the expression of a "return to grace," a reaffirmation of the universal ambition of the Islamic cultural set of referents. Within the successive contexts first of colonial domination, then of the stirrings of the independence movement, and finally of American imperial outreach, this can be ascribed to the will of three or four generations of political actors to rehabilitate "Muslim-speak" and to restore the legitimacy of this lexicon or, more widely, the referents of their cultural legacy (as described in more detail in the next chapter). It seems possible, however, to derive their motives from a common interpretative matrix. Conversely, as to the question of gauging what impact the use of this Islamic set of referents may have had on their behavior patterns, in society or in politics, within their national community or on the international scene, as we shall see, it is far harder to provide an unambiguous answer.

On the origins of the restored political fortune of this Islamic referential, we have long been proposing hypotheses which nothing in the current situation can prompt us to abandon. The return to grace of the lexicon of "inherited" Muslim culture has appeared to us to be a corollary, in the cultural and symbolic field, of the long-term dynamics of an "arm's length relationship" with the colonizing enterprises of the West. Within the context and the sequels of colonial expansion during the nineteenth and twentieth centuries, in order to counter the discourse and the categories of a colonial culture imported and mainly imposed, a generation irresistibly felt the need to restore the visibility and centrality of its inherited Muslim cultural codes.

By gradually confining the areas of expression of "Islamic" (but above all local and endogenous) religious culture to the private sphere of personal status, the introduction of "secularism" has sanctioned a sort of disconnection between endogenous culture and public matters. From Muslim shores, secularism, thus perceived, has plausibly been experienced as the tool of a form of symbolic dispossession. The assertion of imported cultural categories has indeed inevitably worked to the detriment of expressions (institutional and normative, but also aesthetic and scientific) of local (Muslim) culture. In contrast to the Western vision of secularization as facilitating the coexistence of potentially conflictual religious affiliations, it has often been perceived as the Trojan horse of

9

the culture of the occupier. The "defeated" culture gradually found itself marginalized, and in any case forbidden from participating in the production of meaning or in the expression of any values perceived as universal; it imperceptibly became "indigenized" or "consigned to folklore," its jinxed symbolic attributes only serving to highlight the intrusive and humiliating centrality of Western culture.

The diverse expressions of the dismay experienced under the body blows dealt by this "exogenous" modernization have been widely described by the actors themselves. The social costs of the sudden emergence of foreign models of consumption and production are clearly apparent in the biographies of actors of the colonial confrontation, with militant itineraries as different as those of the Egyptian Sayyid Qutb (1906–1966), executed by Gamal ʿAbd al-Nasser, and of the Algerian Malek Bennabi (1905–1973), who steered clear of any confrontational logic. In his biography of Qutb, the British historian William Shepard shows that this modernization, which produced both "winners and losers," has fueled a process of social differentiation but also—once the "effendis" of the modern sector had adopted a more "Westernized" lifestyle and taken to wearing more "Westernized" clothes—a cultural fault-line very close to the fracture which "served as the basis for the 1979 Iranian cultural revolution."[1]

The Islamist leaders-to-be, more often than not, are by no means the "orphans" of economic modernization. It is more the symbolic and cultural impact than the material cost of colonization which most deeply scarified their political memory. Like Qutb, Malek Bennabi, most emblematic of the intellectuals of the Algerian movement, was shielded from economic poverty thanks to his upbringing—even though the latter did not allow him to find an escape route from the ghetto of the jobs reserved for the "Muslim French." Besides, he attaches great importance to the assets to be drawn from the study of Cartesian thought in the colonizer's schools. Yet his *Mémoires d'un témoin du siècle* (Memoirs of a Witness of the Century) enables us to take stock of the symbolic violence of the French colonial model in Algeria and, consequently, of the importance of identity as a component in the reaction of "Islamist" rejection which it has provoked.[2]

Bennabi was born in 1905, in the pivotal years between the infinite inhumanity of the war of conquest and the coming to age of the first mobilizations for independence. He was thus in a position to draw directly on the memory of his close relatives for accounts of the trauma of the initial debacle. During the storming of Constantine in 1852, one of his female ancestors died, "sacrificed on the altar of a destroyed homeland in order to save the honor of a Muslim family": along the breathtaking cliffs of the Rhummel gorges, the ropes with which families attempted to help their daughters flee often snapped. In his personal memory, colonialism emerges, during the first half of the twentieth century, as strictly within the register of a double dispossession: material dispossession, of course, as pauperization was to become brutal and widespread; then cultural and moral dispossession, in a society condemned to "going native," its own symbolic system being gradually reduced to the mere status of a foil for the modernity of the occupier.

The economic and cultural structures of the conquered society buckled one after the other under the weight of such imported models: "We held onto the appearance but were losing the substance." As "the moral order and the social order" were transforming, "the appearance itself started to change." "Society . . . went vulgar from the top down and was impoverished from the bottom up." Even masculine ways of dressing suffered from "this degrading evolution" by irresistibly giving way "to European clothing from fripperies in Marseilles." "The city" itself also "split into two worlds: indigenous life was confined to taking refuge in the back streets and dead ends of Sidi Rached." The world of the arts was not spared the symbolic violence of imported innovations. On the evening of July 14, his grandmother, "hearing the brass, the percussion, and the bass drum of the music whose brazen echo was splitting the enchanted Tebessian summer night through the length and the breadth of the city," kept repeating something like: "How barbaric it is!" Enlisting in the army of the conqueror became the ultimate refuge for all those, be they dispossessed peasants or ruined craftsmen, that the system had rejected to its margins. "Beggary was everywhere on the rise."

To today's Western reader, this evocation of a "downgrading evolution" might recall the conservative discourse of reactionary European elites in the nineteenth and beginning of the twentieth centuries (and of some of their present epigones),[3] calling down fire and brimstone upon the social and cultural upheavals introduced by the modern era. Apart from one difference, which is obviously essential: European reactionary discourse was that of the organic intellectuals of an aristocratic order confronted with drastic internal reappraisals, bourgeois or plebeian, introduced by the champions of a modernity claimed to be mainly concerned with putting an end to the inequalities of the previous order, whereas the discourse of Bennabi (and of his Muslim peers) was that of an intellectual confronted with an exogenous and highly brutal irruption into his own society of a colonizer draped in the virtues of such modernity in order to impose, by fire and by the sword, the worst of unequal orders.

These are the main coordinates of the identity problematic of the dynamics of "re-Islamization." If its genesis is deciphered within this configuration—as confirmed by countless memoirs of actors from one end to the other of the "empire"—the restoration of the categories of the intuitive culture of the Muslim "father," and thus the continuity of a symbolic filiation interrupted by the colonial interlude, figures only as a relative rupture. It reasserts the aspirations of the endogenous culture, following the example of the other cultures of the world and, above all, that of the colonizer itself, to make its own contribution to the expression of universality.

THE AMBIGUITIES AND TURBULENCES
OF RE-ISLAMIZATION

Still, this return has often entailed a new series of deadly traumas. Indeed, closing a "symbolic" interlude is one thing, but reviving an Islamic production of norms interrupted—that is, cut off from the dialectic which every normative system must maintain with real society to stay alive—during the whole period of forced "Westernization" is quite another, as we shall see.

Can this problematic suffice to explain everything? Of course not. It just enables us to understand the reasons for the rising popularity of the Muslim political vocabulary. That is not much, but it is already in fact a lot. It helps greatly to clarify some prevalent methodological misunderstandings. Showing the mainly semantic nature of what all these (Islamist) actors have in common emphasizes just how fragile analyses which take the liberty of capitalizing on the explanatory use of this same lexicon may be.

Highlighting the identity matrix of Islamism does not provide access, indeed, to knowledge in "political" terms of the population which it enables us to identify. We cannot infer from the discourses of the actors the complex and changing modalities according to which they are going to behave in their environment, whether social or political, local or international, facing the ethical, social, or political challenges of their century.

The specificity of their "Muslim-speak" should not mask the methodological necessity of constructing a second object, both different and more complex, this time accounting for the diversity in behavior patterns and in the uses of this common lexicon: the construction of a "social and political" Islamist object must thus necessarily complete that of our "Muslim-speak" object constructed on the identity problematic. Why, within the ranks of those who intend to adopt and promote Muslim-speak, is a process of radicalization destined to manufacture activists of the al-Qaeda breed? Unless we succumb to the shortcuts of essentialism (which is to culture what racism is to ethnicity) when confronting such a question, at this stage of our analysis we can only hazard a cautiously roundabout answer: the radicalization of one segment of users of the Muslim lexicon can by no means be considered the "consequence" of their recourse to such a lexicon.

The methodological requirement of not making the semantic "Islam-ity" alone of al-Qaeda militants, of members of the rest of the Islamist movement, or . . . of the inhabitants of the entire Muslim world the determining or even the main explanation of their political options is, however, far from being commonly acknowledged. This necessary dissociation of religious (or merely cultural) affiliation from the political agenda is in fact commonly considered with reluctance, whether from without, from a lay or even academic vantage point,[4] or from within, by at least a fraction of the players concerned.

In the Western view, the Islamity of the lexicon of the Chechen, Lebanese, Palestinian, or Iraqi activists too often still forecloses the explanation of their resistance or their opposition. The less the observer is embedded in the sociological and political complexity of the "Islamist" terrain, the greater is his propensity to extrapolate from what he knows, or thinks he knows—that is, dogma, terminology (*jihad, fitna, takfir, salafi*, etc.), and the essentialized trends of the long wave history of the actors, thus opting for the comfort of a globalizing culturalist explanation.

To renounce this approach, and such a lethal correlation between the use of a Muslim discourse and political radicalization, is all the more difficult for the cohort of experts in "Islamic" terrorism in that it would deprive them of the backbone of their "explanation." If these terrorists are not attacking the West because they are obeying the commandments of a sectarian ideology or in order to assault "our values," we indeed have to seek another one. The latter, rather than a satellite overview of texts and discourses, would require a far more demanding examination of the sociological and political contexts within which these texts—which often have the bad taste of being written in a language which many of our "experts" are almost totally ignorant of—have been appropriated or such discourses enunciated. It must be sought in a sociological terrain where, far from dovetailing with the monolithic certitudes of our "experts," there reigns a puzzling diversity, an unexpected plasticity of reference, many an exception to the rule, and just as many disconcerting outcomes.

Now let it be said that among Islamist actors, in turn, the thesis of the identity-fueled dynamic of re-Islamization is not necessarily better accepted—far from it. Within the literalist segment of this movement, there is a definite tendency to minimize or to reject it totally, in favor of just as essentialist a reading as produced by the most badly documented Western analysts. In their opinion, by reducing the "Islamic norm" to a simple "lexicon" or to a "symbolic universe of affiliation," by dissolving its principles into the multiplicity of their possible interpretations, such a problematic may indeed tend to throw its intangible character, its specificity, and thus its intrinsic value as a norm into perspective.

PAKISTAN: THE LESSONS OF THE "LAND OF THE PURE"

There is, however, no dearth of examples proving, on the contrary, that the reference which a group claims to represent, albeit religious and reputedly intangible, can by no means prevent the infinite diversity of social standing, political persuasion, or even ethnicity from rapidly asserting its rights.

In the Muslim world, one of these examples has been provided by the fate of a few million citizens of the Raj, the former British Empire of India. In 1947, concerned with preserving their Muslim affiliation when faced with the immense Hindu majority of their fellow countrymen, they decided to found a new nation. This nation, the "land of the pure" or "Paki-stan," was to be "Muslim."[5] Even if the idea of reserving it to Muslims alone became self-evident only with the outbreak of confessional massacres which very rapidly devastated the subcontinent, Pakistan was definitely built "by" and "for" the Islamic reference, which was to serve as its national bond. Historical proximity and unity of place thus make it the model *in vitro* experiment on the construction of political Islamity. We could not dream of a better case study than that of a country which in 1971 made Islamabad—the "city of Islam," built from scratch to that very end—its capital city. What happened to those millions of citizens determined to "speak Muslim" together after having banked on building their destiny on the foundation of a common religious reference?

If we were to grant credence to the nostrums of essentialism, a nation so strongly bound together by a single dogma should, undoubtedly, have marched collectively at the same pace and in the same direction. Naturally, this was by no means the case. Not surprisingly, in Pakistan, neither the founding centrality of the Islamic reference nor its quasi-monopoly in terms of symbolism has prevented a powerful surge of diversification from emerging. Neither the territorial unity of the country nor the Islamic homogeneity of the political scene has resisted the multiple siren-calls of time. In 1971 the territorial unity of the country came brutally to an end: the secession of the eastern province engendered Bangladesh. Even before this rupture, multiple dynamics, political or ethnic, religious or profane, local, international, or regional, had demonstrated the limits of the unifying potential of the shared religious reference.

The first resulted from the schisms that inevitably arise in the course of the exegesis of a referential corpus, albeit religious. The different segments of Pakistani society have, as might be expected, adopted or confirmed substantially different interpretations of the same dogma, along complex fault-lines (social, educational, political, etc.), in the process engendering or reinforcing the existence of just as many religious, intellectual, or political trends: the Sufism of the *pirs*, embedded in a powerful popular tradition, in tension with the punctilious legalism of the *ulamas*, but nevertheless subject to some modernizing vagaries, if not always liberal, in the field of political action; the secularizing reformism of a part of the "Westernized" elites; Deobandi Salafism, whose aim it is to restore a tradition nevertheless constantly reinterpreted. The divisions have also resurrected the old sectarian rifts between Shiites and Sunnis. Pakistan has finally seen the blossoming of a strong minority of Muslims who have read into the Islamic reference "rightly understood" the right to dispense with it in the name of their freedom of conscience.

Another dynamic of diversification, this time external to the religious reference, resulted from the competition with religious identity brought to bear by Pakistan's rich multiplicity of ethnic affiliations.[6] The famous remark by the nationalist Walid Khan excellently illustrates the strength that the ethnic reference can draw from its sense of precedence compared with its religious and, *a fortiori*, national rivals: "I have been a Pashtun for four thousand years, a Muslim for one thousand four hundred, and a Pakistani for forty."[7]

Finally, the united front of the religious reference has recently been put to the test by the regional and international environment. Pakistan's use of its Islamity, by the state or by its opposition, has had to take rapidly changing and often clashing external demands into account. The United States, which "recruited" Pakistan, scarcely born, into its strategy of containment of the USSR, long tolerated the various manifestations of Islamity on the part of its ally. It is well known how deeply, since 1979, in order to counter the Soviet invasion of Afghanistan, the Central Intelligence Agency (CIA) got involved, from inside Pakistani territory, in the mobilization of those who were called the "combatants of faith" by the Western media at the time. Ten years later, however, the withdrawal of the USSR from Afghanistan and its collapse in the regional and international arena abruptly rendered obsolete the need to have recourse to Jihadis as during the Cold War against a Russian enemy henceforth morphed into an ally.

The attacks on September 11, 2001, then precipitated, in a much more drastic manner, the reassessment of the status of the allies or the instruments (the Taliban or the armed groups sent to Kashmir) of Islamabad's "Islamic" diplomacy. Pakistani "Islamity" had to adapt to a comparable evolution in the mood of its closest neighbors: the regimes of the Arabian Peninsula, following the example of quite a few other Arab regimes, also contributed to the evolution of the status of the Islamic reference in Pakistan. After funding anti-Soviet Jihadi mobilizations, the Gulf States, from 1990 on, began to try to put them at arm's length and to implement a vigorous strategy of controlling any militant expressions of re-Islamization. Facing an aggressive upsurge of their own Islamist oppositions, even before the United States took the initiative, they called on Islamabad to drastically reassess its policy, just as Washington was soon to do.

The recourse to the radical resources of religious mobilization, formerly a political resource, has become a source of tension and a zone of relative schizophrenia: while "Jihadism" continues to feature in the arsenal of Islamabad's foreign policy, its eradication is henceforth a paramount objective of global security cooperation. Since its double retreat from Afghanistan and from Kashmir in 2003, Pakistan is thus having to manage its "Islamity" by typically reconciling two contradictory demands: retaining the support of its American and Arab partners without necessarily depriving itself—for instance, against its external enemy, India, or against forms of internal irredentism—of occasional recourse to the precious potential of "Islamism," including its most radical forms.[8]

Without even mentioning countries like Indonesia or Malaysia, where the majority of the Muslim population of the planet is living today, how is it possible to address the complexity of Pakistan other than through the peremptory shortcuts favored by too many of our talk-show analysts, who speak vibrantly of "fundamentalist" Pakistan, "Wahhabi and oil-rich" Saudi Arabia, "Shiite" Iran, "tribal" Yemen, and, *mutatis mutandis,* all other countries that Western media-oriented opinion persists in amputating from their sociology, from their history, from their geography, and, consequently, from . . . their very humanity, under the sole pretext that the people there "speak Muslim"?

A TRANS-SOCIAL IDENTITY

As the example of Bennabi makes abundantly clear, the reactive process provoked by the symbolic and cultural ruptures of colonization was first and foremost of an identity-centered nature. Consequently, the quest for explanations or causalities which are purportedly peculiar to certain social groups, determining the propensity of their members to become "Islamists," has usually turned out to be delusive. In order to explain, within the international context of the North-South arena, the (identity-centered) mechanisms of the renewed legitimacy of "Muslim-speak" and of the dichotomy between "us" and "them" that can ensue, the sociology of groups offers precious little light. When, moreover, it drifts toward some form of sociological determinism (one becomes Islamist because one is "ill" or "young" or "undereducated"), it can become really misleading.

When a "community" mobilizes, in a peaceful mode or radically, against what it perceives to be external political or cultural domination, this mobilization is in fact meant to incorporate, whatever the timeline of adherence, any and all of its diverse components. This is the case for Islamist mobilization as an assertion of the legitimacy of "Muslim-speak" and of the rights of its adepts facing any foreign power as interlocutor, first colonial then "imperial." The inventory of social groups (intellectuals, bourgeois, proletarians, etc.) involved in Islamist mobilization actually proves to be constantly incomplete, partial, or unfinished, for new groups may at any time join the fray and yet none of them, despite the possible effects of leadership, can monopolize the support of all the others alone.

A historian who might intend to "explain" French resistance to the German occupation by reducing it to a strategy of a single social category of the population, thus obscuring its "national" basis (and, moreover, limiting the range of the motivations shared by all its actors), would provoke legitimate incredulity. Without in any way comparing Osama Bin Laden's targets to those of the French resistance fighters of the Second World War, still less George Bush, Ariel Sharon, or indeed certain Arab dictators to the leaders of the Third Reich, it is clear that a mobilization experienced by its actors as the expression of resistance to a process of domination has a certain propensity not to follow the limits of social groups. A social reading of this type of mobilization (which would highlight, for example, in the case of the French resistance, the fact that it was easier to join the underground when one was impecunious than when one stood the risk of having a substantial industrial portfolio confiscated, etc.) can only be cited as complementary, in order to highlight "additional" factors and circumstances, rather than as the main explanatory cause.

Indeed, various field surveys do tend to converge in proving that no such thing as a typical socioeconomic profile of the "partisan of Muslim-speak" exists—no more than in the case of the al-Qaeda activist or the Palestinian suicide bomber.[9] Everywhere, the sociology of the Islamist field lends weight to an identical depiction of reality: that of the social diversity of the actors and the fragility of any solely socioeconomic explanation for their commitment.

The stubbornness with which some observers attempt to disqualify the resurgence of the Islamic referential by reducing it to a sort of pathos, however, still may cause them to want to depict the "evil" as "contaminating" primarily, or even exclusively, certain social categories, in this case the poorest both economically and intellectually. Before admitting, rather belatedly, the decisive role of intellectual elites in the formulation of an agenda subsequently subsumed by all the components of society, numerous authors, as well as conventional wisdom, have tended to envisage Islamists only as emerging from among the ranks of the "young urban unemployed" and the "undereducated" or, more generally, the "have-nots of development."

The resounding victories won early in the 1990s by the Egyptian Islamists in elections in all the trade unions for professionals (the manual workers' unions remaining under the strict control of the state apparatus) amply demonstrated the limits of a thesis both popular and simplistic. The sudden prominence on the Islamist scene of Osama Bin Laden and Ayman al-Zawahiri, a Saudi billionaire on the one hand and an Egyptian surgeon, born into a prestigious family, on the other, should have sufficed to demonstrate the fragility of this approach. The same ex-

planations, according to which the social obfuscates the political, are re-
surfacing today, however, to "explain" the incentives of young Moroccan
or British-born suicide bombers.

Among the ranks of the Islamists, it is a recognized fact that members of the urban proletariat, without necessarily making up the main
contingent, go cheek by jowl with dignitaries of the bourgeoisie (oil-rich,
commercial, military, or tribal), all the nuances of the middle classes,
and/or all ranks of aristocracies far and wide. It has also become apparent that generations as well as professional branches are mingled, not to
mention various levels and fields of education. Last but not least, conventional wisdom itself is starting to acknowledge that the parameter of
"gender" is no longer functional. As widely prevalent as the cliché may
be which would dearly wish to countenance them as merely conceding
to the macho violence of their fathers, brothers, and husbands, Afghan,
Iranian, and Tunisian women indeed have not lagged behind in becoming "Islamists."

Such Islamists are therefore not only deprived people, "orphans of
growth." Neither are they sons of the "rich," intoxicated with profligacy
by oil revenues, or the "young" (products of uncontrollable demography),
or "pious bourgeois," or "intellectuals," or only "civilians," "military personnel," "males" (machos), or "women" (alienated). They are in fact all
these things at the same time, within the spectrum of a diversity comparable to that of the actors of other mobilizations born in reaction to some
form of domination.

The propensity of an identity mobilization to have a "trans-social" basis does not necessarily imply, in either the international or the national
arenas, that economic parameters (even when they occasionally serve
as markers for certain social groups) should systematically be excluded
from the analysis. Protest mobilizations, of course, but also identity
claims (the rejection of one identity in favor of another) are not *a priori*
alien to causalities of an economic type. If one does not start "speaking Muslim" again just because one has "an economic broken leg," the
will to distance oneself from an affiliation in order to lay claim to another may be a means to denounce a frustration that has an economic
dimension.

The will of a group to assert an identity different from that of the
dominant group pinpoints, among other things, a malfunction in the
mechanisms of allocation of political and economic resources within
the affiliation which they have "renounced." More particularly during
colonization *à la française,* the rejection of French identity may at least

partly be explained by the fact that the colonial power which purportedly desired to "share" its identity with the colonized displayed, when
all is said and done, no concomitant will to "share" either its political or
its economic resources. Even within the national entities of the South,
on the very ground of identity assertion, when "Muslim-speak" is mobilized against local elites discredited for their assumed concessions to a
"foreign" environment, the potential role of economic factors cannot be
denied. The sudden fall in the capacity to redistribute on the part of the
petro-states which occurred at the beginning of the 1980s (following the
downturn in oil prices) probably entailed, among people who were then
destabilized by the growing austerity, lending more credence to an "Islamic" membership perceived as an alternative to the affiliation—"secular" (*'ilmani*) and hence "foreign"—of the ruling elites who could no longer satisfy their economic aspirations.

But such nuances can by no means legitimize the social determinism which still often holds sway as an explanation for the whole Islamist
revival. The case of opulent Saudi Arabia—denigrated for its wealth and
regularly reviled at the same time for being the "world's number one ex-
porter of Islamism"—should suffice to demonstrate that all the oil (or
all the gold) in the world will not succeed, any more than all the loans
from the World Bank would, in (re)transforming into "secularists" or
"Marxists" the current partisans of restoring, within their own society
or within the North-South arena, the legitimacy of the symbolic categories of Muslim culture.

BEHIND THE (IDENTITY-CENTERED) TREE OF ISLAMITY, THE SOCIAL AND POLITICAL FOREST . . .

A detailed scrutiny of the various forms of use of the Muslim lexicon
shows that those who have chosen to employ it, including in an "ostentatious" and exclusive way, do so today to further countless "programs,"
using practically all the registers of political action. The keys to their behavior are, in any case, infinitely less simple to access than the binary
certitudes whose function it is to make of the "good Muslim" either, for
some, a patent terrorist or, for others, a perfect humanist. According to
a conviction that I expressed long ago, Islamism is less the product of
one specific political ideology (in this case radical and sectarian) than
of a process of reconnection between the referential of Muslim culture

and the whole landscape of production of political identities. Depending, notably, on their educational trajectories and the social and political contexts, local and regional, within which they have been evolving, depending on the nature and the practices of the people they talk to within the local or international political arenas—we will return to this in the following chapters—Islamists may turn out to be literalists or liberals, democratic or authoritarian, legalist or revolutionary. From the indiscriminate repudiation of Western democratic "technology" (according to the literalist interpretation which states that "divine sovereignty contradicts that of the people") to its over-hyped reappropriation ("the Muslim *shura* 'preceded' French democracy," etc.), a whole spectrum of attitudes and behaviors can be observed, both in oppositional postures and in the various practices of "Islamic" regimes in power.

Concerning the latter, their achievements are obviously less monolithic than conventional wisdom usually perceives them to be. By no means can it be proved that the universally slow and unequal rhythm of the quest for political liberalization and social modernization (that is, for the development of an autonomous political space, the limitation of recourse to the repressive violence of the state, the affirmation of the place of women in the public professional or political sphere) has been significantly more so in the "Iran of the mullahs" or "Hassan Turabi's Sudan" than in Abdelaziz Bouteflika's Algeria, the sempiternal Hosni Mubarak's Egypt, or the Tunisia of a president-general "defender of secularism." As "perfectible" as the sequence of Iranian parliamentary or presidential elections and as problematic as the principle of a double popular and religious legitimacy (*vilayat-i faqih*) may be, the chances of an Iranian voter affecting the balance of the political power ratio at the summit of the state are obviously infinitely more serious today than those of his Algerian, Tunisian, or Egyptian counterpart, condemned to reelect without surprise—without even deserving compassion from the Western political class—the great republican (or monarchic) allies of the West in North Africa.

In order to understand the mechanisms of this ideological diversification within Islamist mobilization, the tools of group sociology recover all their relevance. Hardly enlightening, as stated above, as a means to explain its identity-centered common denominator against the foil of the West, they regain their functionality when it comes to deciphering the social and, naturally, political arcana of "Islamist society" in all its human complexity—that is, when it comes to explaining the diversified uses that the supporters of "Muslim-speak" are prone to make of their lexicon, depending on the social, educative, economic, political, local, or regional configurations in which they evolve. Therefore, sociology's task here is to help explain the diversity in the "ideological" and "doctrinal" itineraries of individual Islamists, from those who confine themselves within the register of "contemplative" pietism and coexistence with the local holder of power, to those who opt for legalist parliamentary action, or, finally, to those who evolve toward revolutionary or even terrorist forms of radicalization.

BEHIND THE SCENES OF AN IDEOLOGICAL ITINERARY: A YEMENI SALAFI BETWEEN "RELIGIOUS" RADICALIZATION AND SOCIAL STRATEGY

Let us take a closer look, for example, at the case of Sheikh Muqbil ibn Hadi al-Wadi'i (1930–2000), who, before becoming the main ideologue of the most literalist of the trends of the Yemeni (and worldwide) Salafi mainstream, long espoused an "Islamist" trajectory.[10] Various motivations, which his discourse presents as being of a doctrinal nature, successively encouraged him to set a distance between himself and his initial Shiite Zaydi membership,[11] to rally to the (Salafi) trend of Saudi Sunnism while simultaneously declaring his opposition to the Saudi regime, to form an alliance for a while with the Muslim Brothers present in Yemen then to combat them, and to accept *de facto* collaboration with the Yemeni regime of President Ali Abdallah Saleh before being reconciled shortly before his death with the Saudi regime.

Behind the doctrinal façade of Muqbil's Salafism, it is interesting to show the importance of the role of more prosaic social and political variables, which contribute to our understanding of so sinuous an itinerary. Without denying Islamist actors autonomy, this complex cocktail of very profane motivations must be systematically taken into account in order to explain their clearly distinct trajectories, as we would do for any of their counterparts in other political contexts. Muqbil's itinerary is therefore not only that of a "Salafi Islamist." Muqbil is also a Yemeni national, a member of a "Zaydi" sect, and finally a man of relatively humble social origin ("a tribesman"). Without any great success, he attempted to ascend the rungs of the social and professional ladder, first of his national environment and then of the neighboring Saudi kingdom. It was only much later, on his return from Arabia, that he was finally to succeed in being inserted into the politico-religious market of his original land, by capitalizing on symbolic resources accumulated abroad.

Born in 1930, not far from the frontier with Saudi Arabia, in a North Yemen governed by the Zaydi Imam Yahya Hamid al-Din, Muqbil soon became aware of the relative weights of his national, sectarian, and social "primary identities." Yemen was at that time one of the poorest countries in the world. It was endowed with a politico-religious system (the Zaydi Imamate, which became a hereditary monarchy in 1926) with a strict hierarchy, where everyone was strictly confined within a certain socioeconomic and political status.[12] It is obviously on this rather material level that some of the explanations for his "ideological" itinerary and for distancing himself from his first affiliations are clearly to be sought. In the social structure of Zaydi society, Muqbil was indeed assigned to a subaltern place in two ways: he was neither a member of the religious aristocracy of the descendants of the Prophet (the *sada*, the only ones empowered to claim the supreme function of the Imamate) nor a member of the juridical aristocracy of the "judges," their main advisors, or even of the aristocracy "of the sword" composed—up to the present day—by the leaders of the great tribes, which have long formed the main armed forces of the Imamate.

As a teenager, Muqbil's first commitment was neither political nor ideological, but rather professional. Following the example of thousands of his fellow citizens, in order to emerge from economic austerity, he emigrated to find employment in Saudi Arabia. In Mecca, he earned a living by working in the building trade, while enrolling for religious training. In a society where the minority Shiites are badly perceived, his Zaydism placed him in an awkward position with regard to the norm of his adopted country. The price of a successful integration into the Saudi religious—but also social and economic—"universal" thus was that he renounce his original sectarian identity. That is exactly what he did.

After Muqbil's first return to Yemen around the mid-1970s, he certainly provided the proof that he had assimilated the Wahhabi creed dominant in Saudi Arabia: he was henceforth to eschew the "sacralization of intermediaries" between the Creator and mankind, be they saints (whose tombs are venerated) or the spiritual leaders of Sufi brotherhoods, a practice which the tradition denounces as "associationism," that is, the sin of raising human creatures to the same rank as God. In his village close to Saada, he denounced the presence of tombs in the mosques and the use of amulets or lucky charms. As he expressed his criticisms very publicly and attempted to win over followers, the Zaydi notables pressured his relatives to "brainwash him," according to his own words. In order to get him back on the right track, they forced him to follow the teachings of the Imam al-Hadi mosque, the cradle of their doctrine.

For three years, Muqbil resisted by agreeing only to study grammar. The isolation and ostracism from which he then started to suffer were not only ideological. They had an obvious social dimension and included the contempt of the *sada* (the descendants of the Prophet) toward him. Whenever he attempted—through his religious and then, potentially, political activism—to escape it, the members of the religious aristocracy reassigned him to his position in the social hierarchy in no roundabout manner: he was no more than a vulgar *qabili* (tribesman) and should not aspire to overstep his rank. They waxed ironical: "Even if rubbed for a long time a floorcloth will never turn white." Handed down by those who, to avoid being confused with farmers, were in the habit of protecting the pallor of their complexion beneath ample parasols, the religious and social call to order was particularly humiliating. "I was to remember it all my life," Muqbil wrote in his autobiography.

By the end of the 1970s Muqbil the Zaydi completed his trajectory toward Salafism. In Arabia, where he had returned to earn a living, the fact of originating from a "Shiite" country brought suspicion of illegitimacy down on him once again. When he aspired to change his status and, bristling with new diplomas, to reach the rank of professor of Muslim law, a committee of investigation again cast doubt upon his orthodoxy. He was particularly questioned on the way he called people to prayer and on the illicitness of praying with shoes on.[13] "I am a Sunni, I think as you do," he declared; and from then on he would always combat the suspicions hampering his career through an ostentatious display of anti-Zaydi zeal.

Briefly imprisoned on the charge of being linked to the Juhayman group, which was soon afterward (November 20, 1979) to occupy Mecca's grand mosque (an action whose repression, with the help of a commando of the French National Gendarmes Intervention Group [NGIG] special forces, was to claim hundreds of lives), Muqbil then took refuge for good back in his native Yemen. Since 1970 the Republic had triumphed over the Imamate. The "materialism" and "communism," though scarcely more than relative, of the regime brought to power in 1962 by the military intervention of Gamal 'Abd al-Nasser consolidated his religious options. On his return from Arabia, it was the Muslim Brothers who were to welcome and financially support him. The Brothers were then, as in the past, the direct allies of the regime. The head of state all the more naturally availed himself of their support in that the Republic, which had to assert itself against a Zaydi theocracy still strongly established in popular culture, had to make up for a deficit of religious legitimacy.

Muqbil the "Salafi" at first displayed an ambivalent attitude toward the trend of the Muslim Brothers. Some of his Saudi masters "warned" him, he explains, "never to entrust [them] with his destiny." But this was not to prevent him from cooperating, when in need, with those who were then strong allies of power. Therefore he accepted being placed in charge of one of their institutes. One year later, in 1982, in a different political context, however, he was to make a spectacular U-turn. In his "ground-breaking" book (*How to Issue Forth from the Dead Ends of Division*)[14] in which he clarifies the lineaments of his "Salafi" vision of Islam, he very abruptly breaks his ties with those he was henceforth to ridicule as the "failed" or "ruined Brothers" (Ikhwan al-Muflissin). His former allies were to become, like almost any other "disbeliever," his favorite scapegoats.

Muqbil's disagreement was obviously justified by arguments of a "religious" nature: all the "modernizations" of the standard reading of the Quran and the Sunna (acts and sayings of the Prophet) attributed to the Brothers were disqualified and likened to just so many innovations contrary to the orthodoxy of tradition (*bid'at*). The Muslim Brothers, upon running in the elections, were accused of fueling the divisions of the community into parties (*hizbiyya*) and thus, finally, its division pure and simple, that is, *fitna*. However, some very profane incentives, simultaneously nationalist, socio-professional, and based on power-brokerage, shed a fuller light on this doctrinal façade.

As it happens, the magisterial aura of the Egyptian *ulama*-schoolteachers—often simple "economic" migrants—was to be exercised in Yemen to the detriment of the local religious elites. The "imported" Brothers were therefore often targeted by forms of criticism not entirely bereft of corporate and nationalist jealousy:

> Those who have corrupted the Muslim Brothers in Yemen are the Egyptians who came to work in the "scientific institutes" and the Bureau of Orientation and Guidance. Most of them are opportunists. They pretend to join the Muslim Brothers with zeal in order to gain the confidence of the leaders of the institutes and keep their jobs. But most of these Egyptians are "chameleons." They are ready to be

Sunni among Sunnis, Shiite among the Shiites, and even Sufi among the mystics. . . . Most certainly, the Yemenis refuse to lag behind the Egyptians and the Sudanese, who still inculcate principles that young Egyptians have already repudiated.[15]

In a tape eloquently entitled *Turbaned Donkeys,* Muqbil extends his verbal virulence to the *ulamas* of the great Cairo university of al-Azhar. The resentment toward those overprivileged clerics—whom the Yemeni government, in the context of the reunification of the country which took place in May 1990, induced to come at great expense in an attempt to reduce tensions—is thus obvious, as is the parallel that can be drawn between the "flexible adaptation" to their environment which Muqbil denounces in these Egyptian immigrants to Yemen and the attitude which he himself displayed as a emigrant to Arabia or, as we shall see, as a "politician" in Yemen.

This competition within the Islamist mainstream is indeed not the only explanation for this sudden radicalization of the discourse of Yemeni "Salafis" against "their" Muslim Brothers. A brief historical flashback is necessary to understand how the rupture occurred, in a way markedly more frontal and confrontational than in the neighboring Saudi kingdom. In the Saudi environment, the Brothers, also "imported" from Egypt (where they had fled Nasser's repression) and the main vectors of a certain religious and political modernization, seem to have avoided any open face-off with the local Salafi movement, very strongly embedded both in the social fabric and among the ruling elites. In Yemen, conversely, local political considerations played a role in the "ideological" self-assertion of Salafism. In 1982 the local Muslim Brothers, heirs, as we have seen, to a long history of cooperation with the regime, had simply contributed once again to its defense by participating in combat against the guerrilla movement of the Democratic Front, established in the southern border region by socialists based in Aden.

At that time, without asserting themselves as potential opponents of the regime, however, they unabashedly refused to be completely identified with it. President Ali Abdallah Saleh had just created a single party, the General Congress of the People, into which he hoped to see all the existing political groups merge.[16] He particularly hoped to rally the Brothers, the main element of the Islamist trend, whose ideological support and tribal intermediation he knew to be essential. 'Abd al-Malik Mansur, one of the senior leaders of the Brothers, was persuaded to join the ranks of the new party, but the majority of the troops refused to follow his lead, and the titular guide of the movement, Ahmed Yasin, ordered Mansur to be boycotted.

Thanks to the new pluralist overtures, the Yemeni Muslim Brothers thus made their entry into politics. In order to divide the Islamist bloc, the regime was subsequently—while maintaining good relations with the Brothers, who were even included in the government when it stood in need of them in 1993 in order to counter the socialists—to do its best to conciliate their potential opponents. It was within this context that Muqbil made a deal with the regime, with which he then initiated a long-standing and multiform cooperation. Very significantly, while violently criticizing the Brothers in his programmatic literature (*Al-Makhraj min al-Fitna*), he cultivated Mansur, who had become a member of the president's party. The main Salafi trend was therefore from then on not only tolerated but supported by the authorities. This cooperation considerably outlived the 1990 reunification and the overture toward pluralist electoral processes which it sanctioned.

During the 1994 civil war (between the former North and the former "socialist" South), the Salafis, along with the rest of the Islamist bloc, fought against the socialists alongside the government troops. After the victory of the North, they went on helping the regime to combat the influence of a greatly weakened socialist party, but they especially became the favorite electoral weapon of the authorities against the Brothers (who were driven from power by the regime, once its victory against the socialists had been assured). Unlike the latter, Muqbil's disciples banned participation in electoral consultations.[17] They hence succeeded in dividing the Islamist voters not into two camps (the opposition and those in power) but into three, inasmuch as the camp of the abstentionists reduced the scope of the electoral opposition to the president's party.

Muqbil died in July 2000. Prior to his death he had been reconciled with the Saudis, who had offered him a medical stay in the United States. Despite the conservative literalism of his teachings, the "Salafi" had therefore more often been an objective ally than an opponent of the regimes of the Peninsula. Such cooperation speaks volumes about the itinerary of a "Salafi" Islamist. The doctrinal radicalization of the Salafis against the Brothers, the opponents to Ali Abdallah Saleh's regime, thus turns out to have been at least partly the product of the benign solicitation of power. Knowing that the Salafis were obviously less committed than the Brothers to the dynamics of political modernization, such support—which had its equivalent in many a country in the region—was wanting in neither realism nor cynicism.

In Yemen as elsewhere, concealed behind the tree of Islamity and ideology, the forest of social issues and politics is thus, as we can see, a somewhat more entangled entity than we had been led to think.

A MULTIFACETED ISLAMISM

Once its identity matrix, the trans-social character of its roots, and the multiplicity and banality of the variables serving to explain the political behavior patterns of its human substratum have been highlighted, the "Islamist object" is hence not susceptible of being understood by extrapolating only one of the domestic or international configurations within which it is today to be observed. Its analysis must weigh the highest possible number of such configurations, each of them, moreover, to be understood within the process of its own historicity. The alpha and omega of Islamism therefore do not reside only in failures or successes—there have indeed been some of the latter, including in the area of social and political modernization—of the governments of Sudan's Hassan Turabi or of Iran's Ruhollah Khomeini, any more than it boils down to the slogan of the Egyptian Muslim Brothers: "Islam is our constitution."

Its modes of action are not only those of Lebanon's Hizb Allah or the Palestinian Islamic Jihad or Hamas struggling against Israel's military occupation. It cannot be reduced to the sectarian tensions which still sometimes rend asunder Sunnis and Shiites, Sufis and Salafis, Marxists and Islamists. A rigorous representation of Islamism can ignore neither the conservative literalism of the Afghan Taliban and the Salafi trend nor the modernizing reformism of Turkish prime ministers Necmettin Erbakan and Recep Tayyip Erdogan. Similarly, it should not restrict itself to the spectacular electoral performances of the leaders of the Algerian Islamic Salvation Front (ISF) in 1990 and 1991 or to their undeniable lack of communication skills: it must also include the terms of the pact of government—against the military authorities established by the January 1992 coup—that this same ISF was in a position to conclude in January 1995 in Rome, under the aegis of the Catholic community of Sant' Egidio, with the Trotskyite Louisa Hanoune, the members of the old National Liberation Front (NLF), and the secularists of the Front of Socialist Forces.

The analysis of Islamism must take into account the icy determination of the kamikaze pilots of the United and American Airlines Boeings on September 11, the outrageous excesses of the Iraqi resistance (especially when, as we are informed, it places bombs in churches). And, no less, the professional cynicism of the torturers of the Algerian junta when they slit throats in the name of their adversaries (military men disguised as Islamists to commit their crimes) or that of the American jailers of the global war on terror. It must include the accomplishments of the ("Islamist") president of Yemen's parliament (and of his "tribal" supporters) and those of Jordanian, Kuwaiti, Lebanese, and Turkish Islamist members of parliament and their obvious capability to contribute, among others, to the reduction of crises in their respective national environments. It must be able to take into account, in their infinite diversity, the sum total of these facts and thousands more. In order to do so, it must therefore have at its disposal not so much an observatory as hundreds of live "sensors" connected to as many political, social, and national configurations as possible.

Finally, a rigorous analysis of the Islamist phenomenon must be placed in a long-term perspective. The quick takes of direct observation must indeed, as often as possible, be historicized, for at all latitudes and at all times the informative value of the discourses and the behavior patterns of a leader or of a political actor depends on the way in which the intelligence they contain is confronted with the flow of time and thus constantly updated: this basic principle of political science is applicable to all, including today's Islamists. In order to be "admissible evidence" in the current debate on Islamism, the phraseology used by the Egyptian Muslim Brothers in the 1940s requires just as great an effort of contextualization as any citation of the discourses of the French Right or Left of that time might require, to clarify their positions today. Similarly, in retrospect, the claims and practices of the radical Algerian ISF leader Ali Benhaj in 1989 are truly explanatory of the current situation of his country and of the political trend that he embodies there only when placed in perspective: they must be confronted with the discourses of other Islamists, in Algeria and elsewhere in the world, who opposed his political line, but also with Ali Benhaj's own discourses and positions, radically divergent on several essential points, which have since subsumed, within an interval of ten or fifteen years, those of the late 1980s.

This is the only feasible approach if we wish to apprehend both the reactive "mechanism" of re-Islamization and the infinite diversity of its expressions within each national context, as in the North-South arena. For all that, establishing the plasticity of the Islamic reference and the diversity of the political usages that its lexicon authorizes should not lead us astray into ignoring or underestimating the earth-shaking transversal trends which are affecting the situation of the geographical spaces where it is predominant today. This is currently the case in regard to the generalized foreclosure which characterizes the distribution of political resources in the Arab world, involving, domestically, the blocking of the quasi-totality of the legal political arenas there and, internationally, the shocking dissymmetry of the prevailing power ratio with the (Israeli and) Western environment.

TWO

FROM NATIONAL STRUGGLE TO THE DISILLUSIONMENTS OF "RECOLONIZATION"

The Triple Temporality of Islamism

The fact that the identity problematic applies more or less to the sum total of actors does not necessarily immunize the latter from history. Even if we can discern a common matrix behind the diversity and elements of continuity within the changes, the modalities of the makeover of an individual between two affiliations ("secular," "French," "religious," "Islamic," etc.) are not strictly speaking equivalent, whether in space (social or national) or in time. Therefore, though it may be legitimate to consider that each member of the successive "generations" of the Islamist mobilization participates in the same assertion of his Muslim identity in the face of the Western alter ego and the regimes accused of pandering to it, it is important to continually reconfigure within each historical context this homogeneity of the identity problematic, in space and time.

THE DIVERSITY OF ISLAMIST ITINERARIES

In the nineteenth century the initial responses of the Muslim world to the thrust of Western hegemony were of an intellectual nature. It was on the pediment of such reformist thought, within the context of enduring British occupation, that the initial expression of the ideas of the Muslim Brothers subsequently crystallized in Egypt during the first third of the twentieth century. The United Kingdom at the time was protecting a fragile parliamentary monarchy, whose elites nonetheless enjoyed a certain pluralism of parliamentary expression. A generation later, the national ideological environment had changed: borders, nations, and mental patterns had been disrupted by the creation of Israel, the thrust of Arab nationalism, and the tripartite expedition organized in 1956 by London, Paris, and Tel Aviv to counter the nationalization of the Suez

Canal. Replenished by the dividends of their nationalist victories, the authoritarianism of the successive regimes grew more pronounced. The entry "into Islamism" is obviously, on multiple levels, tailored to individual histories and national contexts. In their reversion to the fold of religious thought, Nasserists and Egyptian, Syrian, Iraqi, or Arab Baathists did not follow the same itineraries as those who, in Sudan, Egypt, or elsewhere, set aside their traditional membership in Sufi brotherhoods to rally to the reformism of a less passive and therefore more political Islam.

In Yemen, the Muslim Brothers (formed in Cairo by Hassan al-Banna) initially received, in their struggle against an isolationist and conservative religious Imamate, the support of Hassan al-Banna and then that of Gamal 'Abd al-Nasser, at the very moment when the latter was subjecting their counterparts in Cairo to a terrible campaign of repression. While in 1995 Mohammed Atta (1968–2001), an Egyptian architecture student in Hamburg, had so far internalized the categories of Sayyid Qutb's theology that he was ready to place his life on the line to make it triumph, it was in reaction to current events beyond anything Qutb might have known or imagined that he nevertheless forged the death-bent determination which eventually led to the organization of the September 11 attacks.

To render as well as possible both this plurality and the chronological ratcheting up of Islamist logic, I propose here to distinguish three broad contexts and hence three successive overarching sequences in the deployment of its mobilization.

The first sequence was that of the emergence of Islamist mobilization as a foil to direct colonial presence. In order to define its mechanism, it is nonetheless necessary to recall, however briefly, the reformist preambles of the nineteenth century. The second sequence, immediately subsequent to independence, was that of the assertion of cultural options and of the increasingly authoritarian political formulas of the first generation of nationalist elites. The third began in 1990 following the collapse of the USSR with the birth of a so-called world order which increasingly revealed itself to be conspicuously "ordered" around solely American interests. During this third timeline, in the former colonial peripheries, the Western counterpart, with its convergence of interests with the national elites in power becoming more blatant every day, insensibly again became the main foil for oppositional struggle: faced with the progress of a sort of rampant "recolonization," the loss of autonomy of the "independentist" elites stripped them of their ranking as primary adversary, to the advantage of the global superpower.

Iraq after Saddam Hussein provides a paradigmatic example of such a configuration: even more than the new elites elevated into office by the American military occupier, it is the latter that has become target number one for the resistance to a political order justifiably perceived as imposed by the United States.

THE REFORMIST PREAMBLES OF THE MUSLIM BROTHERS: FROM AL-AFGHANI TO ʿABD AL-WAHHAB

During the *first temporality of Islamism,* the resources of the endogenous religious culture were progressively mobilized to fuel the political resistance to the direct stranglehold of the Western colonizer. In 1928, ten years after the carving up of the Ottoman Empire and four years after the dissolution of the caliphate, the last institutional expression of global Muslim unity, eight years before the Treaty of London, which recognized the independence of Egypt in 1936 (while retaining the British military presence in the canal zone), the foundation of the Muslim Brothers by Hassan al-Banna can be considered to be the very first manifestation of the "Islamist reaction."

Nonetheless, the emergence of the Brothers owed much to the heritage of prior intellectual mobilization, which proceeded from a very similar logic. The existential question ("What is to be done to resist Western pressure?") had indeed already been raised by the founders of the trend identified with the thought of Jamal al-Din al-Afghani (1838–1897), Muhammad Abduh (1849–1905), and Rashid Ridha (1865–1935). Essentially, the Muslim Brothers prolonged the first intellectual efforts of their predecessors by transposing them into the political field. The testimony of a large majority of "founding fathers" thus contradicts the existence of any rupture between contemporary Islamists and the reformist thought of their elders.[1]

On this ground, the Algerian experience of Malek Bennabi—already mentioned above—is particularly illuminating. Bennabi paradoxically rediscovered the Arab and Turkish Orient, from which he had been insulated by the dominant north-south flows of colonial exchange, by reading French Orientalist literature. The latter provided him with an aesthetically enhanced image of the Orient. But there was a dearth of the key readings necessary to empower an explanation of its terrible state of decline. As he explained in his memoirs, it was the works of Muhammad Abduh and the Lebanese reformist Ahmed Ridha (1872–1953) which gave him the—political—key to this Oriental decline:

> Finally and above all, I discovered at the En-Nadjah Bookshop the two books that I consider to be the earliest and most decisive sources of my intellectual vocation. I am referring to *La Faillite morale de la politique occidentale en Orient* (The Moral Bankruptcy of Western Policy in the Orient) by Ahmed Ridha and the *Rissalat al-tawhid* by Sheikh Muhammad Abduh, translated by Mustapha Abderrazak, in collaboration with a French Orientalist. These two works, I believe, made an impression on my entire generation at the *madrasa*.[2] In any case, I owe them my turn of mind from then on. Indeed, with an abundant documentation on the splendors of Muslim society at the apex of its civilization, Ridha's work gave me a precise yardstick with which to measure its currently depressing social distress. Abduh's work— I am thinking of the important introduction by its translators, which dwells on the wealth of Islamic thought over the centuries—gave me a point of reference by which to judge its appalling present state of intellectual poverty. This reading chastened my spleen, that nostalgia for the Orient which Pierre Loti, Claude Farrère, and even Alphonse Lamartine and François de Chateaubriand had imparted to me. They revealed to me a historically real Orient whose currently miserable condition I could no longer ignore. They constituted a force, an intellectual call of quite another order which prevented me from lapsing into the romanticism which at the time was so fashionable among that generation of Algerian intellectuals.

There exist numerous other "object lesson" illustrations of this continuity of thought between the reformists and the Brothers. At the other end of the Arab planet, in the Yemen of Imam Yahya, the modernizing movement of the "Free Yemenis,"[3] which we will return to below, never politically distinguished the influence of al-Banna's Muslim Brothers from that of the reformist currents which preceded them.[4]

In this Arabian Peninsula, in Yemen but also in Saudi Arabia, reformist endeavors had certainly been the forerunners of the al-Afghani current. Can they also be associated with the inception of the Islamism of the twentieth century? The least known are the initiatives of the Yemenis Muhammad ibn Isma'il al-Amir (d. 1769) and Muhammad al-Shawkani

(1760–1834).[5] The latter, for almost forty years a Zaydi (Shiite) judge at the service of the imams of the uplands of North Yemen, was one of the first to denounce the bad effects of ill-considered imitation (*taqlid*) of tradition to the detriment of the innovative adaptations rendered possible by *ijtihad*. His thought also contained an embryo of reference to constitutionalism and to a limitation of the powers of rulers, whom he prompts to accept the advice of the nation.[6] His thoughts deeply inspired Abduh.[7] Finally, and above all, he attempted to transcend the divisions between the different legal schools and the Zaydi (Shiite) and Shafii (Sunni) sectarian allegiances.

These reformist antecedents to the colonial shock and the continuity between Abduh and his Yemeni ancestor al-Shawkani relativize the theory of a Muslim world which only confrontation with the West had been able to extricate from its doctrinal stasis. On the contrary, they support the idea that the reformist dynamic already underway before the colonial confrontation was plausibly derailed only when its contributions had been assimilated with possible concessions to the culture of the invader. The wellsprings of this reactive logic, which marked the whole epoch then opening, have been brilliantly demonstrated in the formula of Tariq al-Bishri, an Egyptian jurist close to the Muslim Brothers: "While we resist, do you think it is possible for us to advance?" (quoted by Bennabi).

Whatever the posterity of al-Shawkani's efforts, at least one argument nevertheless suggests not directly associating him with this sequence of a reformist preamble to contemporary Islamism: contrary to members of the later school of al-Afghani, al-Shawkani did not mobilize under the pressure of a clearly identified Western menace. He perhaps only sought to help the Zaydi Imams, whom he served faithfully for forty years, to emerge from the ghetto of their sectarian allegiance to better legitimize their domination over their Sunni Shafii vassals. Above all he sought to transcend the divisions among different juridical schools and their sectarian allegiances.

Among the reformists of the eighteenth century, one whose notoriety has widely survived is "the Saudi" Muhammad 'Abd al-Wahhab.[8] Beginning in 1744, the Najdi preacher undertook a rigorous reinstatement of monotheism and divine unicity. He placed his preaching at the service of the nascent dynasty of Muhammad ibn al-Saud, with whom he threw in his lot, providing what might be called the ideological underpinnings which enabled the sovereign to unify a large part of the Peninsula and to give birth to a stable and autonomous political entity. From the perspective of contemporary Islamism, the status of 'Abd al-Wahhab's approach is therefore somewhat more ambivalent than that of the Yemeni al-Shawkani.

Even if it was not the product of a reaction to the Western threat, its message did indeed have a "nationalist" resonance with international implications. It contributed to help a new Arab nation emerge, to the detriment of the Ottoman Empire. It had a federal dimension, since it enabled a centralized political power to transcend the divisions of the different Sunni schools. It also had reformist implications: the federalism of "Wahhabism" indeed denounced illegitimate political-religious forms, considered to be a challenge to divine unicity. It therefore waged war against Shiism and the "cult" of Ali in the East and, almost everywhere, against the intermediation of the saints advocated by the Sufis. The stamp of Wahhabism, although often caricatured in contemporary literature,[9] left an indelible imprint on later expressions of the dynamics of re-Islamization, including (in its reserve toward certain expressions of Sufism) the thought of the Muslim Brothers.

Essentially, in the context of the colonial confrontation, the first Islamist generation then contributed to reaffirming the place of the religious reference within the lexicon of pro-independence struggles, as not only intellectual but now also political. Even if it was used a lot, the Islamic lexicon did not monopolize the expression of pro-independence anti-Western mobilization.[10] The first generation of nationalists drew heavily on the conceptual arsenal of the colonial power and even more so from its Soviet alter ego and competitor. "Anti-imperialist" socialism as well as "ethnic" nationalism—that is, the so-called secular Arabism, whose original ideologues, first and foremost led by the Syrian Michel Aflaq, included a significant number of Christians—occupied a wide swath of the space traditionally allocated to the religious reference. Many future members of the Islamist generation passed through this universe of "socialist" and "secular" Arabism before experiencing, at the end of highly diversified itineraries, an identical need to restore the religious reference to its place in the expression of the pro-independence project.[11]

The first Islamist generation, notably in Tunisia and Algeria, nonetheless failed to capitalize on the political fruits of its efforts and to control the state apparatus vacated by the departure of the colonizers. Its representatives, be they the Egyptian Muslim Brothers, the trend of Malek Bennabi and the Association of Ulamas founded by Sheikh Ben Badis in Algeria, or the Tunisian Youssefists,[12] were almost systematically excluded from the exercise of power, to the benefit of the so-called secular pro-independence elites. All the complexities of this process, and particularly the role played by the colonial powers in the co-option of their pro-independence "interlocutors," especially in the case of the Algerian NLF, have not yet been completely documented.[13]

THE DISILLUSIONS OF DECOLONIZATION: FROM CULTURAL DIVIDE TO POLITICAL AUTHORITARIANISM

The *second Islamist temporality* stretches from the period of independence until early in the 1990s. This was the period of assertion of the political formula of indigenous elites who had succeeded in coming to power. It was also the period of an increasing calling into question of these same elites. Today the main political opponent of the founders of al-Qaeda appears to be this "Nasserian" or, elsewhere in the region, "Nasserist" generation of pro-independence elites. It was progressively on the receiving end of a double indictment on the part of the rising Islamist generation. One was having betrayed the promises of independence by not having pursued a clear symbolical rupture from the colonizer. The other, which emerged more slowly, was having merely responded to the first demands for political participation with a repressive authoritarianism.

Between the Islamist trends, which were mainly in the opposition, and the elites in power, the dispute focused primarily on a sort of "cultural" deficit observable in the realizations of independence. The Islamists wanted to pursue on the ideological and symbolical levels the process of putting the colonizer "at arm's length," which had just been achieved in the political arena before being extended on the economic level with the "nationalizations" (of oil, arable land, the Suez Canal, etc). They called for a rupture with the mainly Marxist categories of "anti-imperialism" and "Third-Worldism" applied throughout the first temporality of the nationalist dynamic. The modernizing elites in power were therefore criticized for not having carried out the expected cultural and symbolic rupture with the colonial universe—in other words, their inability to perfect the "distancing" of the foreign master by restoring the primacy of the "Islamic," that is, "endogenous," symbolic system. In the Maghreb, the tensions linked to the persistent use of the French language and the state's marginalizing of the religious institutions (notably the universities) inherited from the precolonial "Islamic" system provided the visible part of this process. The elites in power were very soon identified as belonging to "the French party." Indeed, as the Tunisian Rashid al-

37

Ghannoushi, in exile from "Bourguiba's army of the vanquished" to use his own expression, testified, independence, "much more than a victory over the French occupier, constituted instead a victory over the Arabo-Islamic civilization of Tunisia."[14]

The cultural nature of these first claims subsequently expanded to include the more banal denunciation of the growing authoritarianism of regimes and the premises of an "Arab political formula," behind which the pro-independence elites having come to power very soon felt the need to protect themselves. This lock-out of the political field progressively appeared all the less acceptable for benefiting from a watchful tolerance and, often enough, explicit support on the part of the former colonial powers. Beyond any reaction to colonial violence in itself, it was as a stand against the repression brought to bear by the pro-independence elites (Nasser's repression of the Muslim Brothers is paradigmatic here) that the first radical offshoots (above all in the case of Qutb) emerged in the course of this second temporality. In the immense majority of cases, the expressions of Islamist mobilization were very soon denied access to the legal political arena. Hence their members were long confined to clandestine action or, in the most favorable cases, to the associative or trade-unionist institutional outer fringe of political life. The more their capacity for mobilization was asserted, the more the policies of exclusion of the regimes and the ostracism of the Western media cracked down.

Despite the diversity of national configurations, the recipe for the radicalization of part of the Islamist population gelled thanks to the same ingredients: the regimes, having exhausted the capital of nationalist (Algeria, Tunisia, Morocco) or revolutionary resources (gained in the course of popular revolutions following independence, Egypt, Libya), progressively harmonized their governmental practices within the mold of a quasi "Arab institutional norm." Despite the patent discrepancies with all the humanist precepts lionized by the West, they thus benefited from the active support of the latter.

After a phase of nationalist exuberance, an inversion in the trend of oil prices and the mechanisms of global economic integration inexorably led the pro-independence elites to accept, from the 1980s onward, new forms of dependency, making even more concessions to their Western environment as their own popular underpinnings weakened. Progressively, the heroes of independence and the other Third-Worldist revolutionaries—or their inheritors—were accused not only of rehashing the terms of cultural domination but, increasingly, of endorsing, under the most dehumanized arsenal of political repression, a new "re-dependence," first economic and then political (and even military in the Middle East, as soon as the states of the region stopped resisting Israel's demands).

In the conservative oil monarchies which had purportedly remained closest to the religious reference, the passage through a certain "secularization," then through autocracy and (re)dependence, was in fact very real and fueled identical tensions.[15] In Saudi Arabia during the 1980s (to which we will return below) the *ulamas* were reduced to the role of accessories to power, purveyors of financial *fatwas* legitimizing modes of development, or to silent opposition. The expropriation of the religious norm progressively narrowed to the space of mere personal status, conquering only one new field of action, that of so-called Islamic finance. In Arabia, the political price of dependency on the West was revealed to be proportional to the European and American appetite for oil. Authoritarianism and concussion with Western powers inexorably set up the podium from which the first Islamist demands and the subsequent radicalization of some of their members were to be launched.

FACING "RECOLONIZATION": AL-QAEDA AND THE THIRD TEMPORALITY OF ISLAMISM

After years of being perceived as a problem solver, the United States itself has now become a problem for the rest of the world. After having been the guarantor of political freedom and economic order for half a century, the United States appears more and more to be contributing to international disorder by maintaining where it can uncertainty and conflict.

—EMMANUEL TODD, *AFTER THE EMPIRE: THE BREAKDOWN OF THE AMERICAN ORDER* (2004)

Did you ever wonder why it wasn't Sweden that we attacked?

—OSAMA BIN LADEN, MESSAGE TO THE AMERICAN PEOPLE (NOVEMBER 2004)

The *third Islamist temporality*, during which the gravitational pull of al-Qaeda's influence began to come into its own, emerged in the early 1990s. It underwrote a sort of transfer, or better a "return," of the oppositional struggles of the Arab world to the international scene. For a whole political generation, the Western powers, with the United States as self-imposed leader, gradually "reverted" to the status of main adversary, just as they had been during the colonial period.

The image of a new transition "from close enemy to distant enemy"— used by the Egyptian Ayman al-Zawahiri to describe the strategy of his extremist organization—thus amounts to a return to the binary confrontation of the colonial configuration, the overwhelming power of the foreign enemy reasserting itself against the intermediation of local governing elites, reduced to the rank of protected go-betweens for the new holders of the title "empire."

Three great "denials of representation" were fundamentally instrumental in the radicalization and transnationalization of the rebellion which spread through part of the Islamist constituency. The first was the denial endured by a rising generation of opposition to Arab state regimes, which year after year has come up against the great firewall of conservative political engineering which almost everywhere has replaced the fugitive promises of "democratic transition." The second "failure of the political" was regional: it resulted from the exacerbation of the Israeli-Arab conflict, more "asymmetrical" than ever,[16] and from the state of abandonment in which the hopes of the Palestinian camp, already weakened by the collapse of its traditional Soviet ally, ended up when the paralysis of the 1993 Oslo Accords finally locked in. The third political dysfunction has been global: by bringing the division of the "Western camp" to an end, the collapse of the USSR has abrogated an essential means of regulating the bouts of bulimia of Washington, whose foreign policy from then on increasingly lurched toward unilateral interventionism. As Rashid Khalidi emphasizes, the 2003 American war against Iraq was fought

> . . . firstly to demonstrate that it was possible to free the United States from subordination to international law or the U.N. Charter, from the need to obtain the approval of the United Nations for American actions, and from the constraints of operating within alliances. . . . it was a war fought because its planners . . . saw the tragedy of 9/11 as a golden opportunity to achieve this long-cherished goal."[17]

The correlation of these three levels of crisis—national, regional, and global—gradually widened the gap of misunderstanding between, on the one hand, the millions of citizens in an entire region of the world who deem themselves to be its victims and, on the other, the coalition of those who, at the global, regional, or national domestic levels, stand to reap benefit from it: the American administration and its neo-conservative ideological henchmen, then Israel, largely supported by its public opinion and its powerful communication capabilities, and finally the Arab governing elites, more often than not completely devoid of any public support. It was arguably this general failure in political regulation of world tensions which, early in the 1990s, took the lid off the Pandora's box of Islamist radicalization. The al-Qaeda insurgency, that monstrous progeny of the world's most perverse injustices, can be considered one of its most hyperbolical expressions.

In the globally democratic Western environments, the claims of the alter-globalization movement have highlighted, through radically differ-ent means, political and economic malfunctions which, *mutatis mutan-dis,* are not entirely foreign to those which have nurtured the emergence of al-Qaeda. In lands where—oil interests and Israeli security so de-mand—Western domination has intensified to a particularly high pitch and where, above all, conservative local political arrangements have pro-hibited all forms of legal protest, the radicalization has been spun into the emergence of revolutionary rhetoric and practices and the sectarian radicalization of Osama Bin Laden and his operatives.

The Impunity of the "Arab Pinochets"

The grip of the Arab "institutional norm," endorsed by the international order, manifests itself above all through the outlawing and gradual crim-inalization of real political forces.[18] Parties deprived of their existence or of all access to the legal political arena represent in their immense ma-jority the mainstream of the Islamist trend. The regimes have substituted oppositional "partners," tailored to the requirements of a "pluralist" nar-rative intended above all to lend credence abroad to a democratic façade. By refusing to pay the price for the existence of genuine mechanisms of representation, these regimes have reverted to repression to confront the tensions inescapably born of this deep dichotomy between reality and institution.

From Riyad to Rabat, the use of torture has become banal and sys-tematic. It targets not only political prisoners but very often also their close family, male or female.[19] The presence of an extremist fringe—but also its regular, often massive, manipulation in the scenographies of the mass media—provides the pretext for an iron foreclosure of the legal political scene. Egypt, in which President Mubarak could be "elected" again for a fifth six-year term in September 2005, has been living under a state of emergency since 1981. Almost everywhere, the electoral system, dispossessed of any grasp on the balance of power in the upper reaches of the state, or "defused," to adopt the excellent expression coined by the Moroccan political scientist Mohamed Tozy, is in fact running idle.[20]

Last but not least,[21] this "Arab political formula" has been consubstantial with practically unreserved Western support. The first contradiction of the new American world order has therefore been adapting to the profound discredit of the authoritarian regimes that underpin it. This shows an obstinate blindness, born notably from an American propensity, inherited from the 1979–1980 Iran crisis, to indiscriminately criminalize a whole Islamist generation. Or, alternatively, great lucidity concerning the nationalist bearing of the Islamist thrust and the advantages that, albeit at the price of sacrificing a few sacred principles, the present formula bestows on those who are its chief architects.

The wellsprings of the mobilizing resources of Bin Laden's followers therefore are replenished by the frustration of a political generation which perceives itself to be caught between the increasingly heavy hammer of American interventionism and the anvil of the repressive authoritarianism of its own governing elites. During the 1990s the strategies of liberation gradually came to focus on the American hand perceived as wielding that heavy hammer.

The Walling-Up of Palestine

At the dark heart of the malignant dysfunctions of the political regulation of the world there lies, unsurprisingly, the ever-recurrent Israeli-Arab conflict over Palestine. Through the 1990s, as the real contours of the Oslo Accords came progressively to light, the Palestine Liberation Organization (PLO), which had taken the spectacular step of officially recognizing the state of Israel, received only illusory administrative compensation. The image of an archipelago of asphyxiated Bantustans, ceaselessly redefined by colonial excrescences, was inexorably substituted for any viable form of a Palestinian state, whose creation was continually postponed. Long before Likud came to office, the Labor Party, reputedly composed of "supporters of peace," initiated this systematic colonization of the West Bank, which rendered meaningless the proclaimed principle of an "exchange of land for peace."

From the end of 2000 on, the second Intifada gave the hawks of the Sharon camp the pretext purely and simply to reoccupy the Palestinian enclaves and ratchet up the violence to a new level. Refugee camps were

assaulted with heavy armor and bulldozers. Even more than in its principle, it was in its mapping that the "security wall," which authorized the
annexation of hundreds of hectares of Palestinian land, demonstrated
the reality of the Israeli strategy. For all Palestinians, and for those elsewhere in the world who have preserved the privilege of accessing relatively objective sources of information, it quickly became self-evident
not only that the Israelis did not want peace but that they also coveted
the land occupied since 1967. It also became clear that the American administration, whether under Bush Junior or under Clinton, did not harbor the least real intention of opposing this unacknowledged policy of
annexation of great swaths of the West Bank.[22]

"Against God" Rather Than "Against His Saints": Al-Qaeda Attacks the American World Order

At the beginning of the 1990s the postcolonial formula gave way to a new
"imperial" order, even more obviously dominated by the United States
than before.[23] The methods that Washington has employed to perpetuate or to perfect its hegemony are certainly not new. In 1973, in Chile, a
first "September 11" gave birth, on the ashes of a "rebel" democracy, to a
"subserviently" terrible dictatorship.[24] To the objectives targeted by the
subjection of the entire South American continent[25] were added, in the
case of the Middle East, the strategic nature of oil interests and the security requirements of Israel. The principle of the eviction of a government
duly elected but considered excessively nationalist in favor of a more
conciliatory authoritarian regime had been inaugurated in the region by
the overthrow of the Iranian prime minister Mohammad Mossadegh,
with British connivance, in August 1953.

The Second Gulf War in 1991 marked the overture of an American decade of intervention in the Peninsula. Hitherto a major ally of the United
States, the Iraqi dictatorship was to pay the price for its "unfortunate" attempt, in August 1990, to seize the oil wells of Kuwait, bearing the brunt
of a U-turn in American diplomacy and the mobilization of the United
Nations. After the sacrifice of whole divisions of Saddam Hussein's army,
carpet-bombed by B-52s, it was the Iraqi civilian population, by the hundreds of thousands, who would foot the bill for the economic embargo
subsequently enforced by the coalition. The disarmament of the only regional power capable of militarily resisting Israel also gave Washington
the opportunity to perpetuate its armed presence in countries neighboring Iraq, such as Saudi Arabia. The founding episode of the armed

annexation of the largest oil reserve in the world had just been played out.[26] It was at the core of the incipient rebellion to be staged by the al-Qaeda camp.

The theater of operations of the most disputed initiatives of American and Western diplomacy in the 1990s was not limited to the Arabian Peninsula. The decade opened in Algeria with a double electoral victory (June 1990 and December 1991) for an opposition rallied under the umbrella of the "Islamic Salvation Front." The ISF was probably not significantly more democratic than the military whose interests it threatened, but hardly less so either. The all-powerful presidential institution, which forecloses the constitution and controls the armed forces, considerably limited the maneuvering space for its possible parliamentary majority. Under the pretext of "preserving democracy," Europe and the United States allowed the military junta to suppress the results of these first free elections ever and to implement, from January 1992 onward, an unusually perverse repressive strategy.

The silent approbation of the United States was echoed by the open political, economic, and media-hyped support of France under François Mitterrand. In the view of the vast majority of opinion, which, in the Muslim world, gave no credence to the explanation that Paris and Algiers were attempting to legitimize, the conviction of a cynical Western dualism was further reinforced. The same dualism was palpable in 1995, when, in Bosnia, thousands of Muslim citizens were massacred despite the presence of Western troops under a United Nations mandate, supposedly there to protect them.

Finally, beyond the Middle East but still on Muslim lands, the new American world order granted its former Russian enemy *carte blanche* to wage in Chechnya, amid the rubble of its own empire, a colonial war every bit as barbarous as the one which it had just lost in Afghanistan.[27]

From the Transnationalism of Security Policies to the Internationalization of "Islamic" Resistance

In the mind of an entire generation, and not only among Islamists, the political crises within the Arab world and part of the Muslim world are ever more systematically associated with an order that claims to be global but increasingly seems to be solely American. Washington's propensity to resort to "hard power" has grown, in line with that of its Arab puppet states to have recourse to repression. Both convey a common deficit of political legitimacy. Not only is this world order "Americanizing" (due to the collapse of the Soviet counterpower), but it is becoming increasingly confessional as the neo-conservatives make growing use of Christian references. It is also tending more and more to forgo the endorsement of the ever less credible international institutions dominated by Washington.

For millions of citizens of the Arab world (and not only for them), the mirage of a disinterested, pacifist, and universalist global "new order" has irresistibly evaporated before the hard reality of the support which an arrogant and ever more obviously autistic superpower has by all means at its command, including military, granted to one of the camps, whose actors are easy to identify. These are, first, the bearers of its own financial interests and narrowing ideological vision, that is, respectively, a small military-industrial caste closely linked to those in power and a highly coordinated Christian and Jewish electorate; second, the regional state actors who connive in their defense: Israel on the one hand, the Arab authoritarian regimes on the other.

During the 1990s the correlation between American interventionism and the repressive clout of the domestic Arab state orders was becoming increasingly self-evident. Even before September 11, 2001, the systematization and institutionalization of security cooperation endowed it with a heightened expression. The "War on Terrorism" would lead to the identification of certain Arab regimes with the American order and, conversely, of American interests with the durability of such regimes, notwithstanding their obvious unpopularity.

The formula which welds together this illegitimate transaction between the world order and sundry dictatorships rests on an exchange of resources: the authoritarian regimes "repay" Western silence and support with concessions which may range from massive arms orders to help in controlling oil prices, not to speak of more personal emoluments—which will leave lasting scars on not only the history of bilateral American-Saudi relations, of course, but also that of Franco-Algerian relations.

The first major world summit against (Islamic) terrorism at Sharm-al-Sheikh in March 1996 amounted to a particularly emblematic expression of this process. It was held some five months before Bin Laden's first call for "War against Americans," made on August 23, 1996. A significant double convergence in policy and rhetoric locked in, between the titleholders of the American order and their Arab and Israeli allies. The common enemy of the likes of Bill Clinton, Vladimir Putin, and Benjamin Netanyahu, and also of all Arab dictators, was thereafter characterized as "Islamic terrorism." An alliance involving the American and European (including Russian) security apparatuses, the Israeli services, and the repressive machinery of the most dictatorial Arab regimes was forthwith proclaimed. The enemy was indiscriminately dubbed "Islamic terrorism." It encompassed a wide medley of realities: that of Palestine for Netanyahu, of Chechnya for Boris Yeltsin and then for Putin, of the Algeria of the generals and the Tunisia of Zine al-Abidine Ben Ali.

The rhetoric of Sharm-al-Sheikh to some degree sanctioned the criminalization of all resistance, armed or not, to the dysfunctions of a very wide array of national, regional, or global authoritarianisms. All the actors in these oppositions and this resistance thus came, by an identical stigmatization, to be "invited" to identify with one another. Where this symbolic and political coordination had not already taken place, this was indeed what was to happen. In the eyes of many of those who were designated as being "on the receiving end," the transnational extension of the repression of all forms of protest or oppositional expression employing an Islamic lexicon reinforced the legitimacy of and the necessity for a correspondingly transnational extension of resistance.

For the militants of al-Qaeda, the "distant" American "enemy" thus sealed its own fate, henceforth to be shared with the "close" and long top-priority "enemy" represented by the Arab regimes. In the Islamic sphere, the internationalization and the reterritorialization of the armed struggle took shape concomitantly, echoing the American globalization of an increasingly disputed order.

"Mujahidin without Borders" or the Role of Afghanistan

The integration of several thousand young Muslims (between 10,000 and 15,000) into the ranks of the Afghan resistance to the Soviet occupation (from 1979 to 1989) constituted an episode that the analysis of the al-Qaeda generation must obviously take into consideration. This "Afghan factor"—and the opportunity given to several thousand militants to participate in a victorious armed struggle against the second global superpower of the period—clearly played a significant role in the crystallization and self-affirmation of the al-Qaeda generation, just as the conflicts in the former Yugoslavia and, later, in Chechnya also did to a certain degree. It cannot, however, be inflated into the sole or even the central explanatory factor.

More than being just an opportunity for military training, it no doubt facilitated the "path to action" by accelerating the circulation and transnationalization of revolutionary strategy. It also boosted, at the expense of other political strategies, the credibility of the efficacy or simply the feasibility of armed struggle against one of the pillars of the world order. The thrust of the "rejectionist camp," composed of a minority of proponents of armed action, was indeed favored as much by the failure of the struggles waged within the "national" arenas (notably in Egypt and Algeria) as by the blatant absence of any alternative route offered by the world order and its local intermediaries to the legalism of the central nexus of Islamist movements, notably and above all the Muslim Brothers.

The Afghan episode was constructed around successive and relatively different phases and processes. The first, at the beginning of the 1980s, was that of the legal, even official (from both the Arab and the American point of view), mobilization of thousands of young volunteers in the ranks of the resistance to the Soviet occupation. The legal presence of these "combatants without borders," for a long time known as "Arab Afghans" (even if they came from the entire Muslim world), coincided with the victory, which was also theirs, of the coalition of opponents to the Kabul regime and the subsequent withdrawal of Soviet forces.

In 1992 began a four-year civil war between the victors. At first the "Arabs" bore the brunt. The necessity for most of them to fall back on positions outside the Afghan sanctuary coincided with the beginning of a phase of increased repression by the regimes of their respective countries (notably Saudi Arabia and Algeria), which were wary of such operatives too rashly sent or allowed to go abroad for training in *jihad*. In the eyes of the Western media, these "combatants of the faith" abruptly morphed into "God's madmen."

The rise to power of the Taliban in 1996 once again inverted the regional situation. The deal struck with them by Osama Bin Laden received the support of Ayman al-Zawahiri and the members of his Egyptian organization Jihad—the second, with Jamaa Islamiyya, of the two branches of Egyptian radical Islamism in open revolt against the regime—which had survived the particularly effective repression of previous years. Al-Zawahiri then decided to relocate the front of his old (and inconclusive) struggle against the "close" enemy, the Egyptian state, to an admittedly "distant" (American) enemy, against which an exponentially increasing number of malcontents could be recruited. This last phase gave the signal for the "legal" (from the point of view of their Afghan hosts) deployment of the international networks of al-Qaeda.[28]

The accusations and claims that the Islamist generation had long directed at their respective regimes were thus turned in top priority against the former European colonial powers or, more precisely, against the—American—apex of the global power structure, which, following the defeat of the USSR, seamlessly took over their role.

It was in this context that, in April 1996, an Egyptian named Mohammed Atta sat down to write his will. It was also on that date that most of the perpetrators of the September 11 attacks set out with him on the long road which, via Afghanistan, Hamburg, and a handful of American civil aviation schools, culminated one morning in September 2001 in the firestorm of the World Trade Center.

FROM "COLONIAL UNVEILING" TO MODERNIZATION "BENEATH THE VEIL": THE TEMPORALITIES OF ISLAMISM MEASURED BY THE YARDSTICK OF THE "MUSLIM VEIL"

Both during and after the colonial presence, the capital for mobilization represented by Islamic identity has been the stake of passion-fraught strategies. For over a century the debate on the wearing of the Islamic veil has illustrated in its own way the complexity of the clash initiated by colonization as well as the successive temporalities (and the permanence of the stakes) of "Islamist" reaction.

The contemporary "political" history of the veil stems from the context of colonial self-assertion. Under the effect of the ascendancy of the culture of the colonizer and in the name of the modernization which it sought to promote, a sort of symbolic "de-Islamizing" took place. In a second phase, this modernist "de-traditionalizing," largely adopted by the first generation of pro-independence elites, was fought against by the actors of a "re-Islamizing" thrust. Essentially oppositional, this dynamic of "reveiling" was nonetheless caught up by political regimes in a small number of cases, with the concomitant authoritarian excesses which this sometimes entailed.

Begun in Muslim lands at the time of colonization, the debate on the wearing of the veil today has spread beyond its first borders and gone global. It is also taking place, with unrelenting passion, within Western societies where a tumultuous common history has resettled the former "Indigenous of the Republic,"[29] descendants of the former colonized peoples, with their memories, their ambitions, and their rights.

The first tremor linked to the "veil issue" therefore took the form of a sort of "de-traditionalizing/modernizing" process under the influence, from about the 1930s, of a (very) small number of Muslim women, who, like their mothers, "did not wear the veil but had been born and brought up in it"[30] and decided to dispense with it, thus marking a symbolic stage in their emancipation. In 1923 Hoda Shaarawi, the daughter of Muhammad Sultan Pasha, the president of the first Egyptian parliament and governor-general of Upper Egypt, when she was sailing home from Italy, conspicuously threw overboard the square of cloth with which her mother had no doubt unquestioningly covered her head since childhood.[31] Other figures of the first generation of "modern" feminism, notably Maghrebins, subsequently followed this example. In 1924 the Tunisian Manoubia Ouertani solemnly removed her headscarf at the socialist literary club L'Essor.[32] A certain number of women then did the same of their own free will, convinced that this symbol of religious identity overburdened rather than protected their autonomy as women. It was thus their contention that education and emancipation rhymed with reinterpretation of the religious reference and, in the case of a very small number of them, even made a complete break with it.

If some acted on their own initiative, all received the insistent support of the colonial authorities and were consequently disowned by at least one section of the nationalist elites. The first activists of the first generation of Arab feminism were already at stake in strategies which did not all have liberation as their main agenda. Here and there the ambivalence of such colonial benevolence and the insidious analogy between a possible "emancipation" to come and the pretext for the preservation of current "colonization" showed through. For certain theorists of colonialism at the time, the status of the Arab woman, "a victim of backward societies," was in fact "the living proof of the inability of these societies to govern themselves" and hence of the legitimacy of the very presence and beneficial action of the "civilizing" power which had come to emancipate them.[33] In the British Empire, Evelyn Baring, Lord Cromer, had made the veil the symbol of Muslim societies' contempt for women, which enabled him to present himself as the champion of this despised "Oriental" woman. Very significantly, the altruism which he deployed in the empire did not prevent him from resisting to the very last the feminist movements in England itself.[34]

Behind an apparently humanist façade, the discourse on the "liberation of Muslim woman" thus conveyed some of the contradictions of colonial rhetoric: while dreaming of unveiling her, it denied her access to full political citizenship, just like her brothers and fathers. In Algeria or elsewhere, the refusal to lay down the veil therefore progressively symbolized one of the forms of resistance to the modernizing order—and thus to the very order itself—which the colonial powers sought to maintain. Unsurprisingly, none of this coherence between "modernizing unveiling" and the perpetuation of colonial domination was lost on Frantz Fanon: in *L'An V de la révolution algérienne,* he notes: "The decisive battle was launched before 1954, more precisely during the 1930s. The officials of the French administration in Algeria, committed to destroying the people's originality, and under instructions to bring about the disintegration, at whatever cost, of forms of existence likely to evoke a national reality directly or indirectly, were to concentrate their efforts on the wearing of the veil."[35]

In Algeria, these candidates for "liberation" were occasionally prompted by an appeal from the wife of General Jacques Massu, one of the main architects of the military underpinning of the colonial order, just as others were also to do, in Aden, in response to an appeal from British officers' wives. When, on May 13, 1958, on Government Square in Algiers, "Muslim women climbed onto a podium to burn their veils," as Houria Bouteldja analyzes it today,

> [The implication] of such a scene was considerable: the colonial authorities required Algerian women to dissociate themselves from the struggle of their own people. Their exhibition spoke in the language of a colonial power hard at work winning emancipation for women and for the everlastingness of "French civilization." The gut reaction of Algerian society was to maintain—and this was vital—women beyond the reach of the colonial invasion in order to preserve the Algerian way of being. . . . Algerian women who had long since dropped the veil, writes Frantz Fanon, donned the *haik* again, thus affirming that it was untrue that woman liberated herself at the invitation of France and of General De Gaulle.[36]

MODERNIZATION REVEILED

Once past the troubled waters of a first dynamic of modernization "obfuscated" by the meddling of colonial domination, some women of the same generation were later also to lay down their veil, but this time in the new context of Independence. They therefore did so unsolicited by any foreign pressure, with, moreover, the encouragement of a first generation of nationalist elites still haloed by victory over the colonizer. However, this second page of feminist modernization was not devoid of all misunderstanding and contradiction. Even more radically than the colonial authorities had dared to dream, the "modernizing" regimes born from the process of national insurgency were by no means reluctant to disenfranchise themselves from the codes of inherited (religious) culture.

This route was opened during the 1920s in Turkey when the "father of secularism," Kemal Atatürk, abolished the caliphate, thus bringing to an end any concrete institutional expression of supranational Muslim belonging. He then banned the use of the Arabic alphabet, adopted the Christian Gregorian calendar, and imported rafts of European legislation in both private and public law.[37] By a decree of August 30, 1925, he forbade women to wear the veil and simultaneously chose to prohibit their husbands, fathers, and brothers from donning the fez, the "traditional" headgear of their forbears or at least perceived as such.[38] On the eastern frontier of Turkey, some years later (in 1935), the Iranian emperor Reza Pahlavi made not only the uncovered female head but indeed the beardless male face the symbols of the modernity which he intended to impose. He therefore forbade women to wear the veil and had the beards of religious dignitaries ripped off in public places.

In the newly independent Arab countries of the 1950s and 1960s, a good number of secular modernizers, such as the Tunisian Habib Bourguiba, with a greater or lesser degree of authoritarianism, followed in the footsteps of these predecessors. In the name of this same modernization, Bourguiba stigmatized most of the Islamic markers—from the fasting for Ramadan to the sacrifice of sheep at Eid ul-Fitr, including the pilgrimage to Mecca and the Islamic University of Al-Zitouna, which he marginalized—of a society which he wanted to force-march toward progress. This second wave of "modernizing/de-traditionalizing" was assimilated, just as the first had been, with a sort of religious and, more generally, cultural "de-Islamization" by those who progressively undertook to dissociate themselves from it and subsequently protest against it.

A quarter of a century later, the first signs of a new political dynamic were to all intents and purposes to confirm this hypothesis. The question of the veil entered into a new cycle of turbulence, that of "re-Islamization" and the multiple reactions to which it led. Among the small number—a point which must absolutely be kept in mind—of those who had removed the veil, or among their daughters, it was often the focus of a sort of reactive reappropriation. From about the beginning of the 1970s, some women, generally members of the urban elite themselves, claimed the right to wear it.

This was the case in 1974 for Hind Chelbi, an academic from the Tunisian upper class, who decided to don the veil during a ceremony presided over by the head of state, from whom she declined a paternal kiss as well as a handshake. Bourguiba was nevertheless, like the shah of Iran, one of the symbols of the struggle for "women's liberation" in the Arab world— even if, before rallying to the latter, he had for a long time dissociated himself from calls to abandon the headscarf, which he recognized as one of the "distinctive signs and consequently" one of the "last defenses of a threatened national identity."[39] Hind Chelbi thus broke with the dress code (head, arms, and knees uncovered) of a small urban elite immortalized by the first generation of Egyptian cinema, which the West long envisioned as the best evidence of its modernizing influence.

This "reveiling" movement unsurprisingly encountered the hostility of the nationalist elites who had encouraged modernist unveiling in the first place as well as that of their counterparts from the northern shores of the Mediterranean who saw in it a refutation of the universalism of their own heritage. The distinction between "continuity" and "reappropriation" of tradition generally remained possible, the different manners of wearing the veil enabling them to distinguish, more often than not, between the generation of those "who never set it aside" and those who intended to reappropriate it.

From 1980 and the pro-Khomeini revolution onward, the claim and the assertion of this "reactive" veil took a more openly political turn and little by little became associated with the emergence, almost everywhere in the region, of the Islamist opposition. One after another, regimes became conscious of the scope of a phenomenon which they had at one time reduced to a mere reminiscence of a vanishing traditionalism. In "secular" Tunisia, Bourguiba, his successors, and some of his neighbors progressively radicalized their attitude toward this sartorial symbol of "oppositional" affiliation. From then on, women (notably in Morocco and Tunisia) were long to be banned from wearing the veil, upon penalty of being denied access to a large range of professional activities.[40]

As in the case of its banning, the wearing of the veil also led to authoritarian practices. Voluntary "re-Islamization" was not immune from recourse to authoritarianism by individuals or regimes any more than "de-Islamizing modernization" had been. In Iran and in Saudi Arabia, by bringing the religious tradition—or just tradition itself—under state control, the Islamic regimes associated the obligation of wearing the veil, at least in a fraction of these societies, with their own growing illegitimacy. In 1980 the founders of the Islamic Republic of Iran, after having, with the support of millions of men and women, overthrown the emperor who had banned the wearing of the veil, did not have the wisdom to content themselves with reestablishing the freedom to wear it. They imposed the opposite obligation, respect for which became the condition *sine qua non* of the integration of women into legitimate society. Among at least some of those who intended to dissociate themselves from the absolutism of the regimes which imposed it, the "Islamic" reference therefore lost part of its legitimacy. In the kingdom of Saudi Arabia, a small group of women, at the end of a demonstration organized in Riyad in November 1999, thus even publicly trampled on the veil imposed by the self-proclaimed guardians of religious orthodoxy.[41]

While a large majority of Iranian women successfully engaged in the pursuit, under the veil, of a gradual revolution in their status,[42] a minority among them adopted means of resistance, thus several decades later following in the footsteps of the first feminists. After more than twenty years of "Islamic revolution," the Iranian lawyer Shirin Ebadi chose to present herself with her head uncovered to receive her Nobel Peace Prize in Oslo in December 2003. Once she had established her right not to wear the veil, she nonetheless made a point of denouncing what she regarded as the overly variable geometry of the values of that very West from which she had accepted recognition without wishing to be identified with it. She thus seized the opportunity to clearly condemn the French law which was to be adopted in February 2004, which, by banning the wearing of the veil in public schools, applied the same recourse to constraint which she herself was seeking to denounce.

In November 2003, as the war in Iraq was raging and one month before the Iranian intellectual defied the "Islamic" order to veil herself, Khadija Ben Ganna, a famous Algerian journalist from the Qatari channel al-Jazeera, voluntarily decided to "submit" and to flaunt the veil rejected in her time by Hoda Shaarawi and, much later and in quite a different context, by Shirin Ebadi.

Such echoes of the dynamics of imposed or militant unveiling/reveiling have resonated very regularly ever since. Behind the apparent complexity of the ebb and flow, a transversal reading remains possible. The Algerian women who refused, when France stretched "from Dunkirk to Tamanrasset," to follow the injunctions of General Massu's wife to "liberate themselves from their veil" apparently evolved in a different context from that in which, in 1974, the Tunisian Hind Chelbi (re)veiled. Just like the Tunisian academic, they nevertheless wanted to mark their opposition to what Habib Bourguiba and the colonial authorities perceived as a "modernization" and which, for their part, they felt to be "deacculturation" or "Westernization."

Their motivation was again different from but comparable to that which, in 2003, led the al-Jazeera journalist to "join" them. At the hour of globalization, Khadija Ben Ganna had not only closely followed the French debate on the ban on wearing the veil but also, a few months earlier, the expulsion from the French school at Doha (where her children were studying) of a female pupil who refused to obey the ban.

Thirty years after Hind Chelbi, decolonization has no doubt reached its full term. However, the hour has now struck of a global war on terror in which the identity markers of Islam, identified for a time by the Muslim modernizing elites as signs of underdevelopment, are, as they were during the struggle for independence, correlated once again with terrorist violence. Yet the pressure is no longer brought to bear through the same vectors. It is no longer up to General Massu's wife to feel concerned about the modernization of the "French Muslim woman." Other "modernizers," male or female, bristling here with the weaponry required to allay their fears of political protest, there with the rigid self-righteousness of a highly restrictive interpretation of secularism, have taken up the torch.[43] All nevertheless partake of an absolutely identical obsession: namely, forcing her to cast aside her "Islamic" headgear.

THREE

THE ISLAMIST FIELD BETWEEN NATIONAL SPECIFICITY AND TRANSNATIONALIZATION

After placing al-Qaeda's mobilization within the chronology of Islamist temporalities, in order to define its specificity, it must also be placed "horizontally" or "synchronically" in regard to other contemporary expressions of the Islamist field and the dynamics that tend to strengthen or, on the contrary, to weaken the specificities of national configurations. This enables us to reiterate—what amounts to hard fact but is less and less widely recognized—that the network of Osama Bin Laden's sympathizers today is far from representing the sole, or even the main, doctrinal or political expression of the process of re-Islamization (including in the arena of armed activism, where the movements of resistance to Israeli occupation are currently developing). Taking into account the diversity of Islamist positions and of the dynamics affecting them is a task that must be undertaken in several stages.

In this chapter, we will first recall the nature of the national variables, following the historical trajectories of the societies concerned, which map out specific Islamist realities from one country to another. In *The Islamic Movement in North Africa*,[1] I proposed a first typology of these national differentials and, conversely, of the factors of integration and homogenization. What is at stake here is their intersection with the chronology of the temporalities which I have just charted—a problematic which we will scrutinize in depth in the two following chapters.

FROM THE MODALITIES OF THE COLONIAL CLASH TO THE CULTURAL AND POLITICAL MANAGEMENT OF INDEPENDENCE

Carving up the Muslim world into nations has definitely had a deep impact on the forms of Islamic resurgence and, in particular, on the respective role of the different variables which affect its rhythm, its scope, and the modalities of its expression.

It is true that the actors of the Islamist movement have done their utmost to relativize the impact of these divisions, which have at least partly been the outcome of colonization.[2] Moreover, processes of Islamic internationalization or even "globalization" are obviously gathering momentum, contributing to the erosion of national differences. But, even for those who claim to place the uniqueness and timelessness of the religious reference beyond national affiliation, it is clear that the itineraries leading to commitment to Islamist mobilization can vary from one country to another. In 2008 being Islamist does not have the same meaning or entail the same consequences for a citizen of Iraq or Kuwait, of Algeria, Libya, or the United Arab Emirates—and, *a fortiori,* for someone who lives in a Western society with a mainly Christian cultural tradition.

The impact of the identity variable ("Who are we in relation to the West?"), which may be considered to determine the "potential" of Islamist mobilization, has obviously varied, first due to the more or less traumatic circumstances during which the initial encounter with the West occurred. It has then depended on the posture of the pro-independence elites, notably in the cultural and religious fields. On this ground, the characteristics of societies at the time of the arrival of the colonizer must be taken into account, particularly whether a process of "imported" or endogenous modernization had already been initiated or not, defining what Malek Bennabi[3]—and Habib Bourguiba[4] after him—once dubbed their degree of "colonizability."

The differences also result from the relative length and institutional form of the colonial presence, as well as from the distinctive methods and ambitions of French, Italian, and British colonial powers and their respective cultural traditions.[5] On this ground, national differences are complex and polymorphous, the violence of colonial de-culturation giving way to a highly differentiated acculturation, depending on whether the colonizer was French or British: an Islamist intellectual "manufactured" against the foil of French colonization, like Malek Bennabi, who drew widely on the resources of Cartesian thought, substantially differed from his Libyan or Egyptian counterpart, whose intellectual "foil" was by no means comparable.

Local historical settings also play an essential role, and they have often been clearly distinct from one country to another. The French colonial presence was initiated in Algeria by a war of conquest, both long (1830–1849) and particularly devastating (like the war waged by fascist

Italy in Libya). In Syria and in Lebanon, on the other hand, it began under the aegis of an international mandate and by using less systematically destructive methods, though hardly peaceful and respectful of human rights.[6] The length of this colonial presence has also significantly varied: from 132 years in the case of France in Algeria or 128 years for the British in Aden and in all or part of South Yemen to the 26 years of the mandates over Syria and Lebanon or the 75 and 44 years of the French protectorate in Tunisia and Morocco.

At the other end of the Arab-Muslim spectrum, since the departure of the Ottomans in 1918, North Yemen has remained free of all Western inroads. Arabia itself has undergone all sorts of external pressure but no direct colonization; as in North Yemen, the vectors of modernization there apparently have not been as naturally susceptible of being identified with those of the domination of a foreign state.

Next the institutional basis and methods of the colonial powers have played a decisive role. The formulas have, in this field too, significantly varied: in Algeria, a colonization of settlement entailed massive confiscation of the land of the native populations, whose territory was simply politically and administratively annexed to that of the Republic;[7] in contrast, in the protectorates of South Yemen,[8] the British influence was infinitely less strong, often limited to the control of commercial and strategic movements, without directly affecting social hierarchies and cultural practices. Unlike colonization, the formula of the protectorate preserved a possibility of identifying with an authority (bey, sultan), which, even if weakened, was nonetheless symbolically autochthonous. Some colonial actors (Louis Hubert Gonsalve Lyautey in Morocco) chose to assure their power by relying on the existing, notably religious, local elites, whereas others (Thomas-Robert Bugeaud in Algeria) systematically destroyed the latter in order to manufacture mere subordinates entirely devoted to their cause.

After the modalities of colonization, it was the policies of the pro-independence elites which bestowed its national specificities on the Islamist field.[9] From the outset of the nationalist struggle and, even more markedly, following independence, the institutional basis and posture of the regimes in the cultural and religious fields contributed to producing complex configurations, along whose fault-lines the differentials in the potential for Islamist mobilization have progressively deepened. These differentials can be identified by showing how far such nationalist elites have succeeded in fulfilling the expectations in terms of identity of the beneficiaries of "independence" or on the contrary partly left them unsatisfied.

First, the linguistic policies have varied from one country to the next, depending on whether the Arabic language and Arab culture were maintained or reasserted during the march to independence (Libya, Egypt, etc.) or, on the contrary, the Francophone world kept the upper hand (Tunisia, Morocco). Then the reference to Arab ethnic affiliation was diversely brought into play by the newly independent regimes. In contrast to the Algerian Houari Boumediene, the Tunisian Habib Bourguiba was no doubt the leader who retained the most reserve toward it, for, in his opinion, Arabism gave umbrage to the independence and the centrality of his role as the hymnist of "Tunisianness" and might have provided a pretext for intervention to the young Egyptian rival he particularly feared.[10] More clearly still, Bourguiba attacked those of his opponents who were renowned for wanting to assert the Arab and Muslim identity of their country more strongly than he did himself.[11] In Syria, Iraq, Libya, and Egypt,[12] the greater role played by the Arab ethnic reference helped to limit that of the other endogenous, "religious" and Islamic reference.[13] In Libya, the secularism, asserted in particular to combat the vestiges of religious allegiance to the monarchy of the Sanusi brotherhood, was partly compensated by a Pan-Arabist overbid, in both the linguistic-cultural (no Latin script and no translation into any Western language allowed in public places) and political fields, in order to serve Arab unification.[14]

Even more substantial differences were molded by the way in which regimes established themselves institutionally in the religious field. The "state fundamentalism" (meaning the capacity for the holders of power to corner most of the resources of re-Islamization, to the detriment of their opponents) of a Moroccan "commander of the faithful" or of a Saudi monarch, heir to and ally of Wahhabi reformism, contributed, at least for a while, to limiting the protest potential of re-Islamization. All the monarchies (in the Persian Gulf and Jordan) have tended to protect themselves from Baathism and Nasserism by backing the opponents of these ideologies (including the Muslim Brothers). Conversely, the more or less openly secular republics (South Yemen, Tunisia, Libya) have more systematically constrained the political space of the religious reference. Where conservative monarchs could aspire, up to a certain point, "to exploit" the demand for re-Islamization and divert part of its resources to the advantage of their power, Bourguiba, with his openly secular or even irreligious discourse, accepted the risk of depriving himself of these resources. The *mujahid "al-akbar"* (the "supreme" combatant, an adjective which religious terminology normally reserves for the Creator) was undoubtedly the leader who went the furthest in distancing his political discourse from the symbolic categories of the Islamic heritage, thus providing the Islamist generation of his opponents with an undeniable advantage.

Within the aforementioned limits, the additional effect of the economic variable in protest mobilizations has also increased national differences. The abilities of the regimes to reallocate resources, significantly higher for those who benefited from oil revenue, have obviously affected their capacity to "buy" political consensus, at least partly (and for some, like the oil-rich emirates of the Gulf, completely and to this day), and thus to protect themselves from the protest potential mobilized in re-Islamization.

POLITICAL FORMULAS BETWEEN DOMESTIC INTRANSIGENCE AND FOREIGN CONCESSIONS

The other "national" parameters are the product of the differential between the specific political formulas of each state, on the one hand, and between their respective positions in the regional or international arena, facing the challenge of Israel and the rise of American unilateralism, on the other. In many respects, Arab regimes get the (Islamist) opponents "that they deserve": their own performances in the democratic arena have indeed very widely influenced their opponents' modes of action. From the Gulf to the ocean, the political formulas subsequent to independence and the degree and forms of the manifestations of authoritarianism on the part of these regimes are not all identical. Except for a few exceptions to this quasi "Arab institutional norm," however, most of them firmly bar Islamist oppositions, and in particular the Muslim Brothers, from any participation in electoral competition, even when considerably disconnected from any real political stake.[15]

If all these itineraries have today led to a generally shared authoritarianism, the differences are nevertheless salient, both in the pace of the repressive radicalization of the regimes and in their final posture. The imaginary and behavior patterns of the Islamist actors definitely bear their mark. Very early on, the regimes (notably Tunisia and Morocco) that never acquired, as in the case of the Algerian NLF, the monopoly on the resources of the national struggle had to come to political terms of transaction with their opponents. These took on different forms: trade unionism or professional associations (Tunisia), formal pluralism (Morocco, Tunisia, Egypt), and all kinds of associative action. However narrow the limits of the electoral procedure (often marred by vote-rigging) and of the actual powers assigned to the parliamentary oppositions, today a small number of Arab countries nevertheless authorize participation of real political forces: this is the case of Yemen, where the president of the parliament originates from the Islamist party close to the Muslim Brothers,[16] but also that of Lebanon, where Hizb Allah is represented in parliament, and even Jordan, Kuwait, and Bahrain. It will no doubt be true someday of Iraq.[17] As already stated, the conservative regimes tended to tolerate and partly integrate their "religious" opponents, while the Nasserist republics set about criminalizing, torturing, and therefore radicalizing them very early on. Generally speaking, the regimes which, as in Algeria or in Egypt, acquired a quasi-monopoly on "revolutionary" or nationalist resources have tended to hold onto exclusionary political formulas longer.

However that may be, at the beginning of the 1980s nothing could have contrasted more strongly than, on the one hand, the political imaginary of a Jordanian Muslim Brother who had lived since the beginning of the 1950s in peaceful coexistence with the Hashemite throne and that of one of his Egyptian "brothers" who had spent the same period undergoing torture in Nasser's jails, on the other. The state of mind of a Syrian Muslim Brother, after the terrifying repression of the city of Hama under heavy artillery fire from the Alawi Syrian regime in 1982,[18] was just as far removed from that of a Yemeni Brother, after a long spell of cooperation, starting in the same year a period of very temperate opposition to a regime where ideas such as his own were widely represented—but more of that later.

The involvement of states, or of individuals, with or without the consent of such states, in regional conflicts subsequently deepened important differences by initiating or accelerating various dynamic processes, among which the militarization of opposition movements was not the most important—the forces deployed on international battlefields (Palestine, Iraq, Lebanon, Yemen, and, of course, Afghanistan, Bosnia, Chechnya) not being systematically mobilized against the ruling elites in the countries the "Jihadis" originated from. Generally speaking, we can consider that every time an Arab regime gave in to the pressures of the Western environment—European, Israeli, or American—this sparked off a "domestic" popular protest which has since then most frequently been taken up by the Islamist generation. Differences have therefore arisen within the Islamist field, depending on the posture of regimes in the international arena and their variably assertive capacity to resist for a more or less lengthy period the pressures of the international environment. After independence, the regimes of the countries of "the rejectionist front," which accepted a certain margin of tension with the Western environment, and countries of "the battlefield," in armed confrontation with Israel, paid a price in the international arena, in terms of American or European pressure, but accrued domestic resources in terms of legitimacy.

The Israeli-Palestinian conflict has therefore had a massive and systematic influence on the destiny of Islamist movements located in the "battlefield countries" and decisively contributed to the varying degrees of their relations with the ruling elites and their own capacity to mobilize. First and foremost in Egypt, of course, but also in Lebanon and Jordan, Nasser's defeat in 1967 had been a rallying cry for the revival of Islamist mobilization almost everywhere. From the creation of Israel in 1948 to the Oslo Accords in 1993 or the first of the Sharm el-Sheikh summits in 1996, all these turning points in the Palestinian conflict—that is to say, above all, during that period, setbacks to Arab diplomacy and thus to Arab regimes—have set the pulse of national Islamist mobilization.

The political identity of the Egyptian Muslim Brothers was indeed not only formed against the foil of the British colonial presence but just as much in reaction to the creation of the state of Israel and the ensuing first Israeli-Arab conflict. The Brothers were then to play, in particular through the Muslim scouts, a front-line role. The particular virulence manifested against them, to this day, by a section of the Western media influenced by Israel is probably not foreign to this founding event. The birth and the radicalization of other Egyptian movements (notably the Jamaa Islamiyya, which, at least temporarily, supported Anwar Sadat, the victor of the Yom Kippur war) are directly linked to the concessions which, in their view, he later made by signing the Camp David accords in 1978. Similarly, the Lebanese Hizb Allah was created in 1982 in response to the invasion of Lebanon by Israel.[19] The emergence of the Palestinian Jihad and that of Hamas were also direct expressions of the resistance to this occupation.[20]

THE FACTORS OF TRANSNATIONAL INTEGRATION

However, several dynamics have obviously tended to limit the scope of these national parameters. The "Islamist frontiers" of states have tended to be relativized as the circulation of individuals, not to mention information and ideas, has developed and accelerated and as the intellectual and ideological but also tactical and strategic dynamics of transnationalization, or even globalization, have consequently grown stronger.

In the Muslim world as elsewhere, the main factors in harmonizing the Islamist reference have been well documented. Pilgrimages—and not only to Mecca—were historically, with trade routes, the very first; more recently, economic, political, and student migrations and tourist flows have developed. Being, generally speaking, a pioneer, Egyptian Islamism widely exported first the model of the Brotherhood then that of Qutb. Conversely, temporarily influenced by the Brothers, Saudi Arabia itself has probably influenced the Islamist movements by exporting, particularly to Egypt, with or without the Wahhabi logo, a certain Salafi "reaction" to the relative hegemony of the model of the Brothers.[21]

Historically speaking, the Egyptian Brothers, who very rapidly set up an international branch, outgrew the borders of Egypt as early as 1948, as noted above, in order to participate in the first Arab war against Israel. But their first mass exile was the result of Nasser's repression in 1954. This episode constitutes the archetype of this kind of Islamist "migration."[22] At the time, the Brothers left in great droves first for Saudi Arabia and the Gulf then for North Africa (notably Algeria, where they were employed to "Arabize" higher education from 1973 onward), but also for Yemen, where, besides their direct political role, their influence was due to their massive presence, alongside Sudanese primary school teachers, in the educational system. The Brothers from then on significantly and durably influenced, notably by means of education, the alchemy of the nascent Islamist movements regionwide and, as will be seen below, the "endogenous" modernization of the political reference. But Egypt has not only exported *ulama*s and teachers: it has also "imported" thousands of Arab and Muslim students into the religious universities of al-Azhar and especially Dar al-'Ulum.

Since the 1980s, Islamist guerrilla forces have also fueled transnational armed mobilizations, for which the Afghan episode provided the first benchmark. In the same register, Bosnia,[23] Kosovo, and Chechnya successively unfolded. Then the fresh waves of repression in the 1990s (notably in Algeria and Tunisia) boosted the flow of political exiles. The major importance of this phenomenon cannot be overemphasized: as the authoritarian Arab regimes got closer to the "Western bloc" to secure their survival, they toughened up the crackdown on "their" national Islamist movements—here the Algerian general "eradicators" probably deserve the prize for ferocity and manipulative perversity. And thus they helped to fuel a global diaspora which has been one of the breeding grounds for the radical offshoots of the "al-Qaeda generation"—even though many such exiles are far from identifying themselves as such.

Finally, since the middle of the 1990s, the impact of these human, economic, political, or revolutionary migrations has been powerfully relayed by the penetration of new communication technologies: from satellite channels to the Internet, via teleconferencing,[24] they have accelerated the pace and amplified the process of interconnectedness, which in turn has helped to limit the impact of particularistic national identity and confer on contemporary Islamism its "global" character.[25]

FOUR

RED SEA SECRETS OR ISLAMISM
WITHOUT COLONIZATION

Everywhere in the Arab world, disciples of Hassan al-Banna have tried to reassert the presence of Islam in their respective Constitutions; in Yemen, conversely, they have helped to introduce the Constitution within Islam.

—MOHAMED QAHTAN, ONE OF THE LEADERS OF THE YEMENI
UNION FOR REFORM (2003)

The case of the Arabian Peninsula, the cradle of al-Qaeda, fully testifies to this gradual disappearance of national specificities to the benefit of a transnationalization of political imaginaries. In most of Yemen and in Saudi Arabia, the Islamist movements indeed emerged within a space on the whole sheltered from direct colonial pressure, which is a major characteristic in regard to the modalities of the first temporality of Islamism.[1]

Born in 1962 in Sanaa, on a territory often compared to "tribal Afghanistan" or described as the "Tibet of the Red Sea," the Arab Republic of Yemen took over from a religious (Zaydi Shiite) monarchy, which, after its victory over the moribund Ottoman Empire in 1918, had succeeded in protecting itself from any foreign inroads. In all of North Yemen,[2] as modernization could not be related to a foreign presence, Islamists should theoretically have no incentive to claim some "restoration of a symbolic universe" of which they had purportedly been dispossessed and to be seeking their ideological underpinnings, as naturally as their Algerian or Tunisian counterparts did, along the lines of a critique of modernization experienced as synonymous with "de-Islamization."

The main hypothesis which I have always put forward is that the more violent cultural "de-Islamization" has been, the stronger the subsequent propensity to reject the transplant, and the higher the potential for Islamist mobilization. However, in the course of a highly atypical history, the Yemeni and Saudi Islamist movements have indeed represented, as elsewhere in the region, the front-line opposition forces. What clarification can Yemen and, to a certain degree, Saudi Arabia bring to our understanding of the "universality" of this sort of mobilization? Why have these two countries, which were not brought to heel by direct Western colonization, nevertheless become important "radical Islamist-producing" countries, together providing the main contingent of members of the September 11 commandos? How has Islamism here developed outside the purview of the anticolonial dialectic? Have the Islamisms of the Peninsula inherited any specificity from this fact? What lessons are there to be drawn from this peninsular singularity?

NOT SO INSULAR A PENINSULA

The main answer emerges quite clearly if we break down the temporality of Islamist mobilization according to the three historical sequences already posited above.

First, if the history of the Peninsula has been written without the formal presence of the ingredients specific to the first temporality of the colonial face-off, considerable outside influence nonetheless affected these two countries during this period. We should therefore modify the representation of societies which, because they were not colonized, allegedly have only experienced a purely endogenous modernization, consequently circumventing the "deculturation" syndrome. The absence of colonization in the North is first of all considerably qualified by the fact that Yemeni society, since the 1990 reunification, has been the product of convergence with the southern part of the country, which had indeed been colonized for almost 130 years. In the South, the People's Democratic Republic emerged, in 1967, from a nationalist struggle against the British Empire, which had occupied Aden and then its hinterland from 1839 to 1967. This South does not therefore depart to any significant degree from the colonial paradigm. Open to world information flows, like any great port on the route to India after the opening of the Suez Canal, the People's Democratic Republic of Yemen was furthermore, after Independence in 1967, one of the only regimes in the Muslim world to have explicitly implemented the Marxist reference.

Long before the 1990 reunification, the society of the North, fragmentary and isolated as it may have been, was already in contact, notably because of the high rate of migratory flows, with this "British" South, populated by a massive influx of its own migrants, with whom family links had always been maintained. The society of the North was subsequently, through vectors other than the British presence, subjected to Western influence. The Young Turks, the representatives of an Ottoman Empire which even though on the decline was nonetheless the bearer of profound reforms, were probably the first mediators of these European-influenced *tanzimat* (reforms). Such actors of an "imported" modernization were in a significant way denounced by the "nationalist" and religious resistance led by Yahya Muhammad Hamid ed-Din, known as Imam Yahya (ruled 1904–1948), as vulgar disbelievers, accused of "wearing trousers" and imbibing fermented beverages.

Most of the modernizations—not only technological but intellectual and political—which had not been introduced by the Ottomans arrived via Aden. One of the most important was certainly the experimental creation of a modern school directly inspired by Adeni practices by Ahmad Muhammad Nu'man in 1936, south of Taez.[3] The exchanges of students and "technical aid" which Imam Yahya gradually organized with Lebanon and Iraq, then with Egypt, after being forced to recognize, in 1934, the technological backwardness of his troops defeated by his rival 'Abd al-'Aziz ibn 'Abd al-Rahman al-Saud, were the first channels for Arab and foreign intellectual influence. This intellectual modernization prepared the way for the 1948 constitutional revolution, launched by the "Free Yemeni" movement,[4] exiled to Aden but also very close to the Egyptian reformists, especially to Hassan al-Banna's Muslim Brothers.

Beginning in the 1950s, the Muslim reformists lost some ground to Nasserists and Baathists who started competing with them.[5] The Yemeni students enrolled at al-Azhar or at Dar al-'Ulum and then, more and more directly, the written press and the radio waves of the "Voice of the Arabs" broadcast the new ideas. The republican revolution, fueled by the opposition to change and the authoritarianism of the Imamite regime of Ahmad ibn Yahya (ruled 1948–1962), the son and successor of Yahya, would, however, never have taken place as early as 1962, at a time when Muhammad al-Badr, very much the liberal, had just succeeded his father, Ahmad, if Gamal 'Abd al-Nasser, backed and armed by the USSR, had not sought to thwart the political and ideological ambitions of his Saudi competitors and of their American and British sponsors in the south of the Peninsula.

This problematic, which sets the absence of the colonial syndrome sharply into perspective, can, for the most part, be extended to Saudi Arabia itself, where the importance of foreign influences, expanding exponentially from the Ottoman presence to the second Gulf war, has been even greater. Pascal Ménoret has brilliantly demonstrated that the idea of Saudi society allegedly remaining immune from colonial intrusion must indeed be highly qualified.[6] Even if the British did not consider it important enough to colonize, Arabia lived under a colonial-type order, which was actually handed down through three successive titleholders. This "colonization" was first Ottoman, whether in the form of military interventions in the heartland of the Najd from 1818 until the mid-twentieth century or, more frequently, in the form of subsidies paid out to traditional elites, in order to remotely control them as surely as any occupation in due form might have done. Consequently, the colonization was British, before becoming American.

These successive dominations, however atypical in form, were also perfectly functional. After an elusive British protectorate (1915–1927), first British and American diplomats and secret agents and then American oil executives of the Aramco "state" played, until belated nationalization in 1988, the role played elsewhere by more costly colonial state machinery.

The ingredients of the Islamist recipe proper to the second and third temporalities, which witnessed the multiplication of the cultural, economic, then political or even military concessions of the ruling elites to the Western environment, have brought the configuration of the Peninsula closer to that of the rest of the Arab world, when they have not been even more deeply implicated, as in Saudi Arabia under American tutelage. Partially shielded from the norm of colonial acculturation because they had not undergone the implementation of such domination by a foreign state, the countries of the Peninsula, as we will see below, can by no means be exempted from the general explanatory matrix of contemporary Islamism.

YEMEN AND SAUDI ARABIA FACING WASHINGTON OR THE END OF PENINSULAR EXCEPTIONALITY

In Yemen as in Arabia, the partial absence or atypical characteristics of the temporality of the colonial confrontation has been in a way compensated by the very specific configurations of the following two temporalities, where the different forms of foreign pressure were all the more self-evident in that these societies had formerly been less directly exposed to them.

In Yemen, in 1962 (as had also been the case in 1948), the catalyst of "revolutionary modernization" was to originate from a foreign capital, Cairo, the city of the "secular Arab nationalist" Gamal 'Abd al-Nasser, then committed to a violent repressive campaign against the Muslim Brothers. The revolution was even sparked off by Nasser himself. Moreover, he did not even take the time to inform the leaders of the Free Yemenis exiled in Cairo and was not loath to set his face against the opinion of his military intermediaries in Sanaa, the Yemeni "Free Officers." The latter actually were afraid, as in 1948, of suffering the vindictive fury of tribes in the habit of disowning any intervention perceived as "foreign." It was again Nasser who, at the cost of prolonged military presence and under considerable duress, ensured the subsequent survival of the new regime until the 1970 pact that put an end to the civil war. Through proxy elements in the military or sworn henchmen ('Abd Allah Sallal, of "humble origin," or 'Abd al-Rahman Baydani, "born of an Egyptian mother and an unknown father," as their adversaries, including the cofounder of the Free Officers, Ahmad Muhammad Nu'man, delighted in describing them), it was again Nasser, until the June 1967 debacle, who was actually to rule, almost absolutely, over the republic born on the territories of the ancient kingdom of the Queen of Sheba.

A highly emblematic episode provides an opportunity to assess the vigor of this custodianship: when it became apparent to his advisor for Yemeni affairs, a certain Anwar al-Sadat, that the government of the country was toying with the idea of emancipation, Nasser (in September 1966) purely and simply locked up the sixty members of the governmental and diplomatic delegation who had just arrived in Cairo by special plane, including the whole government. Ahmad Muhammad Nu'man, whom he considered responsible for this fantasy of emancipation on the part of his protégés, spent more than a year in jail![7] The consequences of this brutal—and armed—interference by Nasserism in the political imaginary of the North, both before and after the 1962 revolution, should therefore not be underestimated.

If the first of the three "temporalities," the colonial confrontation, is partially missing from Yemeni and Saudi Islamist chronology, the actors of the second temporality definitely underwent a situation comparable to those of territories that had suffered from colonization. At the beginning of the 1960s, memoirs from North Yemen provide accounts of some episodes closely akin to those that citizens of the most secular republics have experienced. Even if the establishment of the Arab Republic of Yemen in 1962 benefited from the support of the Muslim Brothers, and the most radical Nasserist wing was defeated, the fall of the monarchy was indeed felt by many to be the beginning of an intolerable decline in the religious reference. Indeed, the fall of a Zaydi Imamate perceived above all as religious does seem to have legitimized, at least momentarily, the rise of an openly antireligious attitude within certain circles of power.[8] The denunciation of the practice of prayer in some educational institutions, the neglect or even prohibition of the cult in military academies, and the Nasserist ring of political discourse during the first years of the North Yemen Republic obviously introduced a certain disruption in the symbolic continuum.

In the South, during the same period, after Independence in 1967, the problematic of "de-Islamization" was at work, of course, in a more conventional way, despite strong popular resistance on this terrain. The "partisans of Islam" were more or less marginalized from the public sphere and from political representation. The *awqaf* (foundations whose management traditionally guaranteed their resources to religious institutions) came under government control. Typically, the cults of the saints of Sufi brotherhoods were promoted, according to the logic of "retraditionalization" of religious practice supposed to preempt or slow down its oppositional "politicization." Under the influence of the Soviet older brother, civil legislation was strongly "secularized," the wearing of the veil being notably combated throughout the civil service. A section of the religious elites then chose to go into exile toward the North or to Arabia.[9]

In Saudi Arabia, behind the screen of "state fundamentalism," an evolution not unconnected with what was occurring in North Yemen took place. King Saud and King Faisal hired and promoted technocrats educated in the Western style and gradually relegated the *ulama*s to the background to perform purely honorary duties.

The "correct" functioning of the Islamist paradigm in an environment which has not suffered from the impact of colonialism is consequently to be explained in the same way as the presence of some degree of Western modernity in a country which has not been in direct contact with the initial producer of this modernity. Despite the slow pace at which this modernization has been imported, albeit by Arab mediators, the alchemy of the Islamist "reaction" has nonetheless occurred. The third temporality was to "perfect" and accelerate the return of the Peninsula to the mainstream of regional history. Confronted with the interventionist and hegemonic outreach of American superpower, the peninsular itineraries not only have reverted to the mainstream of the history of Islamist mobilization but also have acquired exemplary status therein.

With the second Gulf war, it was indeed in the military register that, only two years after the nationalization of Aramco (in 1988), whose scope it significantly reduced, the irruption of the American imperial order in the Peninsula was manifested. The Saudi princes, fearing for their throne, at that time accepted the insistent invitation of the United States to provide funding for the campaign for the liberation of Kuwait and the subsequent installation of American troops on their territory. We know the decisive role that this episode was to play in the emergence of Islamist protest and spiraling governmental repression.

Yemen was not spared by this situation. As early as 1990, accused of supporting Saddam Hussein's camp, it was brutally ostracized by Washington and its allies, the oil-rich monarchies. The consequences of this financial boycott were tragic for the economy of a country which had just entered the trials and tribulations of reunification: a million emigrant workers were expelled from Saudi Arabia, triggering a terrible economic and social crisis which the country has not fully recovered from fifteen years later. After September 11, American pressure became more direct, Washington by then having taken on the task of "normalizing" Yemen.[10] Arabia and Yemen thus converged at the core of the effects of American unilateralism, with a part of their inhabitants fully reintegrating the "universality" of the Islamist rebellion against what was seen as illegitimate foreign custodianship.

Yemen, formerly the least autocratic of the region's regimes, thus tended irresistibly to join the ranks of the supporters of the "Arab political formula." Its "normalization" was undeniably the direct cause of the crackdown launched, in June 2004, against the partisans of Hussein Badr al-Din al-Huthi, which represented the first major rift in the long-standing transactional status quo between the Islamists and President Saleh's rule.[11] American pressure in Yemen may thus be undermining the subtle balancing act of the transactions among the authorities, the Islamists, and the tribes, which had long been the key to the political stability of the country, enabling it to obviate the tensions inherent in the policies of repression or even eradication of the Islamist generation.[12]

As in Riyad, the regime of Sanaa is today being forced to make security-oriented and diplomatic concessions which are weakening its ideological and political credibility in the face of its opposition. This no doubt facilitates the growing identification of public opinion with the line of "Islamic" resistance, of which Osama Bin Laden, one of Yemen's sons who migrated toward the Saudi North, is emblematic.

The Islamist reaction to the "malfunctions" of a process of "Western-

ization" perceived as threatening Muslim cultural and political affiliation may well therefore have been in a certain sense "imported" into the
Peninsula as it gradually emerged from a status at least partially protected from direct Western pressure. Political globalization has, it may
be said, set back the historical clock by exporting there the reactive dynamics from which it had been preserved for a time. Despite displaying less apparent cultural causalities, due to the absence of "colonial de-
Islamization," Islamist mobilization in the Peninsula has been fueled by
an increasingly "universal" perception, throughout the Muslim world,
of the reality and the cultural, but also economic and political, impact
of Western hegemony. In the course of this globalization of representations, the political imaginary of Yemenis and Saudis quickly became
attuned to the major mobilizations and great regionwide and worldwide
ideological tensions.

THE MUSLIM BROTHERS THROUGH
THE LOOKING GLASS OF YEMEN

Even when fused into the mainstream of the identity problematic, the
trajectories of Islamism in Yemen nonetheless shed new light. The dynamics of re-Islamization, notably as implemented by the Muslim
Brothers, in the very specific context of a society which had not formerly
been . . . de-Islamized, have in fact been closely associated with those of
modernization, that is, the advent of new forms of political organization
(and primarily the adoption of a Constitution), but also the transcending
of barriers erected by the primary identities inherent in social hierarchy
or in sectarian divides.

In Yemen, the Muslim Brothers, under the direct impetus of Hassan
al-Banna, were indeed the active promoters of the introduction of constitutionalism into Islamic thought and therefore of the modernization
of that thought.[13] But, in this domain, the lesson of Yemen does not end
there. When, in 1948, they wanted to introduce the constitutional reference into the institutional and doctrinal fabric of the Imamate, the representatives of the Egyptian organization and their Yemeni allies were
themselves rejected by the traditional political society as unbearably
"foreign," just as the Young Turks, though also "Muslims," had been, for
different but not completely incommensurable reasons.

A threefold conclusion can be drawn from this episode. First, the confirmation that the Egyptian Muslim Brothers, the "founding fathers" of contemporary Islamism, have not reneged on the modernizing legacy of the groundbreaking reformists who inspired them and certainly have not broken off or "regressed" with regard to them, as so many of their recent contemporaries, despite very early warnings against such simplifications, have written.[14] The attitude of Yemen's modernizing intelligentsia toward Hassan al-Banna's envoys is from this viewpoint highly significant: between Abduh, Kawakibi,[15] and al-Banna, the Free Yemenis did not perceive any of the frontiers so complacently drawn today by those who defend the idea of a radical opposition between their thought and that of their reformist predecessors.

When, as in Egypt, their thought was preceded by the emergence of political modernization, the Muslim Brothers indeed tried to "Islamize" it and reintegrate the Islamic reference into the universe of modern constitutionalism—which was to lead some observers, confusing form and contents, to think that it was they who were rejecting this modernization. Yemen as a field of study provides striking proof that history is radically more complex: when the same Egyptian Muslim Brothers, at the end of their own confrontation with political modernization, found themselves in Yemen facing a political system devoid of all modernization, they became the architects of the legitimization of such modernization and not at all the extollers of its rejection.

It is to this Yemeni lesson that the "Islamist" Mohamed Qahtan, an executive of the Islah party, points when, with a view to specifying the historical itinerary of modernization in Yemen, he explains: "Everywhere in the Arab world, the disciples of Hassan al-Banna have sought to reassert the presence of Islam in [. . .] Constitutions," whereas, "in Yemen, conversely, they have helped to introduce a Constitution within Islam."[16] In both cases, their attitude, poles apart from the traditional posture, has had the impact of establishing constitutionalism as a modernized form of politics.

The second methodological conclusion is probably even more important. The "religious" discourse does not necessarily amount to "tradition" or to endogenous forms of inherited culture: it can be the vehicle of all sorts of dynamics, including modernizing or even revolutionary departures. In the thought of the Muslim Brothers in particular, and in the Islamist mobilization in general, Western opinion tends generally to neglect the political dimension and overemphasize the religious dimension. Conversely, whole sections of Yemeni traditional society then perceived their thought as aiming "to introduce politics into the religious to the detriment of the latter" and hence as suffering from a deficit of religiosity. They then proceeded to reject it as such.

Before 1948 Imam Yahya did not have any difficulty in disqualifying the discourse of the Muslim Brothers and passing its authors off as wanting to "summarize" (and so drastically cut) the Quran. For Westerners, the Muslim Brothers have (to this day) remained illegitimate, as they have reasserted the place of the religious reference in the political field and thereby undermined the autonomy of politics; conversely, for the Yemenis of 1948, opposed to the modernizing reforms of the "Free Officers," these same Brothers, "Muslims" though they might be, appeared, together with their constitutional reform, to be illegitimate because their assertion of the autonomy of politics was to the detriment of the centrality of the religious reference. The same was true in 1962, when the military coup, deprived of popular support, only succeeded thanks to the massive support of Nasser's Egypt.

The thought of the Brothers, "religious" though it may have been, has therefore twice been disqualified by a section of the social and political fabric of Yemen as . . . a vehicle of modernizing rupture.[17] The third conclusion, however obvious the thesis that it confirms may be, is the message to reformers and even politicians of all persuasions which the double failure of the Yemeni revolution highlights. The best causes, handicapped by a deficit in communication, can provoke "irrational" rejection by their potential beneficiaries. The repeated lesson of the two successive failures of the Yemeni revolutions of 1948 and 1962 is clear: when the political vocabulary cuts itself off from the symbolic universe of the intuitive cultural matrix, the locomotive of modernization runs the risk of parting company with the rolling stock of the society which it intends to transform. It is this thesis which was adopted by Mahmud Zubayri, one of the co-founders of the Free Officers, whose experience lies at the heart of the Yemeni "demonstration."

In 1962 the Free Officers, initially defeated when they had wanted to reform the Imamate in 1948, feared a repetition, as they were having such a hard time in containing the royalist counterrevolution, strongly rooted in the social fabric. Zubayri, at the time probably marginalized in part because of his proximity to the Muslim Brothers, observed that Yemen's Islamist modernists had just failed once again to mobilize the rural population against a monarchy which everyone nonetheless agreed should be recognized as a dictatorship. Despite—or perhaps because of—the indispensable military support of their Egyptian allies, the Republic (*jumhuriya*), which many from the countryside considered to be merely "Nasser's wife," was confronted with a growing disaffection of the tribes (that is, the majority of rural society), and the Free Officers anticipated that another searing political and military failure was on its way. "Why have Yemen's two revolutions successively failed?" the disaffected revolutionary then wondered. The answer he saw emerging was clear: the "modernists," because they distanced themselves from the most intuitive version of the religious language, were paying the price, through their isolation, for not respecting a universal law of political mobilization.

In 1964, witnessing a dangerous crumbling of the foundations of the republican regime of ʿAbd Allah al-Sallal, Zubayri resigned from his ministerial post and set out, accompanied by a few close friends (one of whom was ʿAbd al-Majid Zindani, future leader of the Muslim Brothers' Islah party), to meet the powerful tribes at the periphery of Sanaa. In order to avoid repeating the past mistakes in communication, he decided this time that the ideological platform of the reconciliation between tribes and republican "modernists," between rural society and urban elite, was to be called neither more nor less than . . . Hizb Allah, the "Party of God."[18] Thanks to the lessons of his double failure, his intention was to appeal to the resources of the most traditional culture of the tribes and discard the modernist shortcut which had led to their uprising against the first generation of reformists. The gradual rallying of the tribes was to prove him right.

More than ever, before being divine, the law "of God" was thus, in Yemen as everywhere else, "endogenous."

FIVE

THE BROTHERS AND THE SALAFIS

*Between Modernization and Literalism, with or
without Radicalization*

In the Muslim world, even those who show empathy with the anger of partisans of direct action and might in case of need lend their support to armed struggle would not necessarily endorse the simplistic dichotomy of the theology of war of Osama Bin Laden or Ayman al-Zawahiri. Anti-Western resentment in general, and anti-American and anti-Israeli *Schadenfreude* in particular, is certainly widespread enough among contemporary Islamist movements. But the essentialist "confessionalization" through which al-Qaeda's discourse tends to account for the causalities, the legitimacy, and the modes of expression of the Islamist backlash is not necessarily shared by all, by a long shot.

Consequently, on this ground, the supporters of al-Qaeda actually only represent one faction among the actors of a dynamic intellectual and political development, and their isolation, though relative, may legitimately be emphasized: they amount to no more than one of the components of a highly diversified Islamist field, which is in constant evolution.

From Bin Laden's Afghan allies, the Taliban—fallen, but not necessarily unpopular in all the rural areas which they formerly managed[1]— to Turkey's Prime Minister Erdogan, to the leader of the Moroccan Party for Justice and Development and the president of Yemen's parliament, to the Lebanese militants of Hassan Nasrallah's Shiite Hizb Allah,[2] Fathi Yakan's Sunni movement,[3] and the Party of Islamic Liberation (founded in 1952 in Jordan by Taqi al-Din al-Nabhani, to restore the caliphate), the dynamic of re-Islamization has split the political field into various trends with well-asserted ideological differences: its supporters today have recourse to the whole gamut of classical modes of political action. And in their vast majority they actively participate in the processes of modernization and development of their respective societies and, more widely, of the surrounding world.

In order to avoid slipping into the very reductionism which we have been doing our best to denounce, it is clear that there can be no question here of presenting them in all their diversity. Each national situation would indeed require a substantial monograph. At the most, we should emphasize the danger of allowing an expression, politically radical but also in a sectarian breach with the general surge of political modernization, to confiscate the total visibility of a dynamic which is certainly not reducible to it.

THE MUSLIM BROTHERS AND THE "ENDOGENOUS" REHABILITATION OF MODERNIZATION

The movements which have been influenced from their outset by the groundbreaking thought of the Muslim Brothers, whether or not organically linked to the Egyptian center and whether they claim this influence or not, can probably be considered to wield the greatest influence in most of the Sunni Muslim world to this day.[4] The great founding themes of al-Banna's thought are still relevant everywhere, even if the logics of modernization and of "nationalization" throughout the Muslim world and the tensions inherent in the intellectual and political self-affirmation of Muslims living in Western countries with a Christian tradition almost everywhere indeed tend to call into question or place in a new perspective the hegemony or even the political and doctrinal centrality of this founding Egyptian nucleus.

Globally speaking, in most of the countries where it has legal existence, the movement of the Brothers, in the wider sense of the term, remains, however, the matrix of Islamist parliamentary opposition. This centrality is all the more easily attested by the polls because its main Islamist challenger, the Salafi trend, generally does not seek to turn out and compete with it in this arena. It is also attested by the fact that all regimes (Morocco, Tunisia, Egypt, Syria) living in fear of the electoral verdict significantly prefer to deny the Brothers access to the electoral scene. Nevertheless, they are often present there, even under assumed names (Morocco, Egypt, Yemen, Kuwait, Algeria),[5] and have been associated, to varying degrees, with the duties of government in several countries (Yemen, Jordan, and, outside the Arab world, Turkey). By accepting the rules of the parliamentary system, they have clearly broken with the literal reading of classical Islamic political thought, having *de facto* been the main architects of its endogenous modernization in the Muslim world. Essentially, they have indeed clearly joined the camp of those who endorse the principle and the demands of the secularization of politics and its autonomization.

It is by no means their statements, nor those of their attorneys, which serve to demonstrate this, but rather the violence with which the Egyptian Sayyid Qutb and his disciples enacted their rupture with them, in particular Ayman al-Zawahiri's virulent attacks on the record of actions carried out by Hassan al-Banna's disciples since their creation in 1928. It was in his book *The Bitter Harvest: Sixty Years of the Muslim Brothers*,[6] published in 1988, that the man who has become al-Qaeda's number two drew up his final indictment. There are several ways of selecting and above all reading and interpreting the texts by al-Qaeda's ideologues. In this case, the recondite but nevertheless essential interest of *The Bitter Harvest* is to enable an assessment of the importance of the modernizing rupture initiated by the Brothers with regard to the literalist reading of Muslim dogma by al-Qaeda's "Qutbist" founders, adamant in their unconditional rejection of the legislative and constitutionalist contributions of Western modernity. For Zawahiri, as in his time for Qutb, Egypt, by importing European constitutional and legislative references, suddenly and drastically amputated a portion of the sovereignty of the Islamic reference itself. And this dependence on the symbolic and normative universe of the West is for him the source of all the social and political problems of the country.

Zawahiri's imaginary here eloquently illustrates the permanence of the reactive problematic between the first and the second of the three temporalities of Islamism. "The British, after stealing Egypt, which they had occupied since 1882, from the Ottoman Empire, urged the class of native Egyptians that they had manufactured to adopt a Constitution establishing the foundations of secularism," he opines, in order to establish the framework for his criticism of the "secularization" of the Muslim Brothers. "It was, in 1923, the first Egyptian Constitution and even the first Constitution of any Arab country, considered today to be the matrix of all Egyptian and later Constitutions as well as all the Arab Constitutions that were subsequently adapted from it." In 1883, one year after the beginning of British occupation, "laws derived mainly from the French codes, replacing the [customary] dispositions [or] Muslim law, . . . among which only a few elements relative to family law or to what we call personal status continued to be upheld," had already been promulgated for Egyptian courts.

To support his line of argument, Zawahiri then lengthily quotes the articles of the 1923 Constitution and their equivalent in that of 1971. The Muslim reference had been excluded in favor of the "positive rights" or "code of law" (*qanun*), whose first characteristic in his opinion is its foreign nature with regard to the Muslim symbolic system. Where the aim of the legislator, every time he refers to "rights" or to "law," is to signify the decline of the arbitrary, the political imaginary of Zawahiri only consents to see yet another sign of the decline of the Muslim symbolic system and its degeneracy: the progress of "law" means "the expulsion of Sharia" and the progress of the influence of "disbelievers' law." "Article 6 of the Constitution," he thus inveighs, dares to stipulate that there is "no offense and no punishment without the law." This shows in his opinion that both offenses and their punishments have fallen under the dominion of foreign "law" and thus are able to elude the regulatory grip of the only legitimate jurisdiction, Muslim law.

The list of misunderstandings follows the blueprint of the whole constitutional structure: does the Constitution not provide that the rulings of the diverse jurisdictions apply "in accordance with the law"? Is this disposition not repeated in the 1971 Constitution? Does article 125 of the 1923 Constitution not stipulate that "judges are independent and answer to no other power than that of the law"? The "misunderstanding" is just as explicit in the area of sovereignty designated as (or purported to be) "popular" by the new system. The legislative power has allegedly been corrupted, in both the 1923 and the 1971 Constitutions, by the introduction of "human" sources: "sovereignty belongs to the people and to it alone and it is the source of all powers." "All these articles," he argues, "hence confer the power to legislate on human beings." This violation of the supreme deity by "associationism," that is, by man's partaking in divinity, is in Zawahiri's opinion the core of "democracy," which he absolutely condemns, for "none other than God holds the power to legislate for a creature of God." "And yet," he concludes, "it is on the basis of these Constitutions that, successively, King Fuad (until 1936), King Farouk (1936–1952), Muhammad Naguib (1952–1954), Gamal 'Abd al-Nasser (1954–1970), Anwar Sadat (1970–1981), and Hosni Mubarak have ruled."

In the other areas, including women's access to professional and political public space, the Muslim Brothers have also—not without some pain[7]—overcome a certain number of major symbolic barriers which remain stumbling blocks in other sectors of the Islamist field.

THE MODERNIZING OFFSHOOTS

One of the possible typologies thus consists in situating the different components of the Islamist movement on a gradual scale of social and political modernization, defined beforehand against a core posited as universal.[8] The relative rhythm with which each trend has set about rewriting "in the colors of Islamic endogenous culture" or "culturally reappropriating" the main products of the modernization which occurred during the nineteenth century within areas where the West had temporarily outdistanced societies of Muslim culture renders visible, on both sides of the Muslim Brothers, two competing trends which tend either to curb or to accelerate the rhythm of this endogenous albeit selective rehabilitation of "imported modernity."

The Islamist subcurrents of the "Brotherhood mainstream" are distinguishable by the magnitude and pace of the social and political modernizations undertaken to date. For some of them, these indigenized modernizations (of which the positions taken by Sheikh Yusuf Qaradawi on the Qatari channel al-Jazeera provide a good sample)[9] were and still remain unacceptable in their principle and in any case far too precipitate in their cadence. For others, however, who have acquired considerably less social clout, they seem, conversely, to be insufficient and incomplete.

The latter, partisans of fast-track modernization, have started to distance themselves, particularly since the 1990s,[10] from what they perceive to be a form of opposition to change on the part of the Brothers. They generally denounce the difficulty that the disciples of Hassan al-Banna, like the USSR's Supreme Soviet in its heyday, had in renewing their leaders, thus creating a generational tension within the movement itself. In Egypt, the Labor Party, and then the Wassat party (which has insisted on associating with Copt Christians), and more recently several young independent offshoots have thus been depriving the "historical" Brothers of their monopoly on "Islamist" protest against the unshakable Hosni Mubarak and on the "endogenous" modernization of the religious reference.[11] Along a line which at least partially coincides with the generational divide, the reformists (such as the team of the Internet site Islam Online) are calling into question the constrictions which in their opinion still impede the modernization of Hasan al-Banna's legacy: the criticisms often concern the penchant for sectarian foreclosure on the part of the senior generation, its secretive culture inherited from the dark years of repression and clandestinity, a certain difficulty in communicating with other Islamic trends, or even a touch of "Egypto-centricity," and so forth.

Media preachers, among whom Amr Khaled is one of the main symbols in Egypt, for their part have adopted a style of media mobilization both pietistic and disengaged from the political field and particularly pragmatic in its relation with the authoritarianism of the regime.[12] Do such "cyberpreachers," whose style is close to that of American evangelists, herald a "depoliticization" of Islamism, whose "surpassing" could thus once more be said to be on the agenda, just as the identity problematic of Islamism allegedly should be? That hardly seems probable. In the case of Egypt (but not only there), the persistent stranglehold of the regime on the social and political fields is a parameter which probably considerably limits the impact of this apparent "depoliticization" of some compartments of Islamist mobilization.

Beyond "Mother Egypt," the groups directly inspired or not by the Egyptian mainstream have all opted in practice for some autonomy of thought and action. In Morocco, Nadia Yassine, the daughter of the founder of the Moroccan association Justice and Charity (al-'Adl wal-Ihsan), is a good example of this active modernization of a line of thought never "submissive" to the Brothers but initially influenced by their legacy.[13] The Moroccan PJD (Party for Justice and Development), which chose to compromise with the demands of the regime, is exploring within the framework of the current kingdom—which the 2003 attacks in Casablanca provided with a pretext to lapse back into its old repressive rut—the possibilities and the limits of legal opposition. In Saudi Arabia, the trend of the Brothers has largely contributed to the modernization of the heritage of Wahhabism, a liberal movement, rallying a handful of Shiite and Sunni intellectuals and continuing to champion a critical reading of the legacy of Wahhabism by also exploring the possibilities of "apolitical" or at least nonoppositional reform.[14] The reformist work undertaken by Rashid al-Ghannoushi, the leader in exile in London of the Tunisian movement En-Nahda and an adamant opponent of Zine al-Abidine Ben Ali's authoritarianism, is on several counts more ambitious than that of al-Azhar's *ulama*s. He has notably been one of the first religious leaders to distance himself from the classically received condemnation of apostasy. The more or less institutionalized reformist trends currently present in Europe and in the United States, moreover, are playing an increasingly important role in the evolution of Hassan al-Banna's legacy.[15] In the vanguard of this reformist surge, the Swiss thinker Tariq Ramadan has audaciously suggested a general moratorium on the implementation of Quranic criminal punishments throughout the Muslim world.[16]

THE FORMS OF THE SALAFI "REACTION"

On the other side of the spectrum, besides long-standing pietistic trends (Tablighis), the main alternative to the Brothers is the Salafi trend, with which the ideologues of al-Qaeda can, in some respects, be associated. The history of the Salafi movement varies from one nation to another, and the concepts which would enable us to document it are indeed probably not all yet available. The Salafis were in some instances engendered by a manifest split from the Brothers' mainstream, such as that of Qutb in Egypt. They may, as in Arabia, have had a basis prior to this trend then subsequently come under its influence. One of the main methodological dangers here would no doubt be to slip into lumping them all together, as "common sense" persists in doing to this day with regard to the whole Islamist phenomenon.

The Salafi trend is in fact diverse and, behind its proclaimed opposition to change, just as "dynamic." Pascal Ménoret has usefully recalled the reductive character of its rigid identification with "Wahhabism" by showing the distinct historicity of its reference to the ideology of the founder of the Saudi kingdom and the multiplicity of the uses to which this is put today.[17] If, however, we have to find a common denominator for this component of the Islamist scene, it will no doubt be by following the line of demarcation which the vast majority of its members traced with regard to the Muslim Brothers. The aforementioned study of the career of the Yemeni Muqbil—even, notably because of the variables peculiar to the Saudi-Yemeni context, if it is by no means to be taken as representative of the totality of Salafism—can facilitate the task of highlighting its main doctrinal markers.[18]

The Salafis have in common their assimilation of the essential concessions made by the Muslim Brothers to political liberalization and social modernization with just as many unacceptable alterations in the Quranic reference and in the tradition of the Prophet of Islam. Even if no other activist expression of religious affiliation (neither the Tablighis which emerged in India in the 1920s nor the Party of Islamic Liberation founded in 1952 in Jordan) has received their stamp of approval, the Muslim Brothers were, during the last century, the main foil to their doctrinal assertions, as Muqbil has shown:

> We have called ourselves "ahl al-Sunna" [people of the Prophetic tradition] only because we have seen that the Muslim Brothers were in *bid'a* and that the same holds true of the Jama'at al-Tabligh. . . . The "people of the tradition" are those who have taken the Prophet as their guide, in his sayings, in his choices, and in his behavior. When the Muslim Brothers reproached us for this and began to be viewed as belonging to a different world, all those who did not swear allegiance to them became the object of their animosity. When their reputation deteriorated within Yemeni society, when a great number of people realized that their *da'wa* [preaching] had become materialist albeit everyone believed that anyone calling on God was a member of the Muslim Brothers, we decided, even though we were afraid of aggravating the situation by generating splinter groups, to choose a name in order to differentiate ourselves.[19]

This Salafi "doctrine," however, is not homogeneous, still less static, notably on the essential ground of the participation in political power and the criteria for the assessment of regimes. Even if they disown the democratic principle in its essence, several Salafi trends in the Arabian Peninsula both vote and present candidates (notably during the 2003 Yemeni legislative elections and during the first municipal elections in Saudi Arabia in 2005). This dissociation from the doctrinal literalism of the founders (who refused anthropomorphic iconography and hence television, experimental science, etc.) obviously moves them closer to the long-standing positions held by the Muslim Brothers. This is the case of the supporters of a Syrian defector from the Muslim Brothers, Muhammad ibn Nayif Zayn al-'Abidin Surur,[20] and of 'Abd al-Rahman 'Abd al-Khaliq, an Egyptian settled in Syria.[21] As a matter of fact, individual links exist all the more naturally in that the movement of the Muslim Brothers itself has retained a "Salafi" strain or tendency. In Yemen, in the Party of Union and Reform, the latter is generally identified with 'Abd al-Majid Zindani. Conversely, the main faultline of the Yemeni Salafi faction, personified in the dissidence of Abu Hassan al-Maghrebi, has been the result of a surge toward "modernization" which has tended to move him closer to the doctrinal positions of the Brothers.

The hypothesis expounded on the basis of field observations in Yemen can therefore probably be extrapolated at least in part to the other national breeding grounds of Salafism: reactive denunciation of modernization conveyed by the trend of the Brothers and a more or less open and more or less confrontational rupture with them, according to national configurations, by no means prevent an identical process of modernization from coming into its own, albeit at a slower pace, along similar guidelines, the most salient of which is probably the legitimization of participation in elections.

A "RETURN" OF THE SUFIS TO POLITICS?

The evocation of the dual "literalist" and "modernizing" offshoots of the historical mainstream of the Muslim Brothers is probably no longer complete enough for an exhaustive inventory of the "Islamist field." Its common frontiers with another form of Muslim religiosity, Sufism, indeed seem to be less clearly drawn than the classical dichotomy opposing the two allegiances would have us believe.

Initially on the social and educative levels and, ever more clearly, in the political arena, Sufi brotherhoods have well and truly been participating in the dynamic upsurge of "re-Islamization." It is sometimes forgotten that, for as long as they resisted colonial penetration, these brotherhoods were initially represented by Western public opinion as the "Islamic peril" of their time.[22] Their role today is not as systematically "apolitical" as Western opinion would often like to believe. Without necessarily adopting the categories of Salafi thought, or foregoing the challenges of their mystical quest, they have not been backward in demanding strict implementation of Muslim law and have not necessarily remained passive in facing the onslaughts of foreign hegemony.

Neither local political involvement nor "Jihadi" armed struggle in fact remains alien to the world of the brotherhoods today. In Pakistan, through the channel of a political party (Pakistan Awami Tehreek), the neo-Sufi movement of Tahir ul-Qadri recently staged an elusive appearance in the parliamentary arena. For several years now, in Pakistani Kashmir, in Afghanistan, and, more recently, in Iraq, brotherhoods have been openly engaging in armed mobilization, reviving a practice which was commonplace in the nineteenth century. In April 2005 the Iraqi members of the Qadiriya order announced the creation of the "'Abd al-Qadr Gilani Jihadi Brigade" (from the name of the founder of the order). Ajmal Qadri, the leader of a faction of a Deobandi Islamist party, Jamiat

Ulema-e-Islam, close to the Jihadi group Jaish-e-Mohammed (itself renowned for being close to al-Qaeda),[23] has turned out to be a Sufi simultaneously initiated in both the Naqshbandiya and the Qadiriya orders. And he claims to be the leader of a new transnational order created under the innovative label "World Khudam a-Din" (Worldwide Network of Servants of Religion). Many "Sufislamist" links[24]—complex though they may be—can thus be established between two forms of mobilization that, despite the overt discourses of the actors from both camps, have never actually been in complete antinomy.

Placing such differences in historical perspective highlights why some of them are today becoming blurred. The initial emergence of Sufism and its reassertion of the mystical dimension of Islam can be considered to be a reaction to the excesses of the legalism and the literalism of some of the doctors of law.[25] The recurrent reformist or "Islamist" criticisms (from 'Abd al-Wahhab to his contemporary Salafi descendants) were always directed less at this mystical dimension of faith than at the practices of venerating human intermediaries—living or dead—in the place of God, undermining the principle of divine unicity, or certain practices used to attain mystical ecstasy. Besides this criticism of some popular rites, the tension between the Islamists and the Sufis was fueled by the apparent passivity of some Sufi orders in the local or regional political field. And yet this apparent docility toward the colonial powers was above all the outcome of the very "efficiency" of the violence of these powers. It was indeed that, and not the "essence of Sufi mysticism," which broke the Sufi orders' ability to resist, making them incapable of asserting their grip on the independence movements within which, in the religious field, the reformist trends were subsequently to take their place. Particularly in the case of North Africa, it was thus this crushing defeat at the hands of the colonial powers which lent credence to the idea of a radical antagonism between "Islamism" and the apolitical passivity of the Sufis.

This opposition was then cultivated, manipulated, and essentialized by all the actors, inside and outside the Muslim world, who hoped to find therein a religious palliative to the vigor of the Islamist protest. Authoritarian regimes, Arab "secular" elites, and Western observers from all quarters, including the academic world, to this day have shared the same propensity to promote a reassuring Sufi alternative to the Islamist threat, to the extent of overestimating its capacity for mobilization or, at times, making a "politically" simplistic reading of it. Admittedly, the distinctive traits of the Sufi and Islamist affiliations remain perfectly perceptible in discourse and in practice. And the condemnation of the veneration of human intermediaries by the Islamists remains intact. However, the nuances in the condemnation of the Sufis currently brought to the fore by a certain number of "Islamist" authors, as well as the modernizing offshoots of the great Sufi orders and their propensity to reconnect with the political field, may throw the unbridgeable gap which allegedly separates them into better perspective.

In any case, this detour beyond the pale of the classically defined Islamist field gives rise to the consideration that political radicalization is not necessarily correlated with the position of actors in one or the other of the compartments of the religious field or with a predetermined place on the gradient of social and political modernization. It is probably not necessary to be a Salafi, or even a Muslim Brother, to decide to oppose the manifestations of excessive Western presence in the Muslim world, through recourse to religious affiliation.

Getting the Bin Laden phenomenon back "into perspective" does not mean—as so many actors, notably Muslim, tend to think—seeing only the tip of the iceberg of world protest, reducing it to a phenomenon confined to territories (particularly the Salafi trend) where the daylight of political modernization has allegedly not yet penetrated. The twofold danger of this position—to which the pleas of the "defenders of Islam" are often tempted to give way—is to minimize the scope of the denial of representation which fuels radicalization and to lend credence to the idea that a cocktail of educational policies would be enough to bring its actors meekly back into the fold of world order and political modernity. Admittedly, the supporters of radical groups represent only a tiny minority of the Muslim world, but the number of those who refuse to criminalize their activity, as George W. Bush and Tony Blair do, is much greater. Hence, for all their moving and shaking, the designers of the global war on terror, in its U.S.-Iraqi or European versions, are hardly likely to abate it—quite the contrary.

SIX

ISLAMIC RADICALIZATION

Between Religious Sectarianism and Political Counterviolence

... Usama Bin Ladin and other Islamist terrorist leaders draw on a long tradition of extreme intolerance within one stream of Islam (a minority tradition), from at least Ibn Taimiyyah, through the founders of Wahhabism, through the Muslim Brotherhood, to Sayyid Qutb.

—THOMAS KEAN, LEE HAMILTON, ET AL.,
THE 9/11 COMMISSION REPORT

Our words shall remain dead, like brides made of wax, stiff and heartless. Only when we die for them shall they resurrect and live among the living.

—AL-QAEDA CHANT, QUOTED IN YOSRI FOUDA AND NICK
FIELDING, *MASTERMINDS OF TERROR* (2003)

Confronted with the threat to the West of a radical Islamist mobilization claiming to be "anti-Western," it is essential to distinguish between two often tightly interwoven dimensions, one sectarian and the other political. If this mobilization is only "sectarian," then, indeed, only frontal opposition (as formerly against Nazism) is conceivable. If it is partly, or even mainly, political, then a frontal repudiation is probably not the most legitimate or even the most efficient solution to reduce and ward off the threat.

The main hypothesis of this book is that, on closer examination, al-Qaeda's rebellion is less religious than political and that "radical Islamism" contains infinitely less religious fundamentalism, sectarianism, and obscurantism than a not always illegitimate defense of more down-to-earth political or economic interests, inextricably interwoven with very banal affirmations of identity. I also intend to establish that deciphering the mechanisms of Islamist radicalization can by no means be accomplished without constantly looking into the mirror of what is going on within the Western context, where sectarian elements that are just as culpable have been playing a role in many political mobilizations.

WHAT RADICALIZATION?

The term "radicalization" has different meanings. It can designate recourse to violence or armed struggle in order to resolve conflicts or disagreements, to the detriment of political negotiations or diplomatic transactions. It can also describe the ideological or "sectarian" tension of a defensive and uncompromising withdrawal behind the borders of primary affiliations, be they national, ethnic, or religious. This radicalization leads those who endorse it to criminalize their opponents not for their actions but simply because of their very "being" and thus bar any affiliations other than their own from access to the universal. By so doing, they refute the existence of any capital of common values which may enable members of different affiliations to coexist and act together and, consequently, to transcend them. Sectarian radicalization fuels racist postures. It is used to legitimize hate crimes in times of peace, ethnic cleansing and "war crimes" in times of conflict.

One of the conditions of living with one's alter ego being the capacity to be . . . different, their respective identities have thus led "Muslims" as well as "Westerners" to essentialize their affiliations (their "culture," their "values," their "civilization"). From inside and outside the Muslim affiliation, the *vox populi* thus clamors in unison—in a register incriminating for some, laudatory for others—for the vindication of the existence of a tangible link between "Muslim-speak" and "Muslim-act," between the Islamity of actors and their behavior in politics or in society—at the risk of going into a dangerous tailspin.

Indeed, what happens when a political actor decides to restore its lost centrality to the Islamic reference? The priority suddenly granted by the Muslim "Other" to "his" referential (to the detriment of "ours") may feed into a twofold sectarian involution. At one end, at least, of the spectrum of re-Islamization, the supporters of a narrow literalism, among whom the members of the Salafi trend and the ideologues of al-Qaeda are undoubtedly well represented, may succumb to a pernicious temptation: indiscriminately rejecting whole swaths of the most universal contents of the Western modernizing heritage under the sole pretext that they were not initially expressed from within the Muslim affiliation and with symbolic materials borrowed from that culture. This incapacity to go beyond primary Muslim affiliation highlights a difficulty that no doubt currently constitutes the main obstacle to the political modernization of the world, that is, the assertion of a humanist common denominator capable of transcending cultural and religious affiliations.

It is hence out of the question to deny or to underestimate the fact that a definite slippage toward communalist withdrawal (only my own cultural or religious affiliation can produce something "good," something "universal") is a factor in the Islamist scene or in some of its subsectors. What remains to be done, however, is to weigh both the relative scale of this withdrawal and the degree of its "Muslim" specificity. And yet the drift toward sectarianism occupies a place in the Muslim world that is absolutely comparable to its place in other identities, including Christian or "Western" identities. And nothing authorizes turning it into the very substance or explanatory essence of the dynamic processes of re-Islamization.

Indeed, the most "literalist" Islamists are not the only ones tempted to irrationally reject all or part of the expressions of the culture "of the Other." The Occidental purview, even in the highest spheres of the intelligentsia and the political classes, also often takes equally reductive shortcuts. The temptation is strong for Westerners to deny those who challenge their privileged status and express themselves otherwise than through their own terminological categories any right of access to the political playing field. The emergence within the global arena of claims or, *a fortiori*, of protests expressed in an unacceptably alien "Islamic" terminology has somewhat unsettled the comfortable conviction that Western "particularism" legitimately occupies the whole field of the universal. Less consciously, the "fear of the vocabulary of the Other" probably also feeds into the feeling that this "retrogradation" within the hierarchies of a "plural world" might herald other, even more unwelcome economic or political declines.

One "fundamentalism," in this field as elsewhere, may therefore be symptomatic of another. The territorial claims of a "neighbor" are never easy to accept. When they are not expressed within the codes of our intuitive culture, they become utterly unacceptable.

And what about the case when they do not originate from this neighbor but are expressed within the territorial "stomping ground" of national identity? When, emerging from the enclosure of their community, the "Muslim" voices of Europe aspire to express universalist ambitions, they provoke a chorus of denial which comes close to irrationality. This may perhaps explain, even if it does not excuse, the pathetic improprieties of the French naysayers of Tariq Ramadan—a "scoundrel," as former minister Bernard Kouchner once saw fit to characterize him[1]—when, to "answer him back," a sort of spiteful and arrogant inanity has usurped the place of ethics and logic. Has not this Muslim intellectual who, while retaining the lexicon, aspired to sally forth from the palisade of his own affiliation forced the "Gaulish" tribe, which for a time had thought to monopolize the expression of the universal, to come to terms with the less flattering and more uncomfortable reality of its own particularism?

DIFFERENT CULTURES, SHARED VALUES

"North America and Europe are two countries which, traditionally, historically, share the same values and hence have the vocation of carrying out the same struggles." Many observers did not miss the opportunity to make fun of President Jacques Chirac's Freudian slip during a press conference held in London on November 18, 2004, with Prime Minister Tony Blair, when he made of "North America" and "Europe" two "countries," and, presumably, made General Charles de Gaulle spin in his grave. No one, however, noticed the very unilateral distribution of "values" which such a formulation implied. Do other continents then not share any of our values? And is it thus to be against those others, Africans and other miscellaneous Asians, that Europe and America will be called on to carry out their common "struggles" to come?

With all affiliations, religious or cultural, confounded, many of us tend more or less consciously to conflate the real and very respectable originality of our respective cultures with the "specificity," or even the ideologically charged "uniqueness," of our values.

Muslims and non-Muslims both experience in reality a common difficulty in establishing an essential distinction: like Atatürk (for whom modernity could only be acquired by donning a cloth cap with a visor identical to that worn by Europeans at the time), they confuse the symbolic apparatus (borrowed from history, religion, or culture) that confers on values (social justice, equality between individuals, etc.) the "endogenous" flavor which makes them legitimate for each ethnic, national, or religious community with the practical, universal, stake of the reference to such "values." Hence they tend to think that the use of different lexicons implies the adoption of values which are just as highly differentiated.

Yet, fundamentally, this is a non sequitur. Humanist values cannot be correlated today with any particular culture. At the most, they may be expressed differently according to the social and cultural context, in a premodern rural agricultural society or in an industrial and urban society. Identical values can be legitimized in the eyes of human groups diversified by very different, or even antagonistic, ideologies (religious or materialist), provided that they have as a functional common denominator the fact of being extracted from the historical heritage, religious or profane, of the group concerned. In every culture, in each religion, in the name of Allah, Jesus, or the Republic, the essential rights of the individual or of the human group can today find the references that justify their respect and their guarantees.

The defense of values is hence not conditioned by that of primary affiliations (religious, cultural or linguistic, national or "continental"), with which it cannot be confused without entailing the risk of discriminating against other affiliations. This difference is not always understood. It is, however, self-evident. When we welcome a guest at our table or when we are invited to dine by a foreign host, we can legitimately wish to share or partake of—and on occasion to defend—the expressions of the widest cultural diversity. The same holds for the living room too, as far as literature or music is concerned, or for the registers of fashion and linguistic expression. It is legitimate to want to preserve this vast range of flavors and resonances, of artistic expressions and modes of socialization. These particular interactions of the individual with the world are just so many necessary resources for his or her transaction with this environment.

But if by ill chance the house caught fire, if food ran out, if one of the residents fell ill, if a bellicose aggressor threatened, the analysis of the problem, the assessment of the situation, and the decision-making which "would be self-evident" would not require any "cultural diversity." Muslim, Christian, Buddhist, atheist, socialist, or liberal, each person, whatever his or her "cultural identity," would adhere to a line of action which would be identical, the values carried by each person's culture converging instantly on a common meaning. What difference would remain then? One person would perhaps want to think that he was "doing good" as he was following the precepts of the Son of Mary, another would convince himself that he was obeying the "commandment to do good" or to "prevent evil" revealed to the Prophet Muhammad, another, an atheist, would not require anything more than the promptings of his own humanist conscience.

When the situation that the international community must confront is called torture, or when it is called famine and disease, or deprivation of freedom, political authoritarianism, blind violence, or intolerance, all "struggles" that France and the United States are probably intent on carrying out "together," the cultural diversity that identifies the bloc "of America and of France" loses currency. Social justice, international justice, and respect for the different rights of persons or of minorities have no truck with "diversity." Or they accommodate themselves to it, but the result is the same. Neither cultural affiliation nor the adoption of a religious reference then determines the field of social or political action.

Admittedly, this universality of values has not escaped everyone's attention, and the idea is slowly gaining ground, moreover, including within the "Islamist" bloc. "If the West had only been able to respect its own values," emphasized Leith Chbeilat, already fifteen years ago, then leader of one of the Islamist groups of the Jordanian arena and a deputy elected with the support of part of the Christian community, "we all would have become . . . Westerners."[2] This simple fact of a universality of values, however, has remained all the more a minority view in that the discourse of Western political leaders does nothing, as just noted, to lend credence to it, having long intimated to their Muslim counterparts that it can only exist in the language and under the clothing of their culture alone. Even before the sectarian radicalization of George W. Bush ("With us or against us") and Tony Blair, already mentioned, those of Ronald Reagan's America and Margaret Thatcher's United Kingdom unsurprisingly played their role in empowering a symmetrically sectarian radicalization, under the banners of Islam, which the political imbalances of the world have since then significantly amplified.

It is thus through the prism of such a twofold "geopolitical" radicalization that we should analyze the two forms of radicalization of Islamist mobilization, the political and the sectarian, which have evolved simultaneously, as seen in many other historical situations, apart from any "Islamic" reference.

POLITICAL VIOLENCE AND SECTARIAN EXCESSES

The "red line" of the sectarian involution of Islamism and the mechanism of its transgression are relatively easy to highlight: they appear each time Israeli or American soldiers are fought against not as occupiers but as "Jews" or as "Christians," in the name of their religion or of their nationality, as "infidels," that is, in the name of their alienness in regard to the community of whoever is fighting them. Obviously, numerous Islamic militants practice the sectarian disqualification of those they intend to fight: Muslims who, in their opinion, are not Muslim "enough," Jews or Christians who are not Muslim "at all"; the condemnations normally encompass, beyond their political agenda, the primary identity of their rival. Confronted with another Muslim, it is the rhetoric of *takfir* (declaring someone an apostate) which is mobilized to deprive the rival of the guarantees of a legitimate affiliation. Confronted with non-Muslims, it is an identical "disbelief" which is invoked to disqualify them. The ultimate foreclosure of Sayyid Qutb and subsequently of Bin Laden and his followers within their religious affiliation, mobilized against the "Crusaders" and the "Jews," stems from such a posture, which must be denounced and combated root and branch.

The vigor of the condemnations which are heard every time a citizen of the Jewish faith is assaulted, in his dignity or in his memory, in the name of his affiliation, is essential. Anti-Semitism, which we sometimes forget is the product of European history much more than of the Muslim world, constitutes one of its darkest pages, which must never be blotted from memory. For the sake of the kin of the victims, of course, but perhaps still more urgently for all the descendants of the actors or witnesses of the abominable. The constant reminder of this principle may suffer no reservation, no half-heartedness, no "nuance."

It is upon the bedrock of such an assertion that, precisely, the right to reflection and to a full and lucid vigilance must be reinstated. The worst way to maintain this antisectarian watch would be to allow its assumed guardians to deprive it of its universal basis, to allow the feeling to set in that humanist effusion is henceforth exclusively reserved to some rather than to others and that the principles which found nations, and the world, thus have a two-tier geometry. Antisectarian vigilance should not be diverted from its function and led astray for sectorial political objectives or to serve the territorial ambitions of one camp or of one tribe to the detriment of all the others.

And yet it is precisely this highly dangerous—and as it happens counterproductive—drift which is enshrined in the essentialist discourse of the American policy on "Islamist radicalism." By reducing it exclusively to its sectarian elements, by refusing to recognize the infinite variety of political revolts, not all illegitimate, which it encompasses, this discourse inevitably leads to ruling out any response other than military. And by ruling out the possible political solutions, it of course contributes to feeding the roots of that very "evil" which it claims to "eradicate." In seeking out really efficient means to reduce the threats that it poses to global peace—if, at least, peace is the real aim pursued by the Western powers—it is, on the contrary, indispensable to produce a realistic and well-documented analysis of the intricate complexities of the sectarian and political elements of this "radical Islamist" resistance, too often considered only in terms of anathema.

Admittedly, all sectarian involutions are not "justified" by the recourse to a logic of counterviolence. But for all that, is it enough to stigmatize the sectarian component of a political mobilization to discredit it as a whole? Is it enough to pinpoint—which it is perfectly possible to do—in the long history of the Egyptian Muslim Brothers or in that, more recent, of the combatants of Hamas some exclusionary religious proclamations, some expressions violating the frontier between anti-Zionism and anti-Semitism, or some other traces of sectarian involution to "scientifically" infer the eternal sectarianism of such political trends and of all those who, at one point or another of their history, have claimed to be their representatives or have supported their struggles?

How acceptable in France would such a criterion of the assessment of the legitimacy of political actors be, if applied to the stances of the immediate ancestors (or the contemporary actors) of any French political family on their relations with Judaism, or their representation of the German population, or, more enlightening still, the representation and the treatment of the populations of the French colonial empire or their descendants? The sectarian component of an identity or political mobilization must surely be identified and, let it be repeated, clearly condemned as such. On the other hand, it cannot be used as the only exegetic tool to define the whole scope of this mobilization. If the sectarian component that we can detect and must condemn in the history of the Muslim Brothers sufficed to exclude them from the contemporary arena of political legitimacy, then a great number of political families in the West, and not the least among them, should long since have been excluded. However, the Western view of the Islamist mobilization continually gives free rein to this confusing amalgamation.

For the indispensable indictment of "Islamist sectarianism" to shed as much light as it regularly raises dust, and for sectarianisms, all sectarianisms, every time and everywhere they take hold and really hold sway, to be condemned and combated as vigorously as they deserve, we must deconstruct the process of their formation. And we must clarify the exact role they play, or do not play, in the alchemy of the incriminated violence, be it within the domestic political order, as in Algeria or in Egypt, in the international arena of the Chechen, Palestinian, or Iraqi conflicts, or in the attacks carried out, since 1998, against American or European targets.

It should thus be possible to confront a twofold question: is sectarian involution an inherent product of the "disease of Islam," is it consubstantial with Islamist mobilization alone, constituting a sort of specific marker that justifies a particular ignominy, or does it partake more ordinarily in a relatively universal "chorus" of identity-based and sectarian involutions, present in variable forms and discourses within other affiliations, be they religious or materialistic, ethnic or cultural, more or less everywhere on earth, including the dominant camp of the West?

The corollary question is probably still more central: has the sectarian excess of the Islamists been the forerunner of political violence, constituting its cause, or, on the contrary, were these manifestations of violence (of political discrimination and repression) rather its source? In the precise case of the two mythic figures of Islamist radicalization, Sayyid Qutb in the 1950s and Bin Laden in the 1990s, can the withdrawal into the Muslim affiliation be considered the prime mover of their violence, or is it only to be seen as the rhetorical accessory of a counterviolence provoked by external and very profane political causes? A closer scrutiny of the concrete historical situations within which this Islamic radicalism was born will enable us to answer this question through two hypotheses which we will now attempt to document.

THE ORIGINS OF SECTARIAN TENSION

The first has already partly been addressed and will be examined in the last chapter, on the supporters of hard power: under different semblances and with distinct semantics, sectarian tension arises just as frequently outside the Islamist scene. Almost everywhere on the planet the metaphors mobilized to discredit the enemy have crossed the red line of racist stigmatization. In France, the "Hun" of the 1914–1918 war and, more recently, the Algerian "wog" from a "dirty race" amply bear witness to that. In the official precinct of the Israeli Knesset, Palestinians have with impunity been likened to "earthworms proliferating everywhere."[3] Russian president Vladimir Putin, extemporizing on the Chechen Muslims ("We will take them out even in the john"), and the president of the Italian Council, Silvio Berlusconi, learnedly discoursing on Islamic civilization ("inferior to the West"), have made distinguished contributions to this field of oratory. The Christian and Muslim Lebanese, behind the palisades of confessionalism, are no laggards in criminalizing their respective affiliations.[4] All these provocations, whether metaphorical or not, must of course be identified as such and roundly condemned. Such things are absolutely not inherent in the universe of Islam, but also latent, and sometimes explicit, in the manifestations of the political and cultural unilateralism of the West.

The second hypothesis is that the sectarian radicalization of the al-Qaeda generation and, before it, that of the generation whose emblem was Sayyid Qutb are the direct consequences of the repressive and violent atmosphere of the national and international political environment in which they have occurred, and not the reverse.

Common sense often tends to believe that sectarian radicalization is the antechamber of political radicalization. The rule, however, is far from being established. Conversely, in many cases, it may well have been political radicalization which was the antechamber of sectarian radicalization, which it paved the way for and required. In the twofold symbolic case of Qutb and Bin Laden, the violence of the local political environment, the exclusion from representation of a whole political generation, and the support of the international environment for the implementation and the legitimization of such violence seem to have played a decisive role, as we will see, in the process of sectarian retreat into religious affiliation.

The difference is essential. Subjected to the violence of his environment, a political actor will inevitably, *before* moving on to counterviolence, come to adopt a rhetoric attesting to the illegitimacy of his adversary and the legitimacy of his own combat. Where their predecessors had drawn on the resources of their ethnic membership (just as the colonizer had drawn on the virtues of the progress which he was intent on imposing on the world of the "barbarians"), Qutb and those who followed in his footsteps selected within the legacy inherited from Islamic culture the categories enabling them to ideologize (that is, to legitimize) the radical condemnation of their nationalist oppressor, who in turn legitimized his own violence by a recourse to Arab ethnic affiliation. Without denying—we will return to this later—that the nitpicking literalism of the Salafis might constitute an antechamber to sectarian involution and that the latter may well accompany the transition to armed resistance, the commitment to direct action of the "Jihadis" and other suicide combatants does not necessarily require that form of ideological justification.

The presence, in the ranks of Palestinian candidates for suicide attacks, of members of the whole local political spectrum (and not only of Islamists) in its own way illustrates the reality that the external view frequently tends to deny. In this connection, the American academic Robert A. Pape recalls what has taken a long time to become self-evident: "It is the occupation [of Palestinian territories], rather than Islamic fundamentalism, which is the cause of suicide attacks."[5] "Islamic fundamentalism," he adds, "is not so closely associated with the suicide attacks as many people think. It so happens that the world leaders in this matter are . . . the Tamil Tigers, from Sri Lanka, who are Marxist and fully secular."

The suicide attacks are not multiplying because, as we hear too often, "Jihadi ideology spreads particularly easily thanks to the Internet," but rather because, from Palestine to Iraq and from Chechnya to Afghanistan, the violence of the Western environment is objectively on the rise. They are multiplying because the simplistic dichotomies of Jihadi ideology, based on an insurmountable antagonism between Muslim affiliation and Western affiliation, are day after day given fresh credence by the arrogant unilateralism of quite a few Western political leaders in regard to the Muslim world. Or by the infinite intolerance of their media shields, authorized to blatantly advocate the perennial presence of the "Arab Pinochets" and their barbaric methods, rather than considering whether to cede one inch of their monopoly.[6]

SEVEN

FROM SAYYID QUTB TO MOHAMMED ATTA

Sectarianism or Political Counterviolence?

We frequently hear that for the founders of al-Qaeda, Osama Bin Laden and, still more, Ayman al-Zawahiri, as for many of their young disciples, the fundamental theoretical reference is not the father of "Saudi Wahhabism," Muhammad 'Abd al-Wahhab (1703–1792), or his distant purported inspirer Taqi al-Din Ibn Taymiyya (1263–1328), renowned for legitimizing the "right to fight the impious ruler." It is rather the Egyptian essayist and activist Sayyid Qutb, sentenced to death by Nasser and executed on May 29, 1966. This assertion is far from being incorrect. Qutb was indeed the man who, within the scope of the last century, in the course of the second temporality of the Islamist reaction, bestowed on the latter a sizable share of its ideological grammar. Self-evident though it may seem at first sight, this pervasive reference to Qutb's theology and to his radical refusal of the universe of political modernity nonetheless is also far from being as truly enlightening as it may appear.

Indeed what is now required is to get a clear understanding of the precise nature and the impact of this genealogy. To do this, we must first recall the context within which this reference was worked out. We must then question whether therein lies the "cause" of the radicalization of one part of the last Islamist generation and, subsequently, the "origin" of al-Qaeda itself or only one of its rhetorical trappings. Did Mohammed Atta, one of the September 11 suicide pilots, really need Sayyid Qutb to set out on the road to radicalization?

THE THEOLOGY OF WAR OF SAYYID QUTB AND
AL-ZAWAHIRI OR THE POLITICAL UNDERPINNINGS
OF AL-QAEDA

The theology of war worked out by Qutb and bequeathed to Muhammad 'Abd al-Salam Faraj and then to Ayman al-Zawahiri, Bin Laden, and the latest generation of "Jihadists" is part and parcel of any real understanding of their generation. It is also necessary to raise the right questions and to avoid confusing effects and causes, ideological referentials and political programs, the exemplariness of the trajectory of Qutb and the "paternity" or *a fortiori* the "causality" of Islamist radicalization. The clarification provided by an overview of the context of Qutb's radicalization at the beginning of the 1960s is doubly important: it reveals the real causes of this radicalization, which were more political than sectarian. From Qutb, and a checkered body of work closely linked to the turmoil of his time, only the ultimate radical formulation of his ideology has indeed been retained today, thus obfuscating the itinerary which gave meaning and necessity, even urgency, to that "war of the words of God" launched against his own friends. Hidden by the categories that express the radicalization of his thought, the human and political underpinnings of this radicalization have hardly received the attention they deserve.

The contextualization of Qutb's rupture thus makes it possible to understand that it is the persistence of the same political factors, rather than its intrinsic ideological strength, which assured the "validity" of this radical rhetoric in the eyes of a segment of the following generations. It shows that it was not solely the intrinsic force of his words and expressions which "contaminated" the minds of a generation, but the stamp of an identical violence, from which they were shielded no better than Qutb himself was, which eventually led them to share his convictions.

Indeed, the violence which fueled Qutb's thought was essentially the same as the anger which, twenty years later, was to fuel radicalization—albeit slowly hatched—in Bin Laden or, thirty years later, in Mohammed Atta. The reality of history gives short shrift to the thesis of a purely sectarian involution which purportedly "corrupted" healthy minds, through the sole baleful influence of a handful of "booklets" which circulated "because" of Johannes Gutenberg's technology (already denounced in its time) and, after the age of the cassette,[1] "because" of the Internet, today placed at the core of all explanations and honored with all the responsibilities that it does not bear. If the descendants of Qutb found the categories of his "theology of liberation" alluring, it is above all because they were confronted with the same denial of representation and the same national and regional political malfunctions as those which drove Qutb to cut himself off from the world of his time.

As for Bin Laden or Atta, the irruption of Israel and the Western powers in the region's internal political game played an essential role in this process. Qutb was a contemporary of the creation of the state of Israel, of the first Arab defeat, of the 1956 tripartite Suez expedition. Bin Laden was later to explain that it was while watching images of the Israeli artillery bombarding the high-rise buildings of South Beirut in 1982 that he conceived the project of one day hitting back in a like manner against Israel and its supporters.[2]

Repression, accompanied by torture, and the denial of politics in favor of violence by both national state and foreign actors in Middle Eastern current affairs were already at the core of this process. Qutb and his heirs have rebelled against what they perceived to be an alliance between domineering and cynical foreign powers, discredited in their values, and the subjugated indigenous elites, who were themselves manipulative and dictatorial. The repression and the manipulation of violence by those in power were already part of this recipe. The "inhuman torture"—the very torture that the United States has cynically subcontracted to this day to its faithful Egyptian allies—a torture undergone by Qutb and by Zawahiri, seen at close quarters by Bin Laden and Atta, does indeed appear, at the end of the day, to be one of the key factors of their radicalization, both sectarian and political, "theological" and "strategic" . . .

There is hardly the shadow of a doubt that it was Qutb who bequeathed the main theological-theoretical resource to the political radicalism of al-Qaeda's founders. To this day, it is by paraphrasing his teachings, notably those of his famous *In the Shadow of the Quran* or *Markers on the Trail*,[3] written in Nasser's jails, that the "Jihadi" Salafis denounce the compromises of Muslims with Western influence and their relinquishing of the divinely revealed in favor of the "pagan" norm.

For Qutb, as for Zawahiri and Bin Laden, the holders of power are not only guilty of the usual profane authoritarian excesses. They are above all accused of having relapsed into pre-Islamic ignorance and exposed to the vindictiveness of the believers for their incapacity to respect the divine norm, this incapacity serving to "explain" their political misconduct. The supreme proof is their compromise with the "secularism" whose very essence is to organize the substitution of "positive law," that is, in their opinion, a norm of purely "human" origin, for the norm inspired by divine revelation, the Sharia and its juridical expression, *fiqh*.[4]

It is indeed this resolve to restore the supremacy of Muslim law, the expression of "divine" will, over democratic law, the expression of a solely "human" will, which has been applied since then by a whole generation of radical Islamists, headed by Osama Bin Laden, in order to discredit their "Muslim" environment—the regimes and, more rarely, Muslim societies as a whole. It was indeed in the name of Qutb's exegesis of the meaning and impact of the Westernization of the normative system that Ayman al-Zawahiri, as we have seen, arraigned Hosni Mubarak and his predecessors with the same charges of which Osama Bin Laden had been accusing King Fahd since 1995, that is, ruling under other laws than those which God has revealed to mankind. Qutb no doubt drew his inspiration from Ibn Taymiyya's anti-Mongol texts (1328) and, through more or less orthodox extrapolation,[5] undertook to attack rulers considered to be insufficiently respectful of their religion.

Almost thirty years after Qutb, Ayman al-Zawahiri attests to the permanence of this rhetorical construction, which he has fully internalized, as evidenced by his aforementioned critical report on the activity of Hassan al-Banna's disciples since their creation in 1928.

In order to understand its later good fortune, it is necessary to recall here the political factors involved in the fabrication of this language by Qutb. How did this middle-class civil servant, a brilliant and successful essayist, come to this? William Shepard has meticulously retraced the stages of Qutb's intellectual progression toward radicalization.[6] He has done so in an original way, by comparing the successive editions of Qutb's first book, *Social Justice in Islam,* written before his return from the United States and his "entry into Islamism." The book was published five times: in 1949, before he joined the Brothers; in 1953, before the "Free Officers" took power and after he joined the Brothers; in 1954, before the rupture between the Brothers and the authorities; in 1958, after his imprisonment and the assassination of his companions in prison; and in 1964, when he had just published, from his prison cell, and one year before his execution, his emblematic *Markers on the Trail.*

The last edition includes the most radical views developed at the end of his life in *Markers on the Trail,* when he was plumbing the depths of the repressive deadlock of Nasserism. The transformations of his thought throughout these sixteen years reveal the withdrawal symptoms of sectarian involution: theocentrism was emphasized, and then Islamo-centrism. External doctrinal influences, notably that of the Pakistani Sayyid Abu'l-A'la Mawdudi, whose works had been translated into Arabic during the 1950s, played a significant role. The gap then widened with the policy of secularization and hence of "Westernization" of Egyptian and Arab rulers, to which the official *ulamas* nonetheless were willing to offer their support. Last but not least,[7] it was to be the long experience of prison, isolation, maltreatment of all sorts, and torture which helped to shape the evolution of his thought. Qutb himself contributed some fundamental explanatory comments, today still sparingly employed in Western analyses of his discourse.

THE POLITICAL UNDERPINNINGS OF QUTB'S RUPTURE

Why Did They Execute Me? is a text by Sayyid Qutb published after his death which has remained generally outside the purview of the curiosity of the exegetes of radical Islamism.[8] This autobiography penned in prison not only possesses the anecdotal interest of encapsulating within the title of one of its chapters—"The Islamic Movement Starts from the Base [*al-qa'eda*]"—a possible genealogy of the expression which today is most frequently used to designate Osama Bin Laden's organization.[9] It especially states the reasons and the objectives—the legitimate self-defense of a movement in his view threatened with violent extermination—of his shift into "direct action." Written after weeks spent personally experiencing the physical torture which goes so notably unmentioned in contemporary "expertise" on "Islamic terrorism," this small text places in sharp perspective the trajectory of a man about to be put to death by Nasser's regime, which had failed to break him intellectually. Qutb's reasoning does not so much shed light on the "philosophical" or "theological" origins of the radicalism of today's Jihadists as lay bare the profane underpinnings of this radicalism, thus highlighting, from Algiers to Cairo via Riyad, the current relevance, unfortunately still topical today, of the "suicide bomber production line."[10]

Sayyid Qutb, a middle-class Egyptian public sector employee at the Ministry of Education, dispatched on a study trip to the United States in 1948, at the age of forty-two, started off as an intrigued but soon to be appalled student at the University of Colorado at Boulder. It was probably above all through his contact with this otherness that a more sophisticated awareness of his own identity and of everything which, in his view, jeopardized its development within his national environment began to take shape, following a common trajectory, which we will identify again particularly in the case of Mohammed Atta. His repudiation of American society was presumably accelerated, or perhaps even provoked, by the racist contempt with which, in the land of the hymnists of democracy, the color of his skin was stigmatized—his mother was a native of Nubia.

However that may be, Qutb soon felt alienated by the theological niceties of the American evangelists of the Trinity Episcopal Church with whom he at first met on a regular basis and, even more, by what he saw as the prevailing economic cynicism and moral permissiveness of Americans, which contrasted so brutally with the prudish atmosphere and the intricacy of social interrelatedness in his native Upper Egypt:

> All these representations of the "hypostases" of the Trinity, of original sin, of Redemption, can but wound reason and conscience! And this capitalism of endless accumulation, monopolies, usurer's interests, gloating with greed! And this selfish individualism which prevents any spontaneous solidarity other than what the laws enforce! This materialistic, mean-minded, desiccated vision of life! This brutish freedom invoked under the name of "co-education"! This slave market called the "emancipation of women," the traps and anxieties of a system of marriage and divorce so contrary to natural life! The racial discrimination, so strong and so ferocious![11]

Back in Cairo in 1950, Qutb was still only an essayist and a prolific columnist. The origin of his interest in the Muslim Brothers, whose very existence had been unknown to him before he left for the United States, is particularly revealing. It was the overweening satisfaction of the Anglo-Saxon press concerning the repression to which the Brothers were being subjected which brought home to him the anti-imperialist impact of their action:

> I knew only very little about the Muslim Brothers until I left for the United States, in spring 1948, with a delegation of the Ministry of Education. . . . I was struck by the great interest that the American press, but also the British press distributed in the United States, displayed in the [Muslim] Brothers and by the joyous satisfaction they manifested during the dissolution of their association, before the beatings they were subjected to, and at the time of the death of their guide. I abruptly realized the threat that this association represented for Western interests in this region and for Western culture and civilization.

Qutb's nationalism had just made the link—at the core of the Islamist recipe—with his religious affiliation. The Orientalist literature of the time consolidated his state of mind: "All this drew my attention to the importance that the association was taking on in the opinion of the actors of Zionism and of Western colonialism." In 1949 it was he who was to attract the attention of the Muslim Brothers, now orphans of their founder Hassan al-Banna, recently assassinated, much more than he felt attracted to them: "It was at that time, in 1949, that I published *Social Justice in Islam,* introduced by a dedicatory sentence,[12] . . . in which the Brothers thought they recognized a reference to themselves. . . . They saw in the author of the book somebody sincere in whom they started to manifest some interest."

After the 1952 revolution, his hostility began to crystallize, as the rivalry between the Brothers and Nasser became more manifest, against the symbolic and soon political concessions that the "secular" regime of Nasser in his opinion granted to the West in combating these Brothers whom he considered to be the strongest rampart for his nation.

On October 26, 1954, under murky circumstances—in which Qutb detected a British manipulation—an assassination attempt against Nasser was laid at the Brothers' door. A descent into the hells of repression then began. The Brothers were only to emerge from this long tunnel three years after Nasser's death in 1970.[13] First imprisoned for only a few months, Qutb was very soon to be incarcerated again, for good this time, accused of being "in charge of the publications department of the secret branch of the Brothers," an accusation which he categorically denied.

From the prison cell that he was never again to leave until his hanging on August 29, 1966, Qutb gradually extended his indictment to all the members of the opposition, including the mainstream trend of the Muslim Brothers. It was in this context that his "theological" rupture with the dominant trend of the Brothers, from which he gradually diverged, occurred. During the long ordeal of isolation and repeated torture, theocentrism, which progressively strait-jacketed his thinking even as it was radicalizing, became self-evident to him. This led him to increasingly "ideologize" the remonstrances hurled against his adversaries, whose number, as the passivity of society toward the treatment inflicted on him was confirmed, grew to include society as a whole. How can the upholder of a regime allowing such repressive practices be a true Muslim, he initially wondered, before broadening the scope and impact of his indictment to the point of generalized sectarian exclusion, finally including all those who tolerate such rulers, that is, the whole of society, which he accused—here it comes—of regressing to "pre-Islamic ignorance."

Several convictions structured his analysis of Egypt's political crisis, among whose victims he was to figure: the Americans, the allies of Israel, were attempting to infiltrate the Egyptian scene through the intermediary of the association they were promoting. One of their objectives was the elimination of the Muslim Brothers (whose volunteer brigades had seen distinguished service during the first war against Israel) through the manipulation of public opinion (counterfeit tracts attributed to the Brothers had allegedly been handed out by Christian clergymen). Thus he suspected those he stigmatized—just like Bin Laden forty years later—as "colonialist crusaders" and their "Zionist" allies of purposely spreading dissension between Nasser and the Muslim Brothers. He was convinced that the intervention of the British services in the attempted assassination of Nasser was only the first of a series of manipulations aimed at trapping the Brothers into committing the error which would provide the pretext for their liquidation.[14]

What happened then justified his fears to a great extent: in jail, he was informed of a planned rebellion, masterminded from the outside, which would provide the pretext for the physical elimination of certain prisoners during collective labor outside the walls. The uprising was halted, but the massacre did take place. In 1957, testified Qutb, in Liman prison in Cairo, in the depth of their cells, twenty-one disarmed prisoners were pitilessly gunned down and just as many left wounded. If they really were rebels, as he emphasized, it would have been enough, under lock and key as they were, to turn off the water mains for twenty-four hours in order to force them to submit . . .

Qutb did not deny, in this context, having participated in working out a plan to attack the regime. But he justified this at length as the sole response then possible to the crackdown initiated against the Brothers. And he limited its political objectives to those of legitimate self-defense: "We finally agreed not to employ force to engineer a coup and impose an Islamic regime from the top down." He actually reiterated several times his principled opposition to the idea of any sort of "Islamization from the top down,"[15] recalling how the Prophet himself had declined to become the king of Medina, because he did not want the idea of the state to be co-extensive with that of religion. "But we also finally agreed on the principle of a response proportional to the attack suffered," he added. "The principle enunciated by God was at hand: 'He who attacks you, attack him in the same manner as he has used against you.'" And yet "the attack did take place, in 1954 and in 1957, and resulted in arrests, torture, murders, and the flouting of all human dignity during torture, and then in the destruction of people's homes and the throwing of women and children out into the streets. To this, we decided not to respond. But the question arose again in the face of new aggressions underway. It is to the latter that we decided to respond."[16]

After an interval of almost forty years, *Why Did They Execute Me?* is very close to the political mindset of Bin Laden's imitators. No more than in the case of the "Saudi millionaire" in his struggle against the repressive corruption of his country's princely Americanized elites was Qutb's imaginary merely fueled by ideologized and caricatured representations of the domination which he denounced: he took a stand in the face of the very real perversities of the political systems of his day. Indeed his entirely nonreligious fears of the 1960s—be they the evolution of the Palestinian issue, the repressive turn of Arab regimes, or the international coordination of "security" policies (that is, repression)—were to prove in large part founded in reason.

The profane underpinnings of the global guerrilla warfare launched against the United States by Bin Laden and Zawahiri and adopted by the young kamikazes of September 11 were produced by strikingly analogous political circumstances. In December 2004 Bin Laden (after recalling that his struggle had not yet, at that point, targeted Saudi Arabia's rulers but only the American occupiers) spelled out the logic of his combat as follows: "What is happening today is just an extension of the war against the coalition of the crusaders, led by America, everywhere waging war against us. We are hence reacting proportionately, and this includes the country of the two holy mosques. We have the intention of evicting them from there, if God wills."[17]

This discourse seems hardly compatible with arguments entailing a "genealogy" and even less a merely ideological "contamination" by the "father of radical Islamism": in lieu of any genealogy, anyone who wishes to seriously approach the political history of the region soon discovers the striking similarity of the political circumstances which have fueled this radicalization.

AYMAN AL-ZAWAHIRI BETWEEN SYMBOLIC FRACTURE AND PHYSICAL TORTURE

Presented since 1998 in his role as al-Qaeda's "number two," Ayman al-Zawahiri considers himself to be the direct intellectual and political heir to Sayyid Qutb, as his former rival Montasser al-Zayyat, an ex-member of the rival organization Jamaa Islamiyya, explains today.[18]

Al-Zawahiri was born in 1951 in the well-heeled and Westernized Cairo neighborhood of Street No. 9 in Maadi. His father hailed from a prestigious family which had provided Egypt with numerous renowned religious clerics, including, on his father's side, a sheikh of al-Azhar, and, on his mother's side (Azzam), the leader of a Sufi brotherhood. Though al-Zawahiri graduated from medical school in 1974, he created his first activist Jamaa in 1966, the year Qutb was hung, which can no doubt be considered one of the first catalysts of his commitment, and one year before the terrible defeat of June 1967. In 1980, after the invasion of Afghanistan by Soviet troops, he undertook what might have been called, were he not a Muslim, a long professional humanitarian trainee-ship in an Afghan hospital, while simultaneously continuing his training in surgery.

After returning home to Egypt, in 1981 al-Zawahiri narrowly escaped a roundup of 1,500 intellectuals of all persuasions launched by Sadat a few weeks before his assassination (October 6) but was arrested soon afterward. Under the horrendous torture sessions, which to this day are common practice in interrogations by the Egyptian police, he was forced to disclose all the names of his friends and subordinates, to participate in their arrest,[19] and to testify against them in a court of law. Once released, probably thanks to the influence of his powerful family, he chose, by the subterfuge of participating in a group tourist excursion to Turkey, to quit Egypt forever and to renew his earlier contacts with Afghanistan.

It is likely that he then had a hard time putting down roots again within this activist environment where, or so he thought, he would be blamed for having shown such a culpable weakness facing torture, to which everybody had not succumbed. Nonetheless, from that point on, nothing was to persuade him (unlike some leaders of the rival organization Jamaa Islamiyya, who in 1996 issued a call to lay down arms) to turn aside from the path of armed revolt. From Peshawar or the territory of Afghanistan he thus began to organize sporadic attacks against well-known Egyptian political figures. A particularly efficient crackdown, however, succeeded in considerably limiting the activity of his organization. Paradoxically, until 1998, Zawahiri himself was never indicted on any charge by the Egyptian government, which, convinced that he was temporarily in hiding in Switzerland, probably did not want to give him a pretext to obtain political asylum.

The conviction, already strongly rooted in Qutb, that a close collaboration was developing between the foreign great powers (the distant enemy) and the Egyptian national regime (the near enemy) is an essential component of his political imaginary, thus encapsulating in embryonic form the ultimate internationalization of his commitment. "It is difficult," he asserted, "to distinguish between King Farouk's role and that of the British, or between that of Nasser and of the Americans (at the beginning of his rule) or later between that of Nasser and of the Russians." In April 1995, in an article published by the (underground) magazine *Al-Mujahidun* under the title "The Road to Jerusalem Passes through Cairo," he nonetheless recalled that the order of his tactical priorities began with the near enemy: "Jerusalem will only be freed after the battles of Cairo and Algiers have been won." It was hence out of the question to grant priority to the Palestinian struggle or, *a fortiori*, to the struggle against the Western backers of Israel. This vision was to remain his until 1998.

When al-Zawahiri changed his vision, in order to join Osama Bin Laden's camp, his reasons for doing so were no doubt legion. Under the influence of Bin Laden, confronted with the repeated failures of his Egyptian strategy and the multiplication of arrests within the ranks of his own organization, Jihad, he had little difficulty in convincing himself to change tactics and to join a common front "against the Crusaders and the Jews," whose top targets were the United States and Israel. Therefore, his motives were at least partly "internal" and linked to the terrible series of arrests that crippled his movement, which was then reeling from repeated failure. But they also were widely "external": the growing U.S. interventionism in the region in his view ever more clearly arraigned Washington as the driving force behind the global repression of the Islamist trend.

And yet, far from the exigencies of the situation in Egypt, Bin Laden could marshal important financial means and had just obtained the support of the Taliban regime, which controlled about 95 percent of the territory of Afghanistan. At the beginning of August 1998, the advance claims by Zawahiri, who "predicted" the attacks against the American embassies in Tanzania and Kenya on August 7, were probably aimed, according to Montasser al-Zayyat, at "renewing his credit" on the Egyptian domestic scene, where his movement had partially lost ground. Thanks to the logistics of the Saudi billionaire, he was able to confer on his ambitions a dimension corresponding to what increasingly had come to resemble a thirst for revenge, echoing the accusations that the young doctor himself had screamed, from behind the bars of the steel cage separating him from the courtroom, at the journalists from all over the world attending his trial in Cairo in 1982:

> [W]e suffered the severest inhuman treatment. There they kicked us, they beat us, they whipped us with electric cables, they shocked us with electricity! They shocked us with electricity! And they used the wild dogs! And they used the wild dogs! And they hung us over the edges of the doors . . . with our hands tied at the back! They arrested the wives, the mothers, the fathers, the sisters, and the sons! . . . So where is democracy? Where is freedom? Where is human rights? Where is justice? Where is justice? We will never forget! We will never forget![20]

BIN LADEN AND THE (NONRELIGIOUS) EVIDENCE OF THE NONRESPECT FOR (DIVINE) LAW

Persian Gulf oil and the lack of serious U.S. alternative-energy development are at the core of the bin Laden issue. For cheap, easily accessible oil, Washington and the West have supported the Muslim tyrannies bin Laden and other Islamists seek to destroy.

—MICHAEL SCHEUER, *IMPERIAL HUBRIS: WHY THE WEST IS LOSING THE WAR ON TERROR* (2004)

In the view of Western media or academic opinion, Bin Laden is primarily and almost exclusively the "preacher" who rants and rails at the princes forgetful of the divine rule, the erring ways of the "Zionists," "Crusaders," and other "infidels." The itinerary of the political actor which he also happens to be is far less well known. For what reasons did the privileged ex-student, erstwhile adept of punting parties on the Thames at Oxford and skillful volleyball player, once he had succeeded as an entrepreneur, abandon the comforts of his prodigious wealth?[21] Why did he grant preference not to the dividends of mutually profitable collaboration with the Saudi princes but to the hazards of oppositional exile and guerrilla warfare in the arid mountains of Afghanistan? We have very little knowledge concerning the long perfectly legalist preamble to his political revolt, the list of his many attempts to peaceably amend the policies of the Riyad regime before making up his mind to take up arms not against the regime as such but against its American backers,[22] and the reasons which then led him to attack, in his own expression, "the United States rather than Sweden." In short, if Bin Laden's rhetoric seems at first sight to confine him within the ghetto of his religious sectarianism, few analysts have seriously attempted to consider his itinerary in all its complexity.

From 1993 on, the Saudi regime, which in 1992 had timidly agreed to tone down its authoritarianism and accepted the creation of a "consultative council" whose members were carefully . . . appointed by itself, nevertheless retreated to a solely repressive solution.[23] Preemptive arrests were no longer limited to former members of the Afghan guerrillas, immediately arrested on their return at the end of the 1980s and systematically tortured, sometimes to death. They also included the most moderate protesters, condemned to heavy prison sentences and also tortured. It was in such a context that Bin Laden—just ousted from Sudan under U.S. pressure—clarified and radicalized his offensive against the regime which had rescinded his Saudi nationality.

In 1995—before his call to oust the United States from the Peninsula (1996) and the creation of the "World Islamic Front" (1998)—Bin Laden published the first of his numerous oppositional speeches addressed to King Fahd. These texts present a twofold interest. First, they provide keys to decipher the articulation between the "theological" and "political" components of the conflict which opposed him to the regime and its foreign protector-despoilers; they also enable us, if we are willing to make the effort to penetrate beyond the veil of this "theology of protest," to get a glimpse of the fundamentally political matrix of his radicalization.

The "Letter to Abu Rughal,"[24] addressed in 1995 by Bin Laden to King Fahd of Saudi Arabia, where the essential is put on record, contains a long, well documented and argued inventory of the monarch's outrages against "God and Islam, the land of Islam and the Muslims, the holy city of Mecca, and the community of Muslims." With special emphasis, Bin Laden first conventionally asserts the religious and theological primacy of his demands, which at the time still mainly concerned reform. If he first lists his political grievances against the monarch ("the political oppression that strikes all the elites, . . . the corruption, the squandering of wealth"), it is in order to assert that it is indeed the outrages against the foundations of religion which he intends to condemn first and foremost.

Just as conventionally, his demonstration is underpinned by references to the Quran, clarified by the exegeses of *ulamas*. Above all, it recalls the obligation of the rulers to build on the rock of Revealed laws and the stigmatization of "false believers" who, in place of the successive Revelations, take the *taghut*—a false god, idol, and demon in the Quran's lexicon—as a reference.[25] This mainly resumes the argument used by Qutb to justify his arraignment of the degeneracy of Nasser's regime: the Saudi monarch is acting in breach of the principle of the unicity of God, for he has allowed secular, human legislation, considered to be infidel and of foreign inspiration, to take the place of the divine reference. Thus the kingdom, as a member of the Gulf Council of Cooperation, accepts being subject to the decisions of international jurisdiction. And yet the decisions of this jurisdiction are founded on a body of references whose hierarchy is the "Constitution of the Council of Cooperation, international law, international norms, and the principles of Islamic law." Here lies the proof, fulminates Bin Laden, of the slight importance granted to divine law, classified in the lowest rank among the kingdom's references. Having established the religious nature of the monarch's transgressions, he turns to the inventory of what appears to him to be merely the logical consequence (true as it is that a "twisted stick cannot produce a straight shadow") of such breaches of the divine law. Much more prosaically, he then goes on to enumerate the political, social, and economic consequences which ensue, all fully profane.

The first consequence of the abandonment of the religious reference by the Saudi rulers was, in his opinion, the very eclectic and, in any event, not very "Islamic" character of the underpinnings of the kingdom's diplomacy. The argument emphasizes what too many talk-show analysts of Saudi Arabia, all too eager to denounce the "fundamentalism" of the princes, do not take the time to observe, namely, the limits of an "Islamic" explanation for the foreign policy of that oil-rich kingdom. He specifically accuses King Fahd of having successively funded or armed many combatants with little claim to the title "Islamic": the "Alawite" (*nusayri*) minority in power in Damascus in 1982, the very year in which it crushed the uprising in the city of Hama under heavy artillery, "assassinating tens of thousands of Muslims"; the Christian Maronite phalanges then fighting against the "Lebanese Muslims"; the Christian guerrilla warfare in Southern Sudan against the Islamic regime of the North; "our old friend Saddam Hussein," funded to the tune of $25 billion, while he was warring against the Iranian revolution; the Algerian regime, "which combats Islam and is flattening Muslims under its jackboot"; the "Communists" of South Yemen during the 1994 civil war, which had just come to an end.

"The Yemen crisis," he continues, "has demonstrated to what degree your support for the Afghan combatants had nothing to do with the cause of Islam: it was only intended to protect Western interests threatened by a possible Soviet victory." "For otherwise," he goes on relentlessly, "an Afghan Communist not being different from a Yemeni Communist, . . . how can you justify your simultaneously supporting Muslims against Communists in Afghanistan and Communists against Muslims in Yemen? . . . This contradiction is incomprehensible if we don't know that your policies are in fact dictated by the world of the Western Crusaders, to whom you have linked your destiny."

The demonstration then shifts to the economic terrain and attempts to answer the question which everyone, within the kingdom itself and throughout the world, had been raising. Knowing that the kingdom, at the end of the 1980s, had accumulated reserves amounting to some $140 billion and had at its disposal daily revenues of about $100 million, how, he asks, was it that by 1995 it had become one of the most indebted countries in the region? Why were its educational and health systems overcrowded, underequipped, and in crisis, 150,000 of its young graduates unemployed, and so many families facing economic insecurity? "Where has all this money been spent?" Bin Laden insists. First and foremost, on the sumptuous expenses of the royal family itself. The narrator "does not know" on this ground "where to begin the enumeration of palaces and other abodes blocking the horizon inside the kingdom and elsewhere in the world." The upkeep of such palaces, the courtyard of a single one of which "could contain the whole of the state of Bahrain,"[26] was to be reckoned in "thousands of millions of dollars." While the governors of the provinces advocated energy-saving measures, the palaces, moreover, remained floodlit day and night.

The core of the indictment, however, does not reside there, but in the terms of a leonine transaction with the Western "partners" of the kingdom: the true aid provided to the West has not been just the occasional funding of its various geopolitical appetites: the kingdom is caught in the stranglehold of two other exceptionally warped systems. The first is the weapons contracts, completely disproportionate with the needs and human resources of the Saudi army, Bin Laden argues. The percentage of the state budget devoted to defense by Saudi Arabia is close to 30 percent, he recalls, surpassing any equivalent on the global scale. And yet the contracts are not drawn up according to the technical needs of the army, but in order "to create revenues for the princes in power," who take up to 60 percent of the amount of each transaction in kickbacks, and in order to give personalized "compensations" to the heads of state (American and British: "Boeing to help get Bill Clinton reelected," "Tornadoes to thank John Major," etc.) who "help them to remain in power." The only results of such expenditures are "stockpiles of weapons with no human resources to use them . . . and huge military bases which appear to be intended for occupation by foreign forces."

The 1991 Gulf war resulted in a sort of upscaling of this military-financial "cooperation." The coalition forces rallied around the United States against Iraq "had hit on the opportunity of their life to blackmail you and exploit your fears and your cowardice." "They have insisted on making you pay the quasi-totality of the expenses for the war, . . . that is, $60 billion, of which $30 billion went into the pockets of the United States and about $15 billion into those of the other allies. . . . The rest was spent on commissions, market kickbacks, and other bribery." "The balance sheet of this Gulf war," according to Bin Laden, "speaks volumes about the efficiency of the armament policy. . . . The [Saudi] air force, which had five hundred planes at its disposal, was only able to shoot down two Iraqi aircraft, devoid of air cover. The navy, despite its thirty warships, of which twenty were equipped with missile-launchers, did not fire once. The army did not do any better: the country had to import technicians from Pakistan in order to be able to put together a single armored infantry division." The end of the war did not, however, bring an end to this wild extravagance: "After the war, your solidarity in regard to the coalition led you to conclude new contracts in their favor, to a tune of more than $40 billion for the Americans alone."

This long list of profligacy and "crazy expenditures linked to the presence of allied forces during the Gulf war," however, is far from bringing to a close Bin Laden's list of contentions: the worst is yet to come. Implacably argued, on the basis of World Bank figures, the inventory and close scrutiny of the consequences of the "deterioration in oil prices" ineluctably leads to a terrible, self-evident fact: Arabia has been ruined solely because its leaders have paid—at the highest price—for the privilege of being . . . militarily occupied. They are paying a still higher price for the right to continue to placate their protectors and therefore to benefit from their protection, by committing for their sake a sort of perpetual financial harakiri: while accelerating the rhythm of the depletion of their reserves, the fear-stricken princes are actively helping to bring about the very overproduction which reduces the financial value of their product, thus handing back a tremendous percentage of their receipts to their protectors. "Even if the West takes care to never kill the goose which lays the black golden eggs, it takes great care that the price of these eggs should remain as low as possible." For Bin Laden, writing in 1995, the kingdom has thus been the victim of the "biggest hold-up in history."

Is the charge that outrageous? Is the posture of the "radical Saudi Islamist" the only one to lead to such damning diagnostics? Nothing is less certain. The most official statistics and the expert appraisals the furthest removed from "terrorist" circles both prompt us to think that everything is not imaginary in this demonstration—far from it: "We pay for the oil at the market price. But this price is based on supply and demand: by increasing supply, the Saudis keep the prices low," Robert Baer, a former CIA operative, admitted in 2003. "It's something the Saudis have paid out of their pockets. We've never reimbursed them for this surplus capacity. We built it in the sixties and seventies; but when they nationalized Aramco they paid for it, they bought it back. We can't simply just sit down and say, 'These guys have always been against us and the Wahhabi fundamentalists have been sent by the royal family to destroy the West.'"[27]

While Bin Laden the Islamist was fulminating his terrible indictment, a French citizen, Jean-Michel Foulquier (the pseudonym of an ambassador stationed for several years in the capital of the Saudi kingdom), had reached a completely identical conclusion, albeit expressed at the time in less theological terms. Concluding a ruthless description of the nature of the relationship between the United States and the Saudi kingdom, he compared it ("you pay and I protect you") to the relationship between . . . a pimp and his prostitute.[28]

"I think the motives of the terrorists are above all of a political nature," concluded the American CIA expert Baer. "And the sooner we will stop intervening in the Middle-East, the better the terms on which we will be able to make a truce with terrorism."[29] Has the message come home to roost? Nothing could be less sure. "I think they are not pumping it all out," President Bush claimed in spring 2005, before entertaining Crown Prince Abdallah at his ranch and . . . obtaining a new spike in the kingdom's oil production in an attempt to restore a more advantageous price. His approach was unsuccessful for once, but for reasons linked more to the inefficacy of Saudi goodwill than to its reappraisal.

Without departing, it is true, from the framework of the most classical Islamic thinking, which granted all the room needed to nonreligious logical reasoning, Bin Laden has actually taken leave of the strictly religious sphere to evolve toward that of the "rational."[30] Nonreligious, political, economic, and financial analysis, once its rank has been grounded in religious rhetoric, occupies even in his rhetoric a pivotal position which too many observers, however, have been slow to take into account.

MOHAMMED ATTA OR THE MURDEROUS TRAJECTORY OF A PILOT OF SEPTEMBER 11

The biography of Mohammed Atta is just as eloquent. His trajectory as an adult militant—much shorter, since he was born on September 1, 1968 (in Cairo) and died at the age of thirty-three—is almost completely in resonance with the third temporality of Islamism. The life of the man who piloted the first of the two Boeing 767s to crash into the World Trade Center in New York on September 11, 2001, has been meticulously pieced together by many investigators.[31] The identity matrix of his "entry into Islamism" is particularly easy to decipher. The markers on his trail to radicalization are no less so.

Atta also did not come from a penniless background but from the universe of the Egyptian urban middle class. His father was a jurist; his sisters, as he himself had done, attended a university. He was granted the privilege of studying abroad. An architect by education, he was a member of an Egyptian engineering union which had been taken over by the Islamist trend in the 1990s. In Cairo, he classically denounced the repressive atmosphere and the regime's propensity to criminalize, with Western support, the Islamist trend in particular and all forms of political opposition in general. President Mubarak's project of violating the integrity of the historic city center of Cairo—by creating what Atta considered to be a sort of Islamic Disneyland for foreign tourists—revolted him just as much.

When, after having graduated from the University of Hamburg, Atta left for Syria in 1995 to carry out the first "fieldwork" for his diploma in urbanism, he claimed to have been outraged that the architectural expressions of Western culture towered over those of his Muslim culture. Everything converges toward the idea that his pious austerity was then already emerging, at least in part, in the wake of Qutb's example during his stay in the United States, in reaction to the repulsive "permissiveness" of German society.[32] That cultural alienation, his rebellion against the endless recital of international injustices, the huge gap in wealth between his chaotic native Egypt and German opulence, and the abject submission of regimes both illegitimate and highly repressive to American demands of all sorts gave Mohammed Atta the icy determination of "Abu 'Abd al-Rahman al-Misri," the *nom de guerre* that he, like all his al-Qaeda counterparts, assumed at the time of his commitment.

The elements of the most classical Islamist alchemy are here combined. It was on April 11, 1996, in Hamburg at the small mosque on

Steindamm, one month after the Sharm el-Sheikh summit (on March 13) against Islamic terrorism, that Mohammed Atta seems to have made the decision to "shift into direct action mode"—and to do so at the peril of his own life, in writing a very detailed will proving his plans to die. The care he put into defining the treatment which was to be bestowed on his mortal remains shows that he already knew then that he was going to die, but not yet that it was to be at the controls of a flying machine filled with thousands of liters of jet fuel.

The four emblematic figures of al-Qaeda whose trajectories in space and time we have just briefly retraced evolved under different historical and territorial circumstances: Sayyid Qutb, the political and ideological ancestor, and Ayman al-Zawahiri, Qutb's direct political heir, who both passed through the mold of physical torture; Osama Bin Laden, the harbinger of the globalization of resistance; and Mohammed Atta, one of his most determined operatives. However, it was strictly comparable formative factors and political mindsets which prompted them to formulate or adopt the categories and strategies of Qutb's rupture.

Qutb conceptualized and ideologized the reasons for his rift with a political environment that he considered illegitimate, because it was under the yoke of foreign custodianship, and whose authoritarianism, under torture, he had been in a position to attest. Zawahiri has taken up Qutb's torch, on the ideological as well as political level. Like Qutb (and unlike Bin Laden and Atta), his itinerary was warped by physical torture. Like Qutb, he has constructed himself by severing ties not only with the regime itself but also with the mainstream of the first Islamist generation opposed to it. He was the man who gave the final touch to the theological nitpicking legitimizing the rupture with the Muslim Brothers, accused of having made unacceptable compromises with the Western symbolic universe, imported by secular regimes, from which he truly intended to distance himself.

Bin Laden, for his part, found this rhetoric ready at hand and has not felt the need to add any major ideological dimension. However, he has contributed a sense of political and military logistics incomparably more sophisticated than anything that Qutb and Zawahiri succeeded in mobilizing, as well as firsthand knowledge of the disruptions engendered by U.S. interventionism in the Arabian Peninsula.

Atta came on the scene when the ideological matrix and the political logistics of the rebellion were both fine-tuned and perfectly functional. His political imaginary, exacerbated by direct contact with the West (which also left a baleful mark on Qutb and Bin Laden), was more

particularly fired by the vagaries of American and Israeli interventionism and thus at the core of the logic inherent in the third temporality of
Islamism. The evolution of the world during the 1990s, from Palestine
to Iraq, seemed to reinforce Qutb's analysis forty years earlier and thus
sanctioned the radicalism of his categories of rupture. Atta, in direct line
from Zawahiri and Qutb, seeing "his own" confronted with political violence comparable to what Qutb himself had suffered and denounced, was
thus to become, forty years later, his best soldier, for the first time, at the
cost of killing close to 3,000 innocent people, transporting the inferno of
war into the symbolic heart of the West.

FROM FEARS INHERITED TO FEARS EXPLOITED

The War of Representations

Are all these countries going to evolve toward democracy or go on . . . speaking Arabic to each other?

—HIGH-RANKING FRENCH OFFICIAL IN CHARGE OF THE
EURO-ARAB DIALOGUE (ADDRESSING A CONFERENCE IN 1990)

It must have helped you to speak French, the language of democracy!

—WELL-KNOWN LITERARY CRITIC ON FRENCH TELEVISION,
SPEAKING TO ONE OF THE MUSES OF THE ALGERIAN
"ERADICATOR" TREND IN 2002

Someone who refuses to drink down his glass like all the others, can he be one of ours?

—FROM A FRENCH POPULAR SONG

Most Muslims are not fundamentalists, and most fundamentalists are not terrorists, but most present-day terrorists are Muslims and proudly identify themselves as such.

—BERNARD LEWIS, *THE CRISIS OF ISLAM* (2003)

Anyone who wants to form a rational judgment in the West concerning Islamism must overcome two stumbling blocks. The first is the accumulation of subconscious, "inherited" fears triggered by our old Muslim neighbor-enemy onto whom, in the alchemy of our identity-building, has been foisted the essential role of telling us who we are. The second, more superficial but nonetheless efficacious, is the deliberate strategies on the part of all those who, in the West or in the Muslim world, have some reason to feel threatened in their momentary privileges and see more point in manipulating these fears than in combating them.

Anyone who has currently succeeded in casting someone who resists him as an "Islamist" knows full well that fear and ignorance of the Other can *ipso facto* turn out to be his most precious allies. The control of information flows being the nerve center of economic and political warfare, the biased manipulation of breaking news and the preference for lurid close-ups to the detriment of explanatory historical perspective are too often the rule. Those who, consciously or not, resort to such devices in the media and in the political sphere have no problem in mobilizing the irrational fears deeply embedded in the public psyche.

Since the 1980s this dual mechanism has been firing on all cylinders in the production of representations of the "Islamist issue" within the societies of the "North" (mainly, in this case, those of Europe and North America). But it is probably in France that it has taken the most grotesque turn: of all the Western powers, France is indeed the only one where a particularly long-standing relation to the Muslim Other—shared essentially with Spain since the Crusades—has been reinforced by the longest-lasting colonization of a Muslim land, Algeria, ruled by France from 1830 to 1962. That is why this chapter devoted to the "war of representations" of the Islamist phenomenon in the Western world is essentially going to focus on the French experience.

FEARS INHERITED

Identifying the origin of such inherited fears in order to have some chance of overcoming them requires a brief recapitulation of the status of this "culture of the Other" that is Islam and its role in the construction of our identity. Our difficulty in accepting the emergence of a lexicon other than that which we have subconsciously inflated into the only one capable of expressing the universal seems to be, as we shall see, at the nexus of our complacency in regard to all sorts of analytical dead ends.

Seen from France, Islam is thus above all the identity marker of the "culture of the Other" and therefore of the Other per se. To discuss Islam, to establish a relationship with it, is therefore, par excellence, to discuss or to communicate with the Other. And yet to discuss the Other, as we have known at least since G. W. F. Hegel, is in many respects to discuss ourselves. It is the Other who tells us "who we are," what place we occupy in space, and, to a large degree, what role we play there. Identity only exists through contact with the Other. It is the second person who reaches the summit of a mountain or the shores of a desert island who determines the consistence of the ego of the first occupier, male or female, black or white, intellectual or blue-collar, fat or thin, and so forth. The terms of our "relativity" depend on the Other, and therefore our "identity" lies in the Other or in opposition to him/her. Even if the person who joins me on the desert island is a native of my village, I will find the feature that specifies him and thus enables me to exist in my necessary uniqueness.

In the case of the relationship to Islam in France, the propensity of the Other to affect the ever fragile inner balance of our ego is all the stronger for not being about "any old Other." This Other does not hail from Mars or evolve in a context devoid of representations. He or she is on the contrary most frequently a native (on the level of representations but also, for once, concurrently in the world of statistics) of a North Africa doubly close, through the narrowness of the Straits of Gibraltar as well as through a history very largely in common for want of having been truly "shared." This long *tête-à-tête*, emblazoned with Saracens and Crusaders, colonists and *fellaghas*, repatriates and immigrants, is attested not only by historical events with their still festering wounds or by technical and linguistic transfers of all kinds but also by fantasies, repulsions, and other phobias.

Emblematically, the relationship with the culture of the Other in its Far Eastern or Buddhist version, to which it is somehow just as necessary to have recourse to determine the frontiers of our identity territory, is less traumatic than with our Arab-Muslim neighbor. In the heart of verdant Morvan, somewhere along the path leading to a Training Center for Imams (at Château-Chinon), whose creation in 1989 fueled so many rampant media fantasies, the wandering visitor has long been struck by the sight of a Buddhist temple whose ornately gilded and scarlet façade trumpets the kitsch exoticism of its architecture. Contrary to the tiniest mosque in our suburbs, this temple of another "religion of the Other" has long enjoyed the silent approbation of the jealous custodians of our national identity.

The Muslim Other also does not hail from Vietnam, which was long buffeted by the storms of colonialism, like Algeria, but whose remoteness has lent a sepia tint to memory and diffused our apprehension. In time as in space, the Muslim is actually (too) close to us in two ways. It is precisely "when difference is lacking that violence most threatens," as the philosopher René Girard has adroitly observed. This neighbor is also too close for comfort on the terrain of religious reference, since, to a large degree, we both lay claim to shared scriptures as well as to common biblical and Quranic figures. Our "old" and "too close" neighbor is therefore logically the most direct agent in the construction of our collective identity, with his diversity in linguistic (his references are not in Latin), ethnic (he does not own to elegant Gaulois or Frankish ancestors), and of course religious strata (his ultimate Prophet is unknown to us and above all he repudiates the "secular" *nec plus ultra* of our French modernity). It has been in counterdistinction to the Saracen or the Moor that a fair share of French ethnic and political identity has been erected, against that of the Mahometan that—without turning a blind eye to our own religious wars all the same—we have wanted to be first Christians, then Europeans and Westerners, and, finally, within the very particular framework of French identity, secular.

It is within this same spatial register that the trauma of the ultimate re-territorialization of getting to know our neighbors is being played out. The perception of Islam is indeed still partly constructed on the territory of the Other, through the intermediation—we will return to this below—of the "news" which flashes so rapidly yet so incompletely back and forth across the seas; but it is accomplished ever more frequently within the "intimacy" of our own public spaces, within the compass of our own society. We no longer erect our cathedrals on the hills of Africa: we are stupefied to discover the existence of mosques in our nearby suburbs. We are no longer "welcomed" by the Other, but, first as a predictable outcome of the cyclone of colonialism, second as a deliberate product of our industrial strategies, it is the Other who today camps among us. The precious distance has been still further reduced. Finally, even if it is today well on the way to diversification, and not only thanks to the soccer player Zinedine Zidane, the first generation of Muslims in France to this day includes more manual workers than representatives of the scientific or artistic intelligentsia, which perhaps has deprived "Islam" of part of the communication skills to allay the fears and misunderstandings raised by its assertion north of the Mediterranean.

Islam is the culture of the closest of our neighbors at a time when the tremendous imbalance born of the colonial relationship is being reduced, albeit very slowly, to the benefit of the southern shore and hence "to the relative detriment" of the northern shore. In 1930, the year of the zenith of colonialism, the "Islam of the colonies," though already the "culture of the Other, our close neighbor," and though already established in France, did not disturb people's mental quietude to the same degree as, from the 1980s on, the "Islam of the suburbs" was to do. The national identity of France then easily accommodated the folklorized Islam of the Great Colonial Exhibition in celebration of the "centennial of the conquest of Algeria." Has the Prophet Muhammad modified his message since that time? Of course not. But the supporters of the religion of the Other have irresistibly risen to eschew the colonial configuration. They henceforth refuse to be merely one of the exotic accessories of our cultural centrality. The sun of the "blessed day" of the unilateral relationship with "our colonies" has set. At the beginning of the twenty-first century, unequal though it may have remained, the relationship between the two shores leaves the North with the vague but not wholly unfounded feeling that the heyday of its secular political and symbolic hegemony lies behind it.

The disenchantment of France is not only the result of the end of the reassuring colonial paradigm. The triumph of economic rationality has indeed, as far as development is concerned, demonstrated its tremendous quantitative potential. But it has gradually also let us catch a glimpse of its contradictions and qualitative limits: high social and ecological costs, the weakening of social links, the loss of ethical landmarks. The crisis, for a time masked by the glitter of technological progress, is today exacerbating to the beat of collapsing growth curves, ever steeper unemployment charts, and the recourse to risky sectarian trajectories as the means to reenchant the world.

If it has obviously been accentuated by the "alien" character of the human vector of the "new religion,"[1] the tension created by the assertion of Islam thus partakes, to a high degree, of the tension that any religious assertion whatsoever would give rise to, in a society which is in fact, *stricto sensu,* much less Christian than de-Christianized and much less "secular" than devoid of all religious meaning. Behind the banner of secularism, it is the creeping desertification of the religious sphere, rather than its separation from the public sphere, that has been the upshot of the century of Jules Ferry's heirs. On this ground, "Islamic tension" may consequently express less the rivalry between two Revelations than the irritation resulting from what may appear—due to the religious lexicon—as a demand for spirituality in a society priding itself on having solved the issue of the social demand for the sacred once and for all. Hence Islam must overcome the reluctance fanned not only by its status as "religion of the Other" but also by its status as a religion per se.

On a second level only, but also fueled by the dynamics of its Eastern alter ego, it is possible to discern the old, purely religious tension of conflict between the dogmas, also exacerbated by their extreme proximity. On closer examination, and if we give credence to "their" Quran, are Muslims not really Christians who have received an extra "coating" of prophecy?

FEARS EXPLOITED OR THE REPRESENTATION OF ISLAMISM IN THE BOOBY TRAP OF POLITICS

The fears inherited from a long conflictual *tête-à-tête* are not always combated with utter determination: they are often very knowingly fueled by all those who can turn them to political profit. The success of the irrational and criminalizing interpretation of the Islamist generation is thus the product of more or less subconscious psychological and psychoanalytical variables; but it is still more the outcome of deliberate strategies, all the more effective because they happen to be those of a conjunction of particularly powerful state actors. Besides the "historical enemies" of the Muslim Other, among their front ranks are found all the Arab regimes devoid of grass-roots support, that is, the vast majority of them.

The international legitimacy of these discredited governing teams tends to be reduced to their talent for criminalizing any alternative to their rule. The Arab dictators have thus adopted since the beginning of the 1980s, and even more grotesquely since September 11, a communication strategy which, in order to turn the dividends of Western fears to their advantage, consists in exporting a demonized image of their Islamist oppositions. And it matters little that they themselves have in fact very widely contributed to the radicalization of such oppositions—in some cases (as in Algeria, as we will see below) even purely and simply stepping in for them, through terrible manipulations of violence, massacring their opponents while placing the blame on them. So long as they display a willingness to flatter its ignorance and foster its fears, the Western public will readily grant "those who fight the fundamentalists" the monopoly on representation of universal values and elevate them to the status of sole legitimate spokespersons.

But the Arab dictatorships are not the only players in this field. Israeli strategists, thanks to their tremendous media power throughout the West, very quickly grasped the scope of the resources that they could draw from a weakening of the PLO and the irruption, within the ranks of Palestinian resistance, of the Islamist generation of Hamas. Russia, which had failed to do so in Afghanistan, has since successfully, from the very outset of the Chechen conflict, turned to swelling the ranks of all those for whom the irrational fear of the Islamist Other has become a source of ultimate legitimacy more than of legitimate concern.

September 11 and the "Binladenization" of "Muslim" political oppositions which it entailed have dispelled the last reservations and swept away the ultimate nuances. "Never" since that date, the Tunisian opposition leader Moncef Marzouki summarizes, "have the dictators had it so good." The image of the Other is no longer today the product of a strategy of knowledge aimed where necessary at overcoming irrational fears: it has become the stake of particularly cynical strategies of power where, from Algiers to Washington via Tel Aviv, top brass and "experts" of all nationalities and religious faiths vie with each other in deploying their talents.

It is true that this repressive drift receives substantial support from the fringe of the Islamist trend which really deserves to be qualified as extremist and which helps by its discourses and its actions to lend credence to the worst manipulations and the most warped Western fantasies, consigning any will to contextualize and all clamors for truth to the realm of naïveté and ingenuousness, even culpable compromise. The existence of this obtuse fringe and the terrorist threat that it embodies definitely are major challenges which must be confronted, with all the force of the law. But these challenges should not make us forget another of a radically different nature, which consists in the astonishing capacity of this extremist minority to highjack all the media visibility of the re-Islamization process. This conjuring trick, however, has its rationale: the thirsting of the radicals of this movement after the media spotlight is all the more easily satisfied in that they enjoy support from all those who take advantage of the fact that the most repulsive fringe of their political opponents eclipses the moderation of the vast majority of them. Whereas it is so difficult to become familiar with the faces of the spokespersons of the moderate trends of the Islamist scene, every European viewer knows ad nauseam all the nuances of the conquering ravings of the most repulsive fringe of Islamist "Londonistan," whose representatives are tracked down by the media in prime time, thanks to the terribly selective sagacity of their "special correspondents."

In the emblematic case of Algeria, the proven counter-performances of such "special correspondents" and other "investigative journalists" expose the full spectrum of the distorted representation of reality systematically allowed to prevail by those who so readily drape themselves in the virtues of objectivity and "completely independent" reporting.

INTOXICATION AND MISINFORMATION: THE PRIME EXAMPLE OF ALGERIA'S "RADICAL ISLAMISM"

In such times of strong "Islamic" turbulence, the factual information which we receive from the Muslim world should be as scrupulous as possible. The emblematic example of Algeria's civil war shows how far this is from being the case. If we were asked to point out, long before the electroshock of September 11, the media messages which, over the preceding decade, had most scarred the subconscious of the French and Europeans in general, in their relationship with the Muslim religion, the horrors laid at the door of the "Islamist terrorists" during the never-ending Algerian civil war would no doubt spring to mind.

Year after year, ever since Algeria's junta canceled the January 1992 elections won by the Islamic Salvation Front, how many thousands of televised images, talk shows and op-eds, news summaries and cartoons, on radio or in the press, have been devoted to the subject? Considerable legitimate energy has been roused to denounce those in charge of the planned elimination of "secular intellectuals," the successive assassinations of foreigners living in Algeria, the spectacular hijacking of the "Algiers Airbus," the indiscriminate bombings in the Paris metro, and the atrocious crimes against nuns, a bishop, monks, sportsmen, singers, writers, and artists. How many times were we sickened by the terrifying way—no figure of speech intended—in which, one after another, each of our cherished humanist references was ruthlessly shot down by maniacal killers who, furthermore, signed their crimes with particularly outrageous statements? And what is to be said about the plight of hundreds of villagers, often defenseless women and children, slashed to death in the depths of the night?

It has since then become possible to write this page of history and so perhaps to turn it. For several years now, piecing together a long trail of clues, perfectly converging revelations have confirmed what for a long time had remained only hypothesis.[2] They have thus enabled a decisive breakthrough in our knowledge of a particularly murky episode of our recent relations with "radical Islam." But oddly enough, as their accuracy and importance have grown, the media attention granted to these testimonies, which, however, fulfilled the double quest for knowledge of the close relatives of the victims and of world opinion, has . . . tailed off. After the turmoil triggered early in 2001 by the first revelations of ex-lieutenant Habib Souaïdia,[3] those of ex-colonel Mohammed Samraoui, albeit the first to emanate from within the secret services of the Algerian army, sparked only a particularly limited response.[4]

And when, in 2004, in *Françalgérie: crimes et mensonges d'États*, journalists Lounis Aggoun and Jean-Baptiste Rivoire, at the end of a particularly fruitful survey,[5] laid out the evidence for massive and systematic army involvement, thus confirming to what a hitherto unsuspected extent the unilateral stigmatization of "Islamist terrorists" was far from being the truth, the silence of the media and politicians became particularly deafening. Except for the unflappable back rooms of pro-Algiers propaganda, assigned the task of discrediting the news, and their usual go-betweens in France or across Europe, no dispatch from the national press agency even found it necessary to inform its French subscribers. Almost no major headline, daily or weekly, gave it a single line.[6] No television channel, except France 3, even mentioned its existence. What was it in these patiently collected testimonies that made everyone so reluctant to hear them?

Quite simply that, since the beginning of the 1990s, the Algerian military regime, behind the pseudo-pluralist façade of massively rigged elections, had not really gone to much trouble to fight the extremist fringe of the Islamist trend. Irrefutable evidence establishes not only that it first protected then systematically manipulated these groups but also that, in many particularly exemplary cases, it purely and simply stood in for them: through their "Islamic Groups of the Army (IGA)," initially controlled then manufactured by the back rooms of the secret services (the Department of Intelligence and Security, DIS), the Algiers generals notably connived in the barbaric assassinations, "in the name of Islam," of members of the opposition as well as their own "secular" allies. In order to discredit all legalist opposition in the eyes of the world and to shift a political struggle that it knew it had essentially lost onto the safer terrain of security policy, the junta made the atrocities of the "IGA" its main mode of action and communication.[7] From 1991 on, even before the appearance of the first "Islamic Groups of the Army," the leaders of an early and elusive radical offshoot of the Islamist trend which had emerged at the end of the 1980s (the Armed Islamic Movement, AIM), after being duly given amnesty at the request of those same semiofficial back rooms, then saw themselves equipped with "government duty vehicles" . . .

According to one of the academics whose forethought it had been that their studies would reveal the key to deciphering the Algerian crisis, the pamphlets of the IGA were written "in a sort of politico-religious cant which rivaled that of the Western Marxist-leaning groups of yesteryear." "What an insight!" ex-colonel Samraoui commented ironically on these conclusions in his book: "The AIG pamphlets [were indeed] written by officers of the DIS whose heads had been trained in Moscow, Prague, or Berlin before the collapse of the Wall." From 1991 on:

> [T]he first pamphlets calling for the seizure of power by the force of arms were issued, in fact, from the Antar barracks at Ben-Aknoun, the headquarters of the Main Operational Command Center (OCC) . . . as for the much touted "blacklists" [of intellectuals to be shot] attributed to the Islamists, they had been drawn up at the Ghermoul center, the headquarters of the Directorate of Counterespionage (DCE). It was Captains Omar Merabet, Saïd Lerari (alias Saoud), and Azzedine Aouis who authored these pamphlets, which elements from the "protection section" and the drivers of the DCE slipped into the mailboxes of the persons concerned.[8]

In Algeria, secular intellectuals easily became convinced—willingly or after seeing so many of their peers assassinated "by the fundamentalists"—of the necessity of zealously relaying the junta's rhetoric. In France and in the world, on the other hand, the generals had to prevent any hostile reaction to the rigging of the ballot boxes and the already disturbingly visible part of the iceberg of the "anti-fundamentalist" crackdown. In order to do so, they had to maintain people's minds in a state close to "post-traumatic stress." The Algerian services were to display a real virtuosity in this field. From the beginning, almost all the sadly famous "emirs of the AIG" were in fact only strawmen in the hands of the services. It is admitted today that Ali Touchent, the person who commanded and manipulated the perpetrators of the Saint Michel metro station bombings in 1995, disappeared . . . into the barracks of the Algerian security services, where it has been proven that he had long been a familiar denizen but where none of our "investigative journalists" ever took the trouble to try to flush him out.

It is true that the architects of this terrible "murder machine"[9] could call on a long tradition of cooperation with their French counterparts.[10] To quote just one example, their alliance worked to such a extent that— in order to justify the huge campaign of arrests which enabled them to send the main leaders of the Algerian opposition who had taken refuge in France into exile in Burkina Faso in August 1994—the French services and Algerian services in the autumn of 1993 jointly organized the fake kidnapping of three French civil servants stationed at the consulate in Algiers by some of their "fundamentalist terrorist" friends.

Many politicians and journalists and just as many academics and well-known intellectuals unconditionally supported (and, in some cases, persist in supporting) this formidable undertaking of intoxication. Some, in the belief that they were making a commitment to a legitimate struggle against obscurantism, did it out of naïveté and ignorance and, in the name of the struggle for secularism, rapturously paraphrased statements issued by the Algerian Military Security. In the case of some others, it seems that the generosity enabled by the bottom line of the generals' oil receipts helped, all caution cast to the winds, to sweep away any ethical or moral considerations.

As difficult as it might be today to render to "Caesar" his share of the violence, this should nonetheless be seen as an urgent task. And the media should do this with the same degree of fervor which some have devoted to laying it at the door of "Allah" or his self-proclaimed representatives.

THE WAR OF REPRESENTATIONS AND THE FAILURE OF INTELLECTUAL MEDIATION: WHERE LIES THE "TRUTH"?

Facing the grievous aberrations of the media and the political sphere, the autonomy of the academic sphere might have been expected to ensure a healthier balance. Academics, however, have been far from displaying performances significantly better than those of the media and the political class. But this failure is less linked to any intrinsic weakness on the part of a generation of "neo-Orientalist" researchers than to the fact that their work only percolates through to public opinion in an extremely selective way. While the Muslim world is one of the great stakes in contemporary knowledge, the media servilely reproduce the political power ratio of the regional and international arenas. On the other hand, they welcome with open arms the representatives of a very specific component of the intelligentsia, at the outer edge of academia. Their production is characterized by never going against the nostrums of received wisdom.

In 1998 Pierre Bourdieu, with a view to exposing the underpinnings of the misinformation obfuscating the Algerian civil war, superbly deconstructed the (mal)functioning of this category of mediators with scientific aspirations by creating expressly for them the category of "negative intellectuals."[11] Just as in most of the accounts by journalists, a large portion of intellectuals had then remained silent concerning the essential thing, that is, the scope of the manipulation of the violence by the military authorities.[12] It was in this context that Pierre Bourdieu denounced those who, in his opinion, combined "the literary avant-garde—or its ersatz—with the genuine political rearguard." The latter had chosen not only a silence of complicity but also a consciously assumed commitment on the side of the junta. Bernard-Henri Lévy and André Glucksmann, the visible part of a particularly well-oiled system, weighed in with rare conviction to obfuscate the degree of involvement of the army in the most appalling collective massacres of civilians. Controlled all along by the collaborators of the regime during an elusive trip to Algeria, the two French "philosophers," whose "insight" was praised by the Algerian press,[13] thought they were informed enough to solemnly bestow their benediction on the perfectly unilateralist arguments of their military hosts.

Scientifically speaking, can the frontiers of Islam be qualified as "bloodstained," as the American essayist Samuel Huntington, for his part, thought himself entitled to write? From the pen of someone whose own (Christian) zone of civilization, lest we forget, more or less directly initiated the modes of converting and settling (or, perhaps better put: . . . unsettling) South America before doing the same in North America, then the transatlantic African slave trade, the expansion of European colonial empires, capitalist or communist, in Africa and Asia, and finally the Nazi Third Reich, the stigmatization of the modes of diffusion of the Muslim religion, whose "performances" in this realm (from the slave trade to military expansionism) are incontestably more modest, such an assessment makes us wonder about the scientific value of the approach on which it is based. Unless we admit the innate "superiority" of Western achievements in the last century (from the Nazi extermination camps to those of communism, via the terrorism of Zionism in its initial phase and those of Euskadi Ta Askatasuna and the Irish Republican Army), the easy recourse to the simplifications of violence at best seems to be the least unequally shared of the political tools of domination. This is the analytical principle which the intellect should lead us to strongly reassert today, in a situation where the camp of the strongest is attempting to mask its responsibilities behind dangerous culturalist explanations. But that is unfortunately by no means the case.

Edward Said has excellently summed up the functional logic of this sort of pernicious mobilization of approximate knowledge, too often drastically devoid of any true sociological understanding of the human territory that it claims to explain to the world:

> Nowadays, book shops . . . are full of doughty volumes with showy titles evoking the link between "Islam and terrorism," "Islam exposed," the "Arab threat," and other "Muslim conspiracies," written by political polemicists claiming to draw their information from experts who supposedly have penetrated the soul of these strange eastern lesser breeds. These . . . have benefited from the support of television channels . . . as well as of a myriad of evangelical and conservative radio stations, of tabloids and even of respectable newspapers, all busy recycling the same unverifiable generalities in order to mobilize "America" against foreign devils. Without this meticulously kept impression that these far away small tribes are not like "us" and do not accept "our" values, all clichés which are the essence of the Orientalist dogma, the war could not have been launched. All the powerful have surrounded themselves with such scholars in their pay, the Dutch conquerors of Malaysia and Indonesia, the British armies in India, in Mesopotamia, in Egypt, and in West Africa, the French conscripts in Indochina and North Africa. Those advising the Pentagon and the White House use the same clichés, the same contemptuous stereotypes, the same justifications in order to use power and violence.[14]

As long as we are speaking of the Muslim Other, there is no end to the list of such ambiguous performances broadcast in prime time. Among a myriad, let us select just one particularly emblematic French example and let us express the hope that one day it will, with hindsight, become the object of a serene and detailed professional, scientific, and political audit.[15] During a leading broadcast on a public television channel, five "heavyweights" on the media, intellectual, and political scene (including the two models for the "negative intellectual" identified by Pierre Bourdieu) one evening in 1993 succeeded in sending into media orbit a perfectly unilateral version of the Algerian civil war. For sixty minutes our heroes of political analysis, thought, and action unreservedly committed their talent and their stature to the presentation of a woman introduced as a courageous Algerian women's rights activist, Khalida Messaoudi. It already required a certain degree of naïveté and ignorance (or cynicism?) not to have known that the person that Pierre Bourdieu was soon to depict as the "Passionaria of the eradicators" was in fact a pivotal element in the interlocking media-police system which the Algerian junta had developed to mask an operation of physical liquidation of its political opponents—next to which, before the tribunal of history, Operation Condor set up by the South American military in the 1970s pales in comparison. Since then, the respective weight of Khalida Messaoudi's commitment to women's rights and to the privileges of the Algerian "Pinochets" has been clarified, the services rendered to the latter having been rewarded in 2002 with a ministerial post.[16] Shortly before her appointment, in Kabylie, a crowd of demonstrators that she was attempting to join, wishing to show that they were not at all in the dark about the nature of her relations with those in power, sent her packing with taunts of "Khalida Lewinsky."[17]

The fact remains. The name of the leading talk show on the French public service channel—which was to be echoed over the following years by several thematic evenings broadcast by its Franco-German counterpart Arte, mobilizing Algerian and French writers and artists—was after all *The Hour of Truth*. Such pseudoanalyses not only taint the credibility of intellectual production: by appearing on the media, they fuel the terrible mechanism of "self-fulfilling prophecy." Factual lies and analytical shortcuts not only fool those Western audiences for whom they are intended. They also contribute to radicalizing those they do their best to criminalize, disqualifying in advance any posture of moderation among their ranks (or among those of their rivals). And when, inexorably, the loop is looped, the heralds of the worst, facing the violence that they have helped to manufacture, can triumphantly witness the most reductive and mendacious of their "prophetic" accusations being fulfilled.

The French channel's historic *Hour of Truth* broadcast illustrates the worst of what the alliance between the two main categories of mediators of our constructed knowledge of the Other can produce: to the "negative intellectuals" too often correspond the distortions produced by the wide spectrum of those we can consider to be their counterparts within the world of the Muslim Other and the vehicles of a second form of distortion in intellectual mediation, the "façade intellectuals."

FROM THE "NEGATIVE" INTELLECTUAL TO THE "FAÇADE" INTELLECTUAL

Luckily for us, the history of the French Revolution was not written on the sole basis of the memories of *émigré* aristocrats. Had it been so, despite the value of their testimonies, the exegesis of the political outcomes of the national "terror" would have been very different, depriving generations of modernizers of the privilege of detecting the rays of light of the Enlightenment behind the deluge of blood of the fallen royalist elites. In terms of revolution or simply the impetus thrusting "Islamic" actors onto the stage (singularly less violent than the French Republican Revolution though they may prove to have been), no such precaution seems to prevail. One of the most effective means to scramble any lucid perception of the Islamists' political arguments thus consists in entrusting analysis or discussion of them only to their fiercest rivals. This is what the Western media often do, by recruiting, within the camp of the Muslim "Other," all those who, for various reasons, which may sometimes be perfectly legitimate, are willing to fan our fears and fantasies. Highly respectable opponents . . . or scarecrows botched together for the occasion do not all share identical motives. But all—especially the female members of the contingent—produce the same collateral damage.

The "Sick Souls of Islam"

The Muslim imitators of Bernard Lewis or of Bernard-Henri Lévy, the defenders of the concept of an "Islamic disease,"[18] support to one degree or another the essentialist hypothesis whose fragility I have attempted, throughout the pages of this book, to demonstrate: the causes of the attacks devised by Osama Bin Laden and Ayman al-Zawahiri are consubstantial with Muslim history and culture. They are predicated as the predictable outcome of a drift whose origins are found not only in the intrinsic nature of the relation that they maintain with their dogma but at its very core. Without denying that improvements in the recognition of the non-Muslim "Other" are still to be achieved within the societies of Muslim culture, I tend to think for my part that this violence could have been fully expressed in a lexicon borrowed from other systems of reference: those of "secular" nationalism, of communism in its diverse versions, of national socialism, or of other religious or fully profane "dogmas," old or new. The pope of the Copts, Chenouda III, and other Christian authorities of the East have granted their "religious" absolution to the suicide attacks of those in despair over Israeli policy. The use of violence (and *a fortiori* that of counterviolence), even when legitimized by a dichotomous, simplistic, or even racist vision of the world, is by no means, in the purview of the past century or any of those preceding it, the prerogative of any one religion or culture.

The assertion of the contemporary Islamist generation very logically interferes with the interests of other components of the intellectual or political Arab and Muslim scene. Opponents for some, more or less direct allies of the regimes for others, whether they have remained in close touch with their society or, on the contrary, have been living in long-term exile (which by no means prevents them from . . . knowing), the "façade" intellectuals have only one feature in common: producing a discourse which is more pleasing to Western ears than that of their Islamist rivals. Accordingly, they obtain not only the attention which is very legitimately due to them but a quasi-monopoly on the representation of their societies and of the political dynamics of which they have been, for one reason or another, the victims. The legitimacy of native informants[19] is all the stronger because the virtue of their family name gives their analysis an endogenous flavor which often suffices to confer authority. Conversely, a more discordant discourse emanating from the holder of a family name just as exotic will very soon cause him to be suspected of being an appeaser or even an accomplice of the "fundamentalists."

The criteria that empower "indigenous" experts from the Muslim world to have access to the world of the media have thus become blatantly simple: they have less to do with any objective knowledge they may possess than with whether or not they offer Western consumers the means for communion in the wholesale denunciation of the "Islamist" Satan. It is consequently out of the question to be too choosy about their political affiliation, how representative their vision of things in their respective societies may be, or even, in some cases, their personal ethics. When discussing Arabism, it has long seemed preferable in Paris to lend an ear mainly to the voice of Berberist activists. When discussing Islamism, Christians or atheists are today particularly welcome. The most fiercely anticlerical Left may well come to adopt the theses of the Arab Christian far Right, even though, in the case of Lebanon, it has only just emerged from its murky phalangist drift. One swallow does not a summer make: the French Right, for its part, can turn to its own advantage the theses of the North African Left, Stalinist fringe included.

The "Muslimists" of the Eleventh Hour . . .

In order to explain their twofold defeat in confronting the Islamists and the authoritarian regimes, different fractions of the Arab Left often attempt today to impose more self-congratulatory, though hardly more convincing, explanations for their current marginalization. They generally attribute it to the rash support which the "secular" authoritarian regimes that they were struggling against allegedly gave to their Islamist rivals. The intellectual options and the political choices of such representatives of the Left and their heirs may, however, be very different in regard to the Islamists. A large proportion of them have made the struggle against the authoritarianism of the regimes their priority. They have thus taken the double risk of running the gauntlet of repression at home and being subjected to the ostracism of the Western media. They have often explored the ideological and political passageways of communication with the Islamist camp and, in the forums where "young Islamists" and "old nationalists" increasingly accept to mingle, they are efficiently helping to restore the communication between the two political generations.

Others, less numerous but more visible, have chosen to make the struggle "against fundamentalism" paramount. They collect the dividends of their struggle either on the national political playing field, by working for the regimes they had formerly fought, or abroad, by providing the communication and the expertise that the Western public is clamoring for. A good many members of the former Algerian Party of the Socialist Avant-Garde (APSAG), a Communist part of the Tunisian secular intelligentsia (including historic figures of the Movement of Socialist Democrats), have thus made the risky bet of rallying around the authoritarian regimes that they formerly fought.

Among the disillusioned members of the Left, some have also reconverted, for media purposes, to a sort of "Muslimism" of the eleventh hour, relocating their struggle against the Islamist challenger inside the religious field. Before European audiences easily persuaded by such a show of "lucidity," they thus defend "the" definitive—most often very recently acquired—version "of Islam," which, in their opinion, lays bare the folly of the whole Islamist generation, whatever their trend may be. The paradox of such a posture is not only that, in terms of essentialism, it does not cede anything to the "religious" challengers to the Left. Such a displacement of the "anti-Islamist" struggle inside the religious field above all serves to prove, though unbeknownst to its hymnists, the reality and the depth of the process of re-Islamization that they are intent on denying or discrediting, without realizing to what an extent they themselves are completely involved in it. On the Western media market, these discourses obviously find a limitless audience, inversely proportional, in reality, to their reception in the societies of the South, for the benefit of which they are purportedly produced.

However that may be, when it comes to discussing the majority, rebel or marginal minorities are particularly welcome. Following the assassination of the Algerian Berberist singer Matoub Lounes in June 1998, Jacques Chirac provided a fine example of this ploy. In order to pay tribute to a man whose twofold rebellion had led him to declare that he was neither "Arab nor Muslim," the French head of state declared: "Matoub Lounes was the voice of Algeria!"

Have the episode of Ahmed Chalabi (the exiled leader of a small Iraqi opposition group and main advisor of President Bush during the campaign against Baghdad from 2001 on) and the way in which the U.S. administration alleges—without protesting too much, when truth is told—that it was lulled by the misleading advice of this native informant been enough to highlight the danger, when building our knowledge of the world, of relying only on those who reinforce our certitudes? Unfortunately, this is to be doubted: unlikely NGOs and dummy associations artificially boosted by the media solely for their talent in vouching "from within" for the criticism of anyone "who refuses to down his drink like all the others" (and for whom the snares of "prepared" or "edited" talkshow interviews in carefully slanted guest setting are reserved) continue to pursue their misleading mission of "information."

The systematic media coverage of stooges of all kinds chosen for their talent in denouncing the "diseases" of the Muslim Other thus thickens the smog of irrationality and fear. As expected, Western opinion consequently slithers toward radicalization in its perception of a complex situation. And as expected, this Western radicalization inexorably reinforces a corresponding spiral of counter-radicalization.

NINE

HARD POWER AND IMPOSED REFORM

The Illusions of the Western Response to Islamism

It is not by reforming the religious discourse that the region will be pacified, but by pacifying the region that the religious discourse will be reformed.

—SAUDI ISLAMIST LEADERS (2005, QUOTED BY PASCAL MÉNORET)

There is no common measure between a terrorism of underground fighters and a state terrorism having weapons of mass destruction at its disposal. Just as there is a disproportion between the weapons, there is a disproportion between the two forms of terror. Should the horror and the indignation in response to civilian victims massacred by a human bomb disappear when the victims are Palestinians and massacred by inhuman bombs?

—EDGAR MORIN, SAMI NAÏR, AND DANIÈLE SALLENAVE,
LE MONDE (JUNE 3, 2002)

And if, . . . more generally, at the core of our secular, democratic, pluralist societies, . . . a tremendous conformism of correct thinking was on the rise? If a terrible mimetic domination replaced the clerical domination of yesteryear? A domination where everyone is socially constrained to conform to a conventional mold of thought, leaving only an illusory freedom of contents. Oh, the sweetness of a totalitarianism of the extreme center.

—JEAN BAUBEROT, LAÏCITÉ, 1905–2005: ENTRE PASSION ET
RAISON (2005)

If Sharon is a man of peace in Bush's eyes, then we are also men of peace.

—AL-QAEDA LEADER, QUOTED IN YOSRI FOUDA AND NICK
FIELDING, MASTERMINDS OF TERROR (2003)

Rising to the challenges that the September 11 attacks have hurled in the face of the Western world would require a doubly attentive and cautious examination of the political agenda of the "aggressors," on the one hand, and that of the camp of the "aggressees" on the other. It would be important to ascertain what motives may, "through our enemies' eyes,"[1] have legitimized such violence. We should also attempt to determine whether all those—American superpower, European middle-weight powers, overprotected Israel, and Arab authoritarian regimes—who sit on the right hand of the domination relationship had anything to answer for in the staging of such a spectacular triumph of the logic of confrontation. But on the political level, neither the lucid scrutiny of the aggressor's motivations nor any realistic introspection into the possible share in responsibility of the camp of the victims of aggression, however, seems to have truly happened.

The "democracies' response" first mainly took the shortcut of massive recourse to military and security-obsessed hard power. Parallel to the language of force, a communication strategy was deployed around two main axes. The first concerned the simple legitimization of a recourse to the devastating and indiscriminate effects of gigantic bombs called Daisy Cutters, used in Afghanistan. The second was deployed at the same time in a more subtle cultural and educational register. It has been aimed to this very day at promoting in the "Greater Middle East"—an audacious conceptual innovation on the part of the American administration to designate the part of the Muslim world between Morocco and Afghanistan—"modernizing overtures," both political and cultural, concerning which *a priori* everyone can only rejoice. An attentive examination of the process introduced by Washington and in the main endorsed by Europe, however, very soon revealed its limits: here again, it was the most pernicious unilateralism which prevailed. It was the Other, and only the Other, who needed to heed the call for change, leaving the imbalance of the allocation of the world's resources safely shielded from any critical scrutiny.

CONFINING THE OTHER IN THE RELIGIOUS ORDER THE BETTER TO EVICT HIM FROM THE POLITICAL

In the eyes of world public opinion, the violence of the September 11 attacks and their spectacular magnitude were enough to legitimize the air campaign launched in October 2001 against the Afghanistan of the Taliban, that protective hotbed of Osama Bin Laden's networks. Accompanied by collective massacres, undertaken directly or through the intermediary of Afghan warlords, this first phase of the American response did not, however, allow for any means to check whether the carpet-bombed human targets really coincided with the perpetrators or the direct or even indirect accomplices of the September 11 attacks. The top leadership of al-Qaeda and of the Taliban, and a substantial portion of their troops, in any case succeeded in melting away during the first round of the confrontation.

The Afghan land campaign and then the ongoing military response—whose main excesses were only to be disclosed much later—subsequently rivaled the most heinous acts for which those it targeted could be blamed. The fate most officially reserved for those "enemy combatants" of the global war on terror caused the laws of war to take a sinister leap back into the shadows of the past: excluded, by virtue of the sole verbal magic of the strongest, from the sphere of application of the Geneva Conventions, these prisoners have been systematically sexually humiliated or tortured under the perfectly official guidelines of the Pentagon, delivered into the hands of private torturers or "extraordinarily rendered" without trace into lands devoid of any rule of law. The Bush administration and the neo-conservative camp, whose propensity to resort to hard power was from the start singularly close to that of the Jihadis they purported to combat, have since then, with their concept of the "Guantanamization" of the enemy, provided a sort of Western counterpart to the Muslim concept of *takfir*.

The treatment reserved, first in places of detention in Afghanistan, then on the island of Cuba, and, in all likelihood, in many other sites of detention in Europe and the Middle East kept secret until recently, is identical to the methods attributed to the propagators of this dreaded ideology.[2] *Takfir*, the rough equivalent of excommunication in canon law, indeed consists in denying opponents their status as members of the human community and in therefore feeling authorized to deprive them of all the rights, protections, and guarantees inherent in this membership. This mechanism, from which, thanks to the Enlightenment, the West believed it had delivered most of the "civilized" world, seems to have found, notably in America, new partisans. Certain more lucid American military personnel became deeply alarmed when they realized that these new norms of the treatment of the Other, reinforced by so dreadful a precedent, might one day be applied to themselves, to their own sons or daughters.

The U.S. administration's communication campaign then set to work, with the help of mass "pieces of evidence," touted as so many established facts by the experts of the major media, denying the enemy's behavior any rationality and even any political coherence. If the question "Why do they hate us?" was sometimes asked in these terms,[3] it was never taken into account as such at the apex of the American power structure, and very rarely in Europe, with all the lucidity deserved. The communication staff of the U.S. administration and its European intermediaries has on the contrary been mobilized to prevent any rational scrutiny of the profane causes of the "religious" violence of the aggressors.

The answer to this question was probably to a great extent already familiar to U.S. decision-makers, involved notably in the co-looting of Saudi resources (by themselves and by the princes they protect) and in the great regional diplomatic and military maneuvers aimed at maintaining the rhythm and the efficiency of this enterprise. For the cohort of self-proclaimed specialists on "Islamic" terrorism, on the other hand, Bin Laden was thus reputed, and peremptorily so, "not to give a damn about Palestine,"[4] Algeria, or Iraq: which convincingly demonstrated that he and his henchmen were mainly out to bring down our democracy, our freedom, our values, as so comfortable an "obvious fact" could only serve to confirm. Only curious Internet surfers, or the too-small number of those who, in the West, have access to the news broadcast by some Arab satellite channels,[5] were in a position to measure the frightening gap which had thus opened between Western representations and those of the Arab world.

The conjuring away of any serious scrutiny of the political agenda of the "aggressors' camp" has mainly proceeded through what might be called the "over-ideologization" of its claims. The eulogists of the official discourse very rapidly succeeded in imposing an analysis both reassuring and simple: if "they hate us," it is because they are "fundamentalists," in the throes of their "anti-Western" or "anti-American" sectarianism (since they are attacking the West and the United States) or their "anti-Semitic" sectarianism (since they are attacking Israel). The rhetorical hat trick consists in confining the aggressor to his religious affiliation alone, to deny him access to the register of politics. In order to be "legitimately" able to ignore the nonreligious claims, it is sufficient to criminalize the exoticism of the vocabulary used to express them. The claims of the Islamists thus end up being confined to a sort of political "off-limits," not only prohibiting them from being taken into account but, more often than not, denying the recognition of their very existence.

The unanimous propensity of caricaturists, editorialists, press agencies, radio and television channels, and a significant part of the academic field to bring to the fore only the religious dimension of their statements rather than their political underpinnings is part of the smooth running of the whole system. Subconsciously, but often also very consciously, the media treatment overdetermines and criminalizes this lexical exoticism, which ends up by providing proof of the illegitimacy of its user. Far from the requirements of social science (which enjoins us to seek out within the actors' history the exact meaning of the markers they use), the dominant approach refuses to lay any semantic or analytical bridges between the two "camps" which are thus locked in confrontation. And any attempt in this direction is inevitably accused of some guilty "understanding" or dangerous "fascination" with the Islamist object, or even of "objective complicity" with the enemy—as if what was at stake was not to reach a better understanding of the wellsprings of this series of anti-Western aggressions in order to find a way to end them but, on the contrary, to fuel them, the better to justify a perennial position of domination. Rather than deconstructing this reciprocal incommunicability in order to try to overcome it, the objective seems to be on the contrary to highlight and thus exacerbate it.

The upshot of all this is that the citizen reader in the grip of his legitimate fear of al-Qaeda is unlikely to wake up to the fact that the *jihad* of his "aggressors" might have an equivalent in the proven penchant of George Bush, and all those who do not oppose his ventures, for the shortcuts of hard power; or that their strange *takfir* might also have found devotees among the designers of the "Guantanamization" of "enemy combatants." It is also out of the question that he be allowed for one second to imagine that this *umma*[6] of the barbarians could have anything in common with any of the collective affiliations with which, throughout the world, a normally constituted individual might legitimately want to identify. It is true that to hear it implied, as an interpretative approach and explanatory principle, that such adepts of an exotic *umma* additionally place the latter in jeopardy of *fitna* (dissension)[7] is probably more "reassuring"—but not necessarily more enlightening—than to recall a fact both massive and banal: the societies of the Muslim world, all composed of human beings, are not immune to the universal rule which decrees that political divisions are the driving force of the dynamics of history. Such an omission obviously does not help our citizen reader to realize what might be at the core of the whole issue, that is, the thousand and one ways in which the "Western camp" has been a party to most of these tensions, without ever in the least acknowledging it.

This strategy does not date from the response to the September 11 attacks. The long civil war born from the cancellation of the Algerian legislative elections in January 1992 had already done most of the fine-tuning.[8] The criminalization of the Palestinian resistance, from the moment that it started being partly identified with the Islamist generation, was then incorporated into the same routine. Vladimir Putin himself excelled in expertly piloting it to disqualify the whole of the Chechen resistance.

Helped by a media quasi-monopoly, the American response therefore had no difficulty in crowding out of the public debate the slightest assessment or even the merest rational statement of the claims of the "adversarial" camp. It is not only the historicized knowledge of the culture, religion, or civilization of the "Islamist" Other which has thus been eclipsed or caricatured but, more fundamentally, the reality of the grievances which he may harbor toward us. Thus operates the "preemptive" disqualification of any resistance to the malfunctions of the political hierarchies and relays of command which found the hegemony of the well-heeled of world politics.

On the part of the American administration, at the time Democratic, the first attacks of al-Qaeda demonstrated how far this strategy of turning a blind eye or burying our heads in the sand, consisting in denying the adversary access to the arena of political expression, was already strongly established. In October 2000, one year before the attacks against Manhattan and Washington, a suicide attack had seriously damaged the American destroyer USS *Cole*, moored in the harbor at Aden (Yemen), and killed seventeen of its sailors. In the opinion of thousands of people in the Middle East (but also in many other parts of the world) of all faiths and all political affiliations, an "act of war" had indeed just caused the death of several soldiers. But this act of war targeted a warship, packed with sophisticated weapons, heading toward the coasts of Iraq, where it was preparing not to participate in maneuvers but to resume its role in the implementation of "strategic strikes" and an embargo responsible for the terrible economic suffocation of an already weakened country. These "young people" were hence waging a real war, as it happens a particularly murderous one, since, without having—as abundantly attested since then—the least efficacy with regard to its stated objectives (the fall of Saddam Hussein and the destruction of his weapons of mass destruction), it was leading to the impoverishment and illiteracy of a whole generation of Iraqi children and to the deaths of tens of thousands of them, not to mention the hundreds of thousands of their parents.

No way! The words of Bill Clinton at the sailors' funerals did not leave room for the slightest doubt, the slightest uncertainty, the slightest reflection on the foreign policy of the United States in the region: without waiting for the pretext of September 11, the deadly impasse of a communication strategy reduced to sign language was already irretrievably engaged. The soldiers who died in Aden were in Clinton's eyes "bonded by the same commitment to the service of freedom" for which America "will never cease struggling": on the part of the aggressors, it could only be a question of "jealousy" toward the values of the young sailors, who came from all the subcultures of the American melting pot. Absolute Evil, monstrously spawned by who knows what perversion or what degeneracy of human nature, had just, once again, attacked Virtue! In conclusion, the president stigmatized the intolerable motto that he attributed to the "fundamentalist aggressors" against the young Americans "in love with freedom." With those people, he exclaimed, it's our way or no way. A few months later, it was similarly in the name of just such a devastatingly oversimplified rhetoric ("with us or against us") that his successor launched the Western world onto the dangerously protracted paths of the great "crusade against terror" in which he has today gone astray.

THE CULTURALIST ILLUSION OR CHANGING THE OTHER . . . AND ONLY THE OTHER

Parallel to the shortcuts of hard power and the campaign of ideological criminalization of the opponent, the American reprisal has mobilized around an equally ideological axis, which upon examination turns out to proceed from the same form of unilateralism. At least partially repudiated militarily by its European partners, the American administration has been rallied almost without misgivings in this culturalist approach to the crisis in relations with the Muslim world. The illusion of an "educational" solution to the tensions with the Other, as widespread as it is intellectually comfortable, rests on a highly simplistic premise. All that is required, once credence has been granted to the culturalist explanation of the origins of the resistance, is to advocate an "educational" solution in order to protect ourselves from it. To deter the aggressors from any further will to protest, the solution is to help them "reform their culture."

The weakness of this approach is, once again, being so curiously selective and thus reinforcing a very unilateralist exegesis of the origins of the malfunctions of the planet. "Change" and "opening" naturally concern those who resist the malfunctioning of the world order rather than the beneficiaries of this order. The U.S. rhetoric of the "Greater Middle East," even if it recurrently mentions the necessity for a peaceful solution to the Israeli-Palestinian conflict, takes the greatest care most of the time to avoid identifying two categories of reforms which are, however, probably the most urgent. The first is that of the institutional systems governing the world order, that is, American unilateralism and the powerlessness within which it confines the UN, especially regarding the Israeli-Arab conflict. The second is that of regimes, notably Arab, which, in exchange for the free rein which is granted them as far as nondemocratic governance is concerned, have opted for the prudent choice of submitting to this "order."

Those who resist or those who oppose it, on the other hand, are required, with much more heavy-handed insistence, to "open up" to the world, to "dialogue," and/or to "change." Under such a logic, "Are you sure that you do not want to dialogue with my civilization?" means "Are you sure that you do not want to compromise with my system?" or "Are you really determined to protest against its imbalances?" "Don't you want to democratize yourself?" should be translated by "Are you sure you do not want to change this regime which is hostile to me in order, in the name of democracy, to promote another which would be less so?" It is indeed to the Other, and rarely to themselves or to their domesticated allies, that the masters of the global war on terror vaunt the expediency of political reform. The "culture of change" which symposiums and seminars have been promoting throughout Western and Arab capital cities since the beginning of this century is to be understood as promoting the culture of change . . . of their adversaries into allies. It is naturally more often to rebellious dictatorships than to those which have willingly submitted that the injunction to "change" is addressed. Of course, infinitely less emphasis is placed on demanding "more democracy" in Algiers or Tunis than in Tehran or in the case of the ruler of Baghdad before he had the suicidal brain wave of seizing Kuwait's oil fields.

On the European level, this policy of very selective education of Muslim actors has its enthusiastic adepts. For them, it would somehow suffice if Muslims decided to make a new reading of their Quran or even to maintain themselves at a more respectable distance, thus completing their modernist metamorphosis, in order to absorb the depth of Palestinian, Iraqi, or Algerian resentment toward us. It is, of course, our duty to help them in achieving this, by knocking into their heads the right way to read their Holy Book. The tools for this cultural policy, with its heavy-duty political ulterior motives, have been honed for a long time. They range from the self-righteous conferences where the sole supporters of the same "secular" camp self-congratulate to the least nuanced of Youssef Chahine's films,[9] which was "shot with a shoulder camera with no cuts" and which the French Republic had no qualms about co-producing, just this once, of course, with the Egyptian Ministry of Culture and the Syrian Ministry of . . . Information.

Will such univocal incantations be enough to bring an end to "fundamentalism," al-Qaeda terrorism, Palestinian suicide bombers, and, while we are at it, car-torching in the Paris suburbs? Such a perspective is wholly misleading. The dynamics of intellectual modernization require, in the Muslim world as elsewhere, a local or regional atmosphere of political liberalism. Any progress of the mind can only occur in a context free from national dictatorships and regional oppressions which fuel and give credence to reactive postures. And yet the whole contradiction originates specifically from the fact that the West is busy with one hand, directly (through British or American cluster bombs) or indirectly (by blind endorsement of the aberrations of Ariel Sharon or the Arab Pinochets), fueling the very radicalism that it claims to be fighting with the other. The apparent (cultural) "disease of Islam" is the consequence and not the cause of this highly political vicious circle within which the Muslim world is trapped and from which the West is so little concerned to really help it emerge.

On April 27, 2004, before shamelessly unrolling the thickest of red carpets before Muammar Qaddafi's first strides in Brussels, was the European Union in the least concerned about the democratic progress made by one of the most authoritarian regimes in the whole Mediterranean region? Certainly not. At the most it had verified that this regime, duly domesticated, no longer possessed the means to have a negative impact on the world order, that is, our vested economic interests. Libya will pump oil at an accelerated rate. It will help us block the path of African migrants seeking passage to Europe. What more could we ask?

For all our rhetoric of "democratic" change, we are thus targeting only the "faults" of our adversaries and other resistance fighters—and theirs alone. It is their education and their culture, so dangerously "Islamic," that is, not "docile," which are to be reformed. What, on the other hand, above all should not be "changed," what should be preserved at any price, is the power ratio that enables the hegemony of the well-heeled of politics, great and small, to be perpetuated. Does the World (of the Other) persist in protesting ever more strongly in the face of the unilateralism of this treatment? We told you so, didn't we? This means that it has become top priority: it must be "changed."

CONCLUSION

Against Terrorism—the Absolute Weapon?

Criminalization, in the media or by Western administrations, of any protest or oppositional expression arising from the "South" as soon as its authors are perceived to be using the vocabulary of Muslim culture has for European diplomacy probably entailed its worst counter-performance: that of the blatant failure of the "Barcelona process," trumpeted in November 1995, whose ineffectiveness everyone today acknowledges.[1] The origin of this obvious setback in North-South communication is presumably Europe's incapacity to recognize the legitimacy of moderate Islamist oppositions and their potential for modernization. The outcome is an ineptitude in establishing any effective contact with the real civil societies of the South, to the sole benefit of partners designated as "secular" and hand-picked—regardless, if need be, of their proximity to particularly illegitimate regimes—for their skill in telling us, in the terminology with which we are familiar, what we want to hear and almost nothing else.

By not wanting to recognize a whole political generation, by bending its principles to the size of the oil incomes managed by its partners, by sacrificing the political long term on the altar of financial and electoral short-term prospects, Europe, with France in its vanguard, has dangerously compromised the range and efficiency of its cultural and political exchanges with its Muslim environment. Unable to negotiate with—or even to accept—representatives other than those close to authoritarian regimes or on the fragile fringe of societies which reflect the comforting image of its own universality, European diplomacy has set itself at loggerheads with a whole region of the world.[2]

It is in this context that, for an ever-increasing number of those to whom the Western powers have denied all political legitimacy, the most radical methods have irresistibly appeared to offer an alternative. To a large extent, this is how we have, on the ruins of a political communication strategy, just as irresistibly entered the era of terrorism.

Conceived with the same prejudices, despite the scope of the means allocated to their development, the weapons employed to struggle against this terrorism have so far demonstrated above all the limits of their effectiveness. Dozens of innocent citizens regularly pay the price for this obvious lack of the protection which political leaders owe to those who have elected them. Yesterday they were living in London, Madrid, or Sharm el-Sheikh. Tomorrow the list may include Copenhagen, Rome, or Madrid. Millions of other citizens are also suffering as a result of the tremendous budgetary waste resulting from the inflation of security expenditures. Moreover, all are affected by the spectacular decline in civic and democratic freedoms, which are another, even more costly aspect of this security option.

Few of the solutions proposed by our experts in counterterrorism to date have been really convincing. Should we "shut down the Islamic universities of the Gulf," as has been suggested by one? Should we intensify the program of reforming the culture of the Other and the rhythm of his "freedom to learn," human rights, and democracy, as another seems convinced we should? Should we build new—ever longer and higher—walls? Should we multiply the wiretaps of the Other and the surveillance cameras pointed solely in his direction? Should we reinforce, time and again, repression and suspicion and, heedless of improving the output of that old repressive "suicide-bomber factory," equip the planet with new "Guantanamos"?

A much more efficient weapon, however, may well exist. It purportedly has already been identified. Only a blind refusal to implement it can therefore be the cause of the resounding and persistent failure of the Western offensive against the terrorist curse of the twenty-first century. It is apparently its cost which hampers those who can afford it from implementing it and thus really protecting their fellow citizens.

It is true that this weapon is particularly costly; and the great and small, "Western" or "Muslim," well-to-do of the world order of the new twenty-first century seem disinclined to pay that price. We can understand them: this mighty weapon is indeed called "sharing." And it targets . . . everything that they specifically have no intention of sharing. That means economic and financial resources, of course, whether oil-related or industrial, on a planetary scale or within each nation. Then political power, monopolized by all the perennial leaders who, from "election" to "re-election," have deprived a whole generation of access to power. Palestine too, where the long-promised sharing has today become so completely fictional.

"Sharing" also means to accept that other discourses and other beliefs than our own have the right to express the Good, the Right, the Just—in short, all the values which we do not always take the time to realize are common to all, even though their defenders do not worship the same icons and use symbolic categories, languages, and codes as multitudinous as the cultures of the world.

More simply, we should also think of sharing and allowing others to share . . . emotion and of bestowing ours on *all* the victims of *all* forms of violence. To do so, we should not hesitate to denounce the hypocrisy of those relativistic humanists who believe that they are endowed with a special dispensation in this field. We may wish to cry over the fate of settlers forced to leave a land which was not theirs and, handsomely indemnified, depart for other colonies. But then let us also not forget the fate of the thousands of those whose houses have been more discreetly demolished, unceremoniously, far from the television cameras, at break of day. We should therefore share, above all, the right to air and assert one's own truth, one's own history great or small, and one's own vision of the world, in prime time, on the screens or over the loudspeakers of a press which we must do everything to help remain—or rather help become again!—an expression of pluralism.

To share, indeed, does not always mean to give. It can also be about taking. That applies particularly to . . . the opinions of others. And yet, if we "invent" our information instead of collecting it, if the voices of the world, and *a fortiori* those of our own societies, only reach us through channels we already have bought out, if we reach the point of only hearing the sound of our own voices, we are depriving ourselves of the benefit of an absolutely vital commodity: the point of view of others, of all others, that very point of view which enables us to get to know ourselves in our own specificity, in our relativity, and hence—who knows?—in our weaknesses and mistakes. Such a foreclosure can quickly take on the aspect of a form of autism. It may be that very condition which afflicts part of the media and political establishment of the planet today.

It is specifically this autism, combined with the demands of politicking and the electoral short term, which might lead—or is already leading—some political leaders down a slippery slope. In Europe, with a rotating light in one hand and a dictionary of the clichés of ordinary hatred in the other, part of the political class seems tempted to amass future electoral victories by cultivating everyone's xenophobic tendencies. For a politician, there are, indeed, two forms of security. The first, which should be the number one priority, is the security of citizens. The second, sometimes more important in the politician's opinion, is securing electoral success. In order to ensure the latter, it could be enough to speak on a gut level to voters, to reinforce their fears, to encourage their ignorance of the Other. And thus to impose a purely securitarian reading of the tensions, underpinned by a one-way handing down of responsibilities and, consequently, by the dominantly repressive nature of the "remedies" to be implemented.

Really protecting the security of the citizens is, on the other hand, an infinitely more costly task. It is indeed less immediately gratifying from an electoral point of view, for its demands lie in the long run. It does not lend itself so much to communication exercises, to the mobilization of shocking images and emotions which "freeze" all perception in an instant. It requires us to address citizens' reason, to calm their fears instead of using them as an oratory springboard. And also to bring them to acknowledge the unpleasant idea of the complexity of the crisis and the fact that each of us obviously bears part of the responsibility, large or small, according to our rank in the world. In 2005, throughout Europe, in the electoral urgency of our democracies, the securitarian politics of the flashing light and the criminalizing shortcuts of the "Karcher" unfortunately seemed to be on track to carry the day.[3] Such victories could, soon enough, take on the bitter taste of a wrong turn leading to the wastelands of real conflict—exactly what we are boasting we want to prevent.

True political courage, which might prepare a real restoration of security, would highlight the necessity of another parsing of international tensions. A reading that would no longer give in to the selective shortcuts of all those who, for one reason or another, refuse to admit that the responsibilities for the terror are well and truly shared and who thus connive, *de facto,* in maintaining it. For as long as it is the only one audible, the chorus of howling wolves reinforces, day after day, the voices of pusillanimous politicians on the make for easy victories.

Sharing or terror. That choice, more than ever, still lies before us.

APPENDIX

The Islamists as Seen by the West in 1992

By locking up thousands of them in the depths of the Algerian Sahara, the leaders of Algeria and Tunisia have probably slowed down the long march of the Islamists toward power. But they certainly have not halted it. Since Nasser and the crushing of the Muslim Brothers, a lot of water has flowed under the bridges of the Nile, and strong-arm tactics, to eradicate from the political scene a trend which is now known to be supported by a wide majority of the population almost everywhere in the Muslim world, might not be enough. In order to prepare itself for a cohabitation which has become inevitable, the North has so far only made a few really small steps. Recent weeks, however, have taught us more about these Islamists than the many thousands of pages written about them over so many years. The activists have once more shown the depth and the solidity of their popular support. Therefore we can jettison the convenient fiction, elevated to dogma by Western wishful thinking, that we are dealing with a small group of activists all the more tempted to seize power by force because they fear being excluded from it at the polls.

Thus the "democrats from the mountains" have nowhere succeeded in convincing their brothers from the plains. We can also jettison the fiction of an alternative other than ethnic—for how is the vote of the Algerian Socialist Forces Front seriously to be qualified?—to the Islamist vote. A very large majority of women, and not only from the depths of the countryside, seem well and truly to have chosen to vote for the ISF. Finally, in an infinitely more complex framework, we can jettison the simplistic shortcut of an Islamist mobilization "against women."

No matter. Failing to find on the political scene the "third force" able to combat its purported enemy, Western opinion (radically encouraged, it is true, by the statements of North African ministries) is nonetheless pursuing its desperate quest for the segment of Arab societies which would be willing to save it from the outcome . . . of their ballot boxes. The most obstinate nonanalysts are currently surveying the battalions of those who abstained from voting.

Do they exist? No doubt. Do they constitute an alternative majority? Certainly not! For how can we forget that the victories of the ISF are the results of the only two polls in all of Algerian history (except the referendum on Independence) in which the regime did not purely and simply invent the level of participation? If we are willing (but who has done so?) to compare them to those (10 percent, 15 percent) who regularly re-elect our great "democratic" allies of the region, the 50 percent or 60 percent of voters of these first real polls amount, for the Islamists, to a tremendous surge of support.

And also nothing, absolutely nothing, enables us to detect in the ranks of those who abstained anything other than the echo of the majority which emerged in 1990, that is, relatively speaking . . . an extra reserve of Islamist votes.

So? No ray of hope on the horizon? No other ship in sight than that of boat people overloaded with women fleeing the tyranny of the Quran? No other outcome, finally, than the martyrdom of our holy secularism? A less tragic and more likely scenario nevertheless exists. It would only cost at present the price of a few ingredients that we must urgently reintroduce into our analyses, in which they have left, on departing, just as many loopholes in the form of shortcuts.

Even if they supposedly shared a few referents in common, it would first be urgent to stop extrapolating the mindset of the assassins of Sadat onto the whole spectrum of forces emanating from the Islamist trend. Then we must accept no longer confining the 1990 and December 1991 Algerian polls within the negative limits of some die-hard "rejection of the NLF" that any of the other parties involved could in fact have expressed. We must also cease to see in the Islamist upsurge only a consequence of the deterioration of the Arab economies: if, on a par with the progress of democratization, the recovery of North Africa's economies must be made, on both sides of the Mediterranean Sea, an absolute priority, neither of these two objectives should be considered to be solely a means to transform the vocabulary of the political actors. How could these dollars, which we are regularly told serve to "export Islam" under other skies, be used here, in North Africa, to . . . make the Islamists disappear?

Help Algeria? Of course! But as it is and not, for once, as we would like it to be. Indispensable for a thousand other reasons, economic aid should not be considered a means of struggling against these "sons of the nationalists," which the Islamists of Tunisia, Algeria, or elsewhere in fact are. Whereas the blowbacks of an elusive revolutionary Islamization "from the top down" had not yet begun first to mesmerize then to blind the West, a slow, deep—and very natural—process of reconnection with the symbolic universe of "precolonial" culture was already at work in every segment of the social, cultural, and political Arab universe.

It is the ultimate political expression of this process which the Islamists' arrival at the threshold of power today demonstrates. If we are to try to assess their capacity to pursue the difficult process of constructing a tolerant society timidly initiated by their elders, one marker must guide our analysis: under Arab skies, if there is to be drawn a clear line of demarcation between good and evil, democrats and antidemocrats, the tolerant and the intolerant, the defenders of the rights of men, or of women, and those for whom they are of less than modest concern, and so forth, it certainly has to be more sinuous than the line between the Islamists and the rest of the political class.

First of all, of course—since what is elsewhere needless to say is better said twice here—because it is not enough to be an Islamist to measure up to the promises of tolerance waived by a large majority of the leaders of this trend. But because it is also not enough to be an anti-Islamist—like Saddam Hussein or Hafez al-Assad or those whose prisons, in North Africa, are no longer vast enough to contain their opponents—to automatically become part of the purported "democratic camp," whose representation the Western political class today grants as a monopoly to such discredited regimes and to those of their opponents who have been marginalized by the upsurge of Islamism.

Last and not least, because one can be an Islamist and not identify with the discourse of rejection put forth here and there by the radical periphery of a trend which is far from identifying with it as a whole. Someday we will end up by having to realize this. The sooner the better.

NOTES

Epigraph. Before resigning from the Central Intelligence Agency, Scheuer used the pen name "Anonymous."

1. Since June 2005 Condoleeza Rice's advisors have suggested the adoption of a new terminology: "SAVE" (Struggle against Violent Extremism) should from now on replace "GWOT" (Global War on Terror), as launched after September 11.

2. Pierre Bourdieu, "L'intellectuel négatif," *Liber* (Paris, January 1998).

3. François Burgat, *The Islamic Movement in North Africa* (Austin: University of Texas Press, 1993) and *Face to Face with Political Islam* (London: I. B. Tauris, 2003).

CHAPTER ONE

1. William E. Shepard, *A Child from the Village* (Leiden/New York: E. J. Brill, 2004).

2. Malek Bennabi, *Mémoires d'un témoin du siècle* (Algiers: Éditions Nationales Algériennes, 1965).

3. See, for instance, Alain Finkielkraut, *La Défaite de la pensée* (Paris: Gallimard, 1987).

4. As shown by the works of the American "essentialist" trend represented by Bernard Lewis, Martin Kraemer, and Daniel Pipes, opposed in different registers by those of Edward Said as well as John Esposito, James Piscatori, Richard A. Norton, John Entelis—and, fortunately, many others—and in France by those of Maxime Rodinson.

5. See in particular Christophe Jaffrelot (ed.), *Le Pakistan* (Paris: Fayard, 2000). The term "Pakistan" is formed by adding different segments of the names of five of its provinces: Punjab, Afghanistan, Kashmir, Sind, and Baluchistan.

6. The country was even built by an "imported" ethnic group that has no roots in its territory. It was indeed the East Indian refugees, the *muhajir,* who succeeded,

even though they could not claim a common ethnicity, in establishing themselves as the national political elite and in making an imported language, Urdu, the official idiom.

7. Quoted by Ian Talbot, *Pakistan: A Modern History* (New York: St. Martin's Press, 1998); also see Christophe Jaffrelot, *Le Pakistan, carrefour de tensions régionales* (Paris: Complexe, 2002).

8. Olivier Roy and Mariam Abou Zahab, *Réseaux islamiques: la connexion afghano-pakistanaise* (Paris: Autrement, 2002); English translation: *Islamist Networks: The Afghan-Pakistan Connection* (New York: Columbia University Press, 2006).

9. Ariel Merari (University of Tel Aviv), "Social, Organizational, and Psychological Factors in Suicide Terrorism," paper presented at the International Expert Meeting on Root Causes of Terrorism, Norwegian Institute of International Affairs, Oslo, June 9–11, 2003.

10. François Burgat and Mohamed Sbitli, "Les salafis au Yémen ou la modernisation malgré tout," *Chroniques yéménites*, 2002, cy.revues.org.

11. The Zaydi doctrine is linked to Shiism and derives its name from Imam Zayd ibn Ali Zayn al-ʿAbidin (who died in 740), a descendant of Ali ibn Abi Talib, the Prophet's son-in-law. It was in 897 that Imam Yahya al-Hadi ilaʾl-Haqq ibn al-Husayn founded a "Zaydi" power hub in North Yemen. According to Zaydi *ulama*s, the legitimate Imam must fulfill fourteen conditions, the first of which is to be a descendant of the Prophet through the two sons (Hassan and Hussein) of his son-in-law Ali and his daughter Fatima.

12. Franck Mermier et al. (eds.), *Le Yémen contemporain* (Paris: Karthala, 2003).

13. Among the "markers" of Salafism in relation to Zaydism, some Salafis consider it legal to keep their shoes on while praying. They just remove the dust with a gesture of the hand, even in a mosque. Unlike the Zaydis, who keep their arms lowered, they pray with their arms crossed and say a resounding *amin* at the end of the recitation of the *fatiha* (Profession of Faith at the beginning of the Quran).

14. Muqbil ibn Hadi al-Wadiʿi, *Al-Makhraj min al-Fitna* (How to Issue Forth from the Dead Ends of Division) (Sanaa: n.p., 1982).

15. Ibid., p. 102.

16. Hence using a *jamahiriyan* terminology, which may have been suggested to him by Colonel Muammar Qaddafi, who was then one of the economic partners of Yemen. When he inaugurated his "power to the masses" theory, Qaddafi wanted to distinguish himself from the previously existing terminology. He coined the word *jamahiriya*, derived from *jumhuriya* (republic, the thing of the public) by making *jumhur* (the public) into the plural *jamahir* (the masses).

17. Within the General Congress of the People in power or in its orbit, a first "Islamist" component thus supported the regime (some *ulama*s close to the seat of power, then the portion of the Brothers rallied in 1982, as well as the big Sufi brotherhoods of the Hadramawt). The "real" Islamist opposition was then represented by the Muslim Brothers, organized since 1990 within the Yemeni Union for Reform, led by the sheikh Abdallah Hussein al-Ahmar and, to a lesser extent, by the mem-

bers of the political revival of Zaydism united within the small Hizb al-Haq party. Finally, the "Muqbilians," the main Salafi trend, supported the regime by simply advocating abstention.

CHAPTER TWO

1. See, above all, the thesis of Tariq Ramadan, *Aux sources du renouveau musulman, d'al-Afghani à Hassan al-Banna: un siècle de réforme islamique* (Paris: Bayard/Centurion, 1998).

2. An educational establishment for Algerian Muslim students. [The French edition gives no source for this quotation—Trans.]

3. Leigh Douglas, *The Free Yemeni Movement, 1935-1962* (Beirut: AUB, 1987).

4. François Burgat and Mohamed Sbitli, "Les 'Libres' yéménites, le courant réformiste et les Frères musulmans: premiers repères pour l'analyse," in Chérif al-Maher and Salam Kawakibi (eds.), *Le Courant réformiste musulman et sa réception dans les sociétés arabes,* Aleppo Symposium marking the hundredth anniversary of the death of Sheikh 'Abd al-Rahman al-Kawakibi, May 31–June 1, 2002 (Damascus: IFPO, 2003).

5. See in particular Bernard Haykel, *Revival and Reform in Islam: The Legacy of Muhammad al-Shawkani* (Cambridge: Cambridge University Press, 2003).

6. See in particular Franck Mermier, Bernard Haykel, and Gabriele Vom Bruck, in Franck Mermier et al. (eds.), *Le Yémen contemporain* (Paris: Karthala, 2003). "On the one hand, he who governs in the name of Islam has a responsibility toward the nation. On the other hand, the nation itself has obligations toward him. One of the former is obedience. The other is to provide council."

7. He wrote: "I raised my voice to call for two very great undertakings . . . The first was to liberate thought from imitation [*taqlid*]. The second . . . was the necessity to differentiate the obedience that the people owe to the government and the right of the people to justice from the government" (quoted by Ahmed Amin, *Zu'ama al-Islah fi al-'Asr al-Hadith* [The Fathers of Reform in the Contemporary Era] [Beirut: Dar al-Kitab al-'Arabi, 1979], p. 84).

8. See Natana J. Delong-Bas, *Wahhabi Islam: From Revival and Reform to Global Jihad* (Oxford/New York: I. B. Tauris, 2004); Alexei Vassiliev, *The History of Saudi Arabia* (New York: New York University Press, 2000); Guido Steinberg, *Religion und Staat in Saudi-Arabien: Die wahhabitischen Gelehrten, 1902-1953* (Würzburg: Ergon, 2002); see also *La Pensée* 335 (July–September 2003).

9. Pascal Ménoret, "Wahhabisme, arme fatale du néo-orientalisme," *Mouvements* (November 2004).

10. Albert Hourani, *Arabic Thought in the Liberal Age, 1798-1939* (Cambridge: Cambridge University Press, 1983); French translation: *La Pensée arabe et l'Occident* (Brussels: Naufal, 1992). For Algeria, see, for example, Jean-Robert Henry and Claude Collot, *Le Mouvement national algérien: textes* (Paris: L'Harmattan-OPU, 1978).

11. See Henry Laurens, *L'Orient arabe: arabisme et islamisme de 1798 à 1945* (Paris: Armand Colin, 1993).

12. The modernity of this is perfectly illustrated by the thought of Malek Bennabi (see Malek Bennabi, *Vocation de l'islam* [Paris: Seuil, 1954]).

13. One of the most emblematic situations is no doubt that of certain future high-ranking Algerian military officers: young officers in the French Army, many of whom only deserted to join the freedom struggle a few months before Independence. They then succeeded in taking a very firm hold on power and, in the 1980s and 1990s, played a well-documented role in foreclosing the political system.

14. Quoted in François Burgat, *L'Islamisme en face,* 3rd ed. (Paris: La Découverte, 2002), pp. 48ff.; English translation: *Face to Face with Political Islam* (London/New York: I. B. Tauris Publishers, 1999).

15. See Pascal Ménoret, *L'Énigme saoudienne* (Paris: La Découverte, 2004).

16. Bertrand Badie, "Palestine, quelles perspectives?" conference held at the Paris Institut d'Études Politiques (IEP), January 19, 2004.

17. Rashid Khalidi, *Resurrecting Empire: Western Footprints and America's Perilous Path in the Middle East* (Boston: Beacon Press, 2004), p. x.

18. See in particular François Burgat, "De A comme Arafat à Z comme Zîn al-'Abidîn Ben Ali: la pérennité de la formule politique arabe," in *L'Islamisme en face,* pp. 244ff.

19. Other than the converging reports of Amnesty International, see in particular Comité pour le Respect des Libertés et des Droits de l'Homme en Tunisie, *La Torture en Tunisie 1987–2000: plaidoyer pour son abolition et contre l'impunité* (Paris: Le Temps des Cerises, 2004); Mahmoud Khelili, *La Torture en Algérie (1991–2001),* Algeria-Watch, October 2001; Youcef Bedjaoui, Abbas Aroua, and Meziane Aït-Larbi, *An Inquiry into the Algerian Massacres* (Geneva: Hoggar, 1999); Lahouari Addi, "La torture comme pratique d'État dans les pays du Maghreb," *Confluences* 51 (October 2004).

Egyptian human rights organizations named around twenty people killed under torture in 2003 and 2004 and 292 avowed cases of torture between January 1993 and April 1994. The Egyptian state refused to allow the visit of the UN special envoy on torture (which the Egyptian National Council for Human Rights, in its first report in April 2005, emphasized was "normal investigation practice").

20. Mohamed Tozy, "Représentation/Intercession: les enjeux de pouvoir dans les 'champs politiques désamorcés' au Maroc," in Michel Camau (ed.), *Changements politiques au Maghreb* (Paris: CNRS, 1991), pp. 153–168. In a manner less academic but quite as eloquent, Mohamed Qahtan, one of the leaders of the Yemeni opposition, close to the Muslim Brothers, described electoral competition in the Arab world as being like a football match in which, "unlike the opposition team, the team in power is allowed to use its hands." "But we like the sport," he adds, "so we play anyway" (interview with the author, Sanaa, March 2003).

21. In English in the original—Trans.

22. Jean-François Legrain, "La Palestine, de la terre perdue à la reconquête du territoire," *Cultures et conflits*, "L'international sans territoire," 2005; Laetitia Bucaille, *Génération Intifada* (Paris: Hachette Littératures, 2002).

23. The phrases "Against God" and "Against His Saints" in the subhead derive from the commonly used French idiom: "Il vaut mieux s'adresser à Dieu qu'à Ses Saints" (i.e., when in urgent need, it is preferable to circumvent the intermediate levels of a power structure or a hierarchical bureaucracy)—Trans.

24. It was on September 11, 1973, in Chile that General Augusto Pinochet overthrew, with the help of the CIA, the regime of the elected president, Salvador Allende. The junta, with renewed American support, subsequently tortured and liquidated many of the members of this "Marxist" opposition, who supposedly threatened Washington's economic interests.

25. "The United States has never officially owned colonies in Latin America, but it has owned *de facto* colonies. From the beginning of the nineteenth century until the 1930s, the 'big stick' policy—armed interventions and occupation of sovereign states—enabled Washington to prepare the ground for the dictators who would later, to the great woe of their peoples, behave as perfect auxiliaries" (Maurice Lemoine, "Du 'destin manifeste' des États-Unis," *Le Monde Diplomatique* [May 2003] 20).

26. "The Iraq War was fought secondly with the aim of establishing long-term American military bases in a key country in the heart of the Middle East . . . America saw these as replacements for the increasingly contested bases established in Saudi Arabia in the wake of the 1991 Gulf War. It was a war fought thirdly to destroy one of the last of the third world dictatorships that had at times defied the United States and its allies (notably Israel). . . . It was a war fought finally to reshape, along the radical free-market lines so dear to Bush administration ideologues, the economy of a country with the world's second-largest proven reserves of oil." (Khalidi, *Resurrecting Empire*, x–xi).

27. See Comité Tchétchénie, *Tchétchénie: dix clés pour comprendre* (Chechnya: Ten Keys for Understanding) (Paris: La Découverte, www.editionsladecouverte.fr).

28. Since December 2001 Ayman al-Zawahiri has argued his strategy in a tract whose essential tenets have been reported, in eight issues (nos. 8405 to 8411), by the London Arabic-language daily *Al-Sharq al-Awsat*, under the title "Knights under the Prophet's Banner."

29. This refers to a contemporary French social movement, mainly composed of second- or third-generation descendants of immigrants from former colonial territories, in favor of Republicanism, nondiscrimination, civil rights, and integration—Trans.

30. To paraphrase Mona al-Munajjed, *Women in Saudi Arabia Today* (London: Macmillan, 1997), Chap. 4 (quoted by Ménoret, *L'Énigme saoudienne*, p. 201).

31. Hoda Shaarawi (1897–1947), during the 1919 revolution, presided over the first demonstration of three hundred women against British occupation. She played a role in the creation of the first Egyptian feminist association in March 1923.

From 1934 to her death, she was the vice-president of the International Union of Women.

32. "Taking wing"—Trans.

33. Declarations quoted by Hoda al-Sadda, "Le discours arabe sur l'émancipation féminine au xxᵉ siècle," *Revue d'Histoire* 82 (April–June 2004): 85 (translated from the Arabic by Ghislaine Alleaume).

34. Leila Ahmad, *Women and Gender: The Historical Roots of a Recent Controversy,* translated from the Arabic by Mona Ibrahim and Hala Kamal (Cairo: Higher Council for Culture, 1999) (quoted by Hoda al-Sadda, "Le discours arabe sur l'émancipation féminine au xxᵉ siècle").

35. Frantz Fanon, *L'An V de la révolution algérienne: sociologie d'une révolution* (Paris: La Découverte, 2001) (quoted by Abu Bakr Haroun, "Fanon, le foulard, et les démons de l'irrationnel," Oumma.com, January 25, 2004); English translation: *A Dying Colonialism* (New York: Grove Press, 1965).

36. Houria Bouteldja, "De la cérémonie du dévoilement à Alger (1958) à *Ni Putes Ni Soumises:* l'instrumentalisation coloniale et néo-coloniale de la cause des femmes"; see the list "Les mots sont importants" and the site Oumma.com, October 13, 2004.

37. Unlike the Arab world during the 1950s and 1960s, where nationalist affirmation was the product of a break with the European colonial presence, this affirmation in Turkey took place against the "Muslim" Ottoman Empire.

38. As an irony or continuity of history, the fez itself had been imposed in 1826, to the detriment of the turban, by Sultan Mahmud II. After having rejected the "colonial" three-cornered hat—his advisors having pointed out that it could be construed as a symbol of the Holy Trinity—he opted for the fez, which to his mind embodied an open break with the traditionalism conveyed by the turban and a clear willingness . . . to open up to Europe (see in particular Jeremy Seal, *A Fez of the Heart: Travels around Turkey in Search of a Hat* [London: Harcourt Brace and Co., 1995]).

39. Quoted by Michel Camau and Vincent Geisser, "Les limites du féminisme d'État bourguibien," in *Habib Bourguiba, la trace et l'héritage* (Aix-en-Provence: Karthala/Centre of Comparative Political Science, 2004), p. 101. He then defined his position: "On the day when Tunisian woman, by emerging from her veil, will no longer experience the strange impression which is like the cry of revolt of her subconscious atavism, on this day the veil will disappear of its own accord, without danger, as that which it symbolized will have disappeared." Or indeed: "We are in the presence of a habit that for centuries has been one of our customs. . . . Is it in our interest to hasten, without managing the transition, the disappearance of our customs, our habits?" (quoted by Larbi Chouika, "La question du *hijab* en Tunisie: une amorce de débat contradictoire," in Françoise Lorcerie [ed.], *La Politisation du voile en Europe, en France et dans le monde arabe* [Paris: L'Harmattan, 2005], p. 159).

40. As early as 1981, soon after the pro-Khomeini revolution, the Tunisian government adopted the following measure: "We have observed recently that female

pupils have presented themselves in their establishments dressed in a way totally foreign to our sartorial traditions by wearing a garment—which could be confused with 'confessional' clothing—which marks affiliation with a trend which distinguishes itself by sectarian clothing, contrary to the spirit of our times and to the healthy evolution of our society."

41. See Mamoun Fandy, *Saudi Arabia and the Politics of Dissent* (London: Palgrave/Macmillan, 1999), p. 49. These groups nevertheless only represented a small part of the spectrum of political opposition, another (Islamic) component of which expressed itself from within the religious field (see Ménoret, *L'Énigme saoudienne*).

42. Fariba Adelkhah, *La Révolution sous le voile: femmes islamiques d'Iran* (Paris: Karthala, 1991).

43. On this point, see especially the critical points of view expressed by Jean Baubérot, *Laïcité 1905–2005, entre passion et raison* (Paris: Seuil, 2005); and Alain Gresh, *L'Islam, la République et le monde* (Paris: Fayard, 2004).

CHAPTER THREE

1. François Burgat, "Ghannouchi, Yassine and the Others: The Logic of Differentiation," in *The Islamic Movement in North Africa* (Austin: University of Texas Press, 1993).

2. On the formation of national frontiers, see in particular Albert Hourani, Philip S. Khoury, and Mary C. Wilson (eds.), *The Modern Middle East* (London/New York: I. B. Tauris, 2000); and Jean-Paul Chagnollaud and Sid-Ahmed Souiah, *Comprendre le Moyen-Orient* (Paris: L'Harmattan, 2004).

3. Malek Bennabi, *Vocation de l'islam* (Paris: Seuil, 1954). Also see the article by one of the best experts on Bennabi: Sadek Sellam, "Le FLN vu par l'écrivain Malek Bennabi: les relations malaisées d'un penseur non conformiste avec le pouvoir algérien naissant," in *Guerres mondiales et conflits contemporains,* April 2002 (article available online on the site Oumma.com).

4. Michel Camau and Vincent Geisser (eds.), *Habib Bourguiba, la trace et l'héritage* (Paris: Karthala, 2004).

5. See Charles-André Julien, *Histoire de l'Afrique du Nord* (Paris: Payot, 1994).

6. Élizabeth Picard, *Liban, État de discorde: des fondations aux guerres fratricides* (Paris: Flammarion, 1988). Also see Jean Charaf, *Documents diplomatiques français relatifs à l'histoire du Liban et de la Syrie à l'époque du mandat français,* vol. 1, *Le Démantèlement de l'Empire ottoman et les préludes du Mandat, 1914–1919* (Beirut/Paris: Éditions Universitaires du Liban/L'Harmattan, 2004); Georges Corm, *Le Liban contemporain: histoire et société* (Paris: La Découverte, 2003; paperback edition: La Découverte, 2005).

7. Charles-Robert Ageron, *Les Algériens musulmans et la France (1871–1919),* 2 vols. (Paris: PUF, 1968). Also see Benjamin Stora, *Histoire de l'Algérie coloniale (1830–1954),* coll. "Repères" (Paris: La Découverte, 1993).

8. Paul Dresch, *A History of Modern Yemen* (Cambridge: Cambridge University Press, 2000).

9. See Ernest Gellner and Jean-Claude Vatin (eds.), *Islam et politique au Maghreb* (Paris: Éditions du CNRS, 1981).

10. This was not to prevent him, in January 1974, at a point when his mental health had probably already deteriorated, from signing an elusive fusion with Qaddafi's Libya, within the framework of a Union whose presidency, it is true, was to go to him.

11. See in particular Souhayr Belhassen, "Les legs bourguibiens de la répression," in Camau and Geisser, *Habib Bourguiba, la trace et l'héritage*, pp. 391ff.: "Bourguiba's opponent was Salah Ben Youssef, who preached the future of a totally independent Tunisia, an integral part of the 'Arab nation' and deeply rooted in Islam. . . . The practice of repression took on an exceptional dimension on the occasion of the Youssefist dissent" (400 "rebels" would be killed).

12. See Olivier Carré, *Le Nationalisme arabe* (Paris: Fayard, 1993).

13. In the Maghreb in general, and in Algeria in particular, it is within this context that the complex role of the Berberist reference must be assessed. In an environment favorable to multiple government manipulations, it has also possibly sometimes but certainly not always (many Islamist leaders have originated from berberophone zones) played the role of a "competitor" with the religious reference and hence for the Islamist mobilization.

14. François Burgat and André Laronde, *La Libye*, coll. "Que sais-je?" (Paris, PUF, 2003).

15. The "first pluralist presidential elections" organized by Cairo in September 2005 to legitimize the fifth mandate of Hosni Mubarak perfectly illustrate this.

16. Where the "first presidential elections under universal suffrage" of the only republic of the Arabian Peninsula, in September 1999, however, only saw one candidate run against President Ali Abdallah Saleh . . . from his own party.

17. See Pierre-Jean Luizard, *La Question irakienne* (Paris: Fayard, 2002).

18. A little-known narration of this from within is given by one of the actors of the revolt, Mahmud ʿAbdelhakim, *Al-Thawra al-Islamiyya al-Jihadiya fi Surya* (The Islamic Jihadi Revolution in Syria), 2 vols. (n.p., n.d.).

19. See Walid Charara and Frédéric Domont, *Le Hezbollah: un mouvement islamo-nationaliste* (Paris: Fayard, 2004); and Judith Palmer Harik, *Hezbollah: The Changing Face of Terrorism* (London: I. B. Tauris, 2005). This author studied the "transformation" of a "radical militia" into a mainstream party; she also emphasizes the capacity of Hizb Allah to muster support from outside the Shiite or even the Muslim community.

20. See Jean-François Legrain and Pierre Chenard, *Les Voix du soulèvement palestinien: édition critique des communiqués du Commandement national unifié et du Mouvement de la résistance islamique* (Cairo: Centre d'Études et de Documentation Économique, Juridique et Sociale [CEDEJ], 1991); Graham Usher, "The New Hamas: Between Resistance and Participation," Merip.org, August 21, 2005.

21. But certainly not, as Pascal Ménoret emphasizes, by "exporting" Wahhabism to the world: "In a way it is more pertinent to speak of 'globalization of Saudi Islam' to mean that the world has spread into Saudi Islam (and not that Saudi Islam has been disseminated in the world)" (Pascal Ménoret, *L'Énigme saoudienne* [Paris: La Découverte, 2004], p. 82).

22. One of the precedents is probably the exile to newly created Pakistan of Mahmud Zubayri, co-founder of the Movement of the Free Yemenis, himself close to the Muslim Brothers, from 1948 to 1952, after the failure of the constitutional revolution. There he attended, in 1951, the inaugural conference of the World Islamic Congress, another instrument for the international confrontation of "Islamist" sensibilities and experiences.

23. See Xavier Bougarel and Nathalie Clayer (eds.), *Le Nouvel Islam balkanique: les musulmans, acteurs du postcommunisme, 1990–2000* (Paris: Maisonneuve et Larose, 2001).

24. Some Salafis are particularly fond of these: refusing to let themselves be photographed, they prefer to do without a passport and compensate for the impossibility of leaving their national territories by collectively listening to the voice of preachers residing in countries other than their own.

25. According to the relevant expression documented by Olivier Roy, *Globalized Islam: The Search for a New Ummah,* CERI Series in Comparative Politics and International Studies (New York: Columbia University Press, 2004).

CHAPTER FOUR

Epigraph: Mohamed Qahtan is one of the leaders of al-Tajamu' al-Yamani lil-Islah (Yemeni Union for Reform), created in 1990 in Yemen by the Muslim Brothers; interview with the author, Sanaa, March 2003.

1. See Joseph Chelhod (ed.), *L'Arabie du Sud, histoire et civilisation* (Paris: Maisonneuve et Larose, 1985): vol. 1, *Le peuple yéménite et ses racines;* vol. 2, *La société yéménite de l'Hégire aux idéologies modernes;* vol. 3, *Culture et institutions du Yémen;* Paul Bonnenfant (ed.), *La Péninsule arabique aujourd'hui,* 2 vols. (Paris: Éditions du CNRS/CEROAC, 1982); Fred Halliday, *Arabia without Sultans* (London: Al Saqi Books, 2002).

2. North Yemen was, at the time of reunification in 1990, three times more populated than the South.

3. See *Les mémoires d'Ahmed Mohamed Nu'man,* text (in Arabic) edited by Ali Zayd (Sanaa/Beirut/Cairo: CEFAS/CAMES/Madbouli, 2004). On the iconography of this period of Yemeni modernization, see François Burgat (ed.), *Le Yémen vers la République (1900–1970): iconographie historique du Yémen* (Beirut/Sanaa: CEFAS, 2004).

4. Leigh Douglas, *The Free Yemeni Movement, 1935–1962* (Beirut: AUB, 1987).

5. "Some are well-known, such as Afghani, Kawakibi, Shakib Arslan," recalls Mohamed al-Ahnaf, "and others less so, like the Palestinian M. Ali-Tahir and the

Tunisian 'Abd al-'Aziz Tha'alibi (founder of the nationalist party Destour). Their scope of action was not restricted to their homeland but covered all the terrain where chance and the necessities of combat led them" (Mohamed al-Ahnaf, "Al-Fudhayl al-Wartilânî, un Algérien au Yémen: le rôle des Frères musulmans dans la Révolution de 1948," *Chroniques yéménites*, 1999, CEFAS, Sanaa [cy.revues.org]). Also see François Burgat and Marie Camberlin, "Yémen: aux sources de la révolution républicaine," in Rémi Leveau (ed.), *Les Monarchies arabes, transitions et dérives dynastiques* (Paris: Institut Français des Relations Internationales/Institut des Études Transrégionales; Princeton University, La Documentation Française, 2002), pp. 121–140.

6. Pascal Ménoret, *L'Énigme saoudienne* (Paris: La Découverte, 2004).

7. See *Les mémoires d'Ahmed Mohamed Nu'man.*

8. See François Burgat, "Le Yémen islamiste entre universalisme et insularité," in Franck Mermier et al. (eds.), *Le Yémen contemporain* (Paris: Karthala 2003), pp. 221ff. One of the editorials in the magazine of the Yemeni Union for Reform, *Al-Nur*, thirty years later recalled this episode: "It did not occur to anyone that the revolution of 1962 could be far from the light of Islam. . . . Two days after the revolution, however, we had the surprise of hearing a 'nonbelieving' voice singing full volume on the national radio: 'From now on, the religious zealots won't rule anymore.'"

9. Mermier et al., *Le Yémen contemporain;* Paul Dresch, *A History of Modern Yemen* (Cambridge: Cambridge University Press, 2000); Sheila Carapico, *Civil Society in Yemen: A Political Economy of Activism in Modern Arabia*, Cambridge Middle East Studies No. 9 (Cambridge: Cambridge University Press, 1998).

10. François Burgat, "Dans l'engrenage de la guerre: la normalisation du Yémen," *Le Monde Diplomatique* (February 2003).

11. The son of a good family from North Yemen, Hussein Badr al-Din al-Huthi is a former member of parliament, co-founder in 1990 of the al-Haqq party, one of the vestiges, in the republican framework, of the political expression of the Zaydi rite. In 1997 the head of state encouraged him to create an association (Believing Youth), which he probably expected would divide the ranks of the religious opposition. In 2002 tensions arose between himself and the regime, or, more precisely, the regime expressed its disapproval, as his discourse against American and Israeli politics in the region radicalized. Following a request from the American authorities, in June 2004 the army set about putting an end to his campaign of mobilization and accused him of wanting to reestablish the Imamate. After his demise, in November of the same year, following a gas attack launched against the cave where he had entrenched himself, his father took over from him in a conflict which so far has caused several hundred deaths in the ranks of the army as well as among the "rebels."

12. The long-standing historical legitimacy acquired by the Islamist trend—first through its struggle against the Imamate (in 1948) and then through its support for the Republic (and the mobilization of the tribes by Zubayri and his Party of God) and for President Ali Abdallah Saleh's regime (through the struggle against the

"Marxists" of the South before and after reunification)—resulted in the fact that the Islamists, accepted in the legal oppositional system and, for a while, associated with those in power, until this episode avoided both prison and the temptation of revolutionary opposition (see Ludwig Stiftl, "The Yemeni Islamists in the Process of Democratisation," in Mermier et al., *Le Yémen contemporain*, p. 247; Jilian Schwedler, "The Yemeni Islah Party: Political Opportunities and Coalition Building in a Transitional Polity," in Quintan Wiktorowicz [ed.], *Islamist Activism: A Social Movement Theory Approach* [Bloomington: Indiana University Press, 2003]).

13. The emblematic figure of the Brothers' interventionism is the Algerian nationalist al-Fudayl al-Wartilani. Arriving in April 1947 in the guise of a trader, the emissary of Hassan al-Banna was the lynchpin of the 1948 revolution. It was al-Wartilani who drafted the Sacred Charter, a programmatic document with constitutional value which was to be the instrument of the reform of the Imamate (see al-Ahnaf, "Al-Fudhayl al-Wartilânî, un Algérien au Yémen").

14. In particular Olivier Carré and Gérard Michaud, *Les frères musulmans* (Paris: Gallimard, 1983); and Olivier Carré, *Mystique et politique: Sayyid Qutb* (Paris: Presses de Sciences Po, 2002), pp. 27ff.

15. See in particular François Burgat and Mohamed Sbitli, "Les 'Libres' Yéménites, le courant réformiste et les Frères musulmans: premiers repères pour l'analyse," in Chérif al-Maher and Salam Kawakibi (eds.), *Le Courant réformiste musulman et sa réception dans les sociétés arabes,* Aleppo Symposium marking the hundredth anniversary of the death of Sheikh 'Abd al-Rahman al-Kawakibi, May 31–June 1, 2002 (Damascus: IFPO, 2003).

16. Mohamed Qahtan, one of the leaders of the Yemeni Union for Reform party, created in 1990 in Yemen by the Muslim Brothers; interview with the author, Sanaa, March 2003.

17. In *Face to Face with Islamism*, I mainly proposed the hypothesis that, "by reconnecting the process of modernization with the symbolic universe of intuitive culture, [re-Islamization] empowers this process, until now reserved to the urban acculturated elites, to affect the whole of society."

18. Abdelmalek Tayyib and François Burgat, "Muhammad Mahmûd Zubayrî et la fondation du Parti de Dieu," *Chroniques yéménites 1998–1999* (Sanaa: CEFAS, 2000), pp. 63–65.

CHAPTER FIVE

1. See Gilles Dorronsoro, *La Révolution afghane: des communistes aux tâlebâns* (Paris: Karthala, 2000); English translation: *Revolution Unending: Afghanistan, 1979 to the Present,* trans. John King (New York: Columbia University Press, 2005).

2. See Karin Kneissel, "Il faut distinguer entre terrorisme et résistance" (followed by an interview with Hassan Nasrallah, "La nouvelle question d'Orient"), *Confluences Méditerranée* 49 (May 2004).

3. On the vision of the Lebanese Sunni leader, see in particular Fathi Yakan, *Islamic Movement Problems and Perspectives* (Indianapolis: American Trust Publications, 1984) and *Que signifie mon appartenance à l'Islam* (Lyon: Tawhid, 1999).

4. On the twofold ground of modernization and political radicalization, it is difficult to prove a structural specificity of the Iranian Shiite world or of the Shiite components of the Lebanese, Iraqi, Saudi, or Yemeni scene. If sectarian tensions persist (and continue to be manipulated, notably in Iraq) everywhere, political links and intellectual convergences, albeit not doctrinal, with the Sunnis can be demonstrated. For a Yemeni example of the modes of intersectarian communication, see Samy Dorlian, "Les filières islamistes zaydites au Yémen: la construction endogène d'un universel politique," master's thesis in comparative politics, Aix-en-Provence, Institut d'Études Politiques, 2005.

5. The participation of the Muslim Brothers in the Algerian parliament is only the result of the rupture that soon occurred between the Islamic Salvation Front and their representative, Mahfoud Nahnah (the founder of the Hamas movement), and the fact that the latter preferred, in order to emerge from his isolation, as proven twice by the polls in June and December 1990, to compromise very quickly with the military regime.

6. Its concluding pages were translated into French by Jean-Pierre Milelli with comments by Stéphane Lacroix, preceded by a useful biography of the author, in *Al-Qaida dans le texte,* introduction by Gilles Kepel (Paris: PUF, 2005). See also Dominique Thomas, *Les Hommes d'Al-Qaida* (Paris: Michalon, 2004) and *Le Londonistan, la voix du jihâd* (Paris: Michalon, 2003).

7. As attested by the tensions within the movement in Yemen, where many women have been elected as leaders of the Islah party, but where their candidacy for an elective mandate is not yet on the agenda.

8. As I proposed to do in *Face to Face with Political Islam,* by considering this modernization to be the result of the development of an autonomous space of politics, a necessary prerequisite to the acceptance of the demands of democracy (institutionalizing the modalities of the transmission of power, limiting recourse to the repressive violence of states, asserting the equal rights of confessional minorities, affirming the autonomy of women within the family space and their access to professional and political public space, etc.).

9. See, for example, Yusuf al-Qaradawi, *Priorities of the Islamic Movement in the Coming Phase* (Swansea: Awakening Publications, 2000). The preacher of the Qatari channel, supervisor of the site Islam Online, notably develops his differences with the reactive distortions of Qutbism and the main expressions of the Salafi literalist trend claiming to be the representative of an author, Taqi al-Din Ahmad ibn Taymiyyah, who says that they do not know him.

10. Even if we can, of course, find such signs earlier on: the Egyptian intellectual Mohamed Amara thus explains that he preferred to become affiliated with the party Young Egypt rather than with the Muslim Brothers, who, in his opinion, were not eclectic enough in what they read.

11. See Xavier Ternisien, *Les Frères musulmans* (Paris: Fayard, 2005).

12. See in particular Patrick Haenni, "L'Islam branché de la bourgeoisie égyptienne," *Le Monde Diplomatique* (September 2003).

13. See Nadia Yassine, *Toutes voiles dehors* (Épinay-Sur-Seine/Casablanca: Alter Éditions/Le Fennec, 2003); Malika Zeghal, *Les Islamistes marocains: le défi à la monarchie* (Paris: La Découverte, 2005); Mounia Bennani-Chraïbi, Myriam Catusse, and Jean-Claude Santucci (eds.), *Scènes et coulisses de l'élection au Maroc: les législatives 2002* (Paris: Karthala, 2004); Frédéric Vairel, "Nouveaux Contextes de mise à l'épreuve de la notion de fluidité politique: l'analyse des conjonctures de basculement dans le cas du Maroc," dissertation in political science, Aix-en-Provence, Institut d'Études Politiques, 2005.

14. See Mamoun Fandy, *Saudi Arabia and the Politics of Dissent* (London: Palgrave/Macmillan, 1999); Stéphane Lacroix, "Between Islamists and Liberals: Saudi Arabia's New 'Islamo-Liberal' Reformists," *Middle East Journal* 58, no. 3 (2004): 352.

15. See Jocelyne Cesari, *L'Islam à l'épreuve de l'Occident* (Paris: La Découverte, 2004); Tariq Ramadan, *Les Musulmans d'Occident et l'avenir de l'islam* (Paris: Sindbad, 2003).

16. The diversity of registers in which the reactions to this proposition coming from the Muslim world were expressed—reluctance or condemnation of principle rather than support—is a good prism through which to read the impact and the limits of the reformist dynamics underway. Tariq Ramadan replied to the malicious insinuations of all those who, in Europe, had reproached him with proposing only a "moratorium" on the implementation of Quranic penalties by reminding them that this was the same expression that Jacques Chirac had used about the implementation of the death penalty in the world: "Le noble 'moratoire' de Jacques Chirac, l'ignoble 'moratoire' de Tariq Ramadan: 'double discours' ou 'double audition'" (article available on the sites Oumma.com and Tariqramadan.com, among others).

17. Pascal Ménoret, "Le wahhabisme, arme fatale du néo-orientalisme," *Mouvements* (November 2004).

18. See Chapter 1 above; and François Burgat and Mohamed Sbitli, "Les 'Libres' yéménites, le courant réformiste et les Frères musulmans: premiers repères pour l'analyse," in Chérif al-Maher and Salam Kawakibi (eds.), *Le Courant réformiste musulman et sa réception dans les sociétés arabes,* Aleppo Symposium marking the hundredth anniversary of the death of Sheikh 'Abd al-Rahman al-Kawakibi, May 31–June 1, 2002 (Damascus: IFPO, 2003).

19. Muqbil Ibn Hadi al-Wadi'i, *Al-Makhraj min al-Fitna* (How to Issue Forth from the Dead Ends of Division) (Sanaa: n.p., 1982), p. 20.

20. Born in 1938, al-'Abidin Surur first got closer to the Muslim Brothers and to their leader 'Isam al-'Attar during his law studies in Damascus (1963–1968), before teaching in secondary schools in Saudi Arabia until 1973 and then working in Kuwait for the magazine *Al-Mujtama'a* and the al-Arqam circle. When he left Kuwait in 1984, he distanced himself from the Muslim Brothers and moved closer to the

Salafis before breaking off with his new associates to found within the Salafi movement itself a reformist tendency which publishes the magazine *Al-Sunna* from Birmingham in Great Britain.

21. ʿAbd al-Khaliq is notably the author of *Al-Hadd al-fasil bayn al-imam wa-l-kufr* (The Boundary between Faith and Unbelief) (Alexandria: Dar al-Iman, n.d.) and of *Al-ʿAmal al-siyasi ʿind al-muslimin* (The Political Action of Muslims) (n.p., n.d.).

22. "No Muslim order," writes Jean-Louis Triaud about the Sanusi order, "has been the subject of a surveillance and a hostility as durable on the part of the French administration and publicists. The dread of the Sanusiyya, the denunciation of this order, and the open struggle against it play a very special role in the colonial drama" (Jean-Louis Triaud, *La Légende noire de la Sanûsiyya: une confrérie musulmane saharienne sous le regard français [1840–1930]* [Paris: Éditions de la Maison des Sciences de l'Homme, 1995], vol. 1, p. 2).

23. Yosri Fouda and Nick Fielding, *Les Cerveaux du terrorisme: rencontre avec Ramzi Binalchibh et Khalid Cheikh Mohammed, numéro 3 d'Al-Qaida* (Paris: Le Rocher, 2003); English translation: *Masterminds of Terror: The Truth behind the Most Devastating Attack the World Has Ever Seen* (New York: Arcade Publishing, 2003).

24. To take up the interesting expression coined and documented by Alix Philippon, "Le soufislamisme: l'invention paradoxale d'une nouvelle modernité politique en islam? Le cas du Minhaj-ul Quran pakistanais," dissertation in political science, Aix-en-Provence, Institut des Études Politiques, 2004. Alix Philippon has highlighted the intricate and changing character of the links between Sufism and political action. Also see, concerning this same terrain but in the case of Yemen, Amira Kotb, "La Tariqa Ba'Alawiyya et le développement d'un réseau soufi transnational," dissertation in political science, Aix-en-Provence, Institut des Études Politiques, 2004.

25. See in particular Anne-Marie Schimmel, *Le Soufisme, ou les dimensions mystiques de l'islam* (Paris: Cerf, 1996).

CHAPTER SIX

1. The editorialist Alain Duhamel for his part called Ramadan a "juggler," the socialist deputy Julien Dray publicly expressed his wish to "punch him in the face," and so forth.

2. Amman, interview with the author, March 1990.

3. Quoted by Pascal Boniface, *Vers la quatrième guerre mondiale?* (Paris: Armand Colin, 2005).

4. Ugharit Yunan has listed the surprising contours of popular parlance in this field in *Kayfa nataraba ʿala al-Ta'ifiyya* (Confessional Education) (Beirut: Dar al-Jedid, 1997).

5. Robert A. Pape, *Dying to Win: The Strategic Logic of Suicide Terrorism* (New York: Random House, 2005). Concerning the motivations of candidates for "death to win," see also the very realistic film *Paradise Now* by Hani Abou-Hassad (September 2005), radically more credible than many op/ed columns or the investigations of some of our "investigative journalists" or "special correspondents."

6. As a symbolic example among a thousand, see Alexandre Adler's profession of faith in the epigraph to the introduction of this book. One of the most overwhelmingly broadcast editorialists in France there explains his tranquil preference for "the most enlightened—or even not enlightened at all—dictatorships possible in Egypt and in Saudi Arabia," over any victory of the Muslim Brothers in free elections, which would enable them to set up "someone like Tariq Ramadan as Minister of Culture" (*Le Figaro*, September 6, 2004).

CHAPTER SEVEN

1. So many experts have long wanted to believe, and to make the world believe, that they "explain" the speed with which the Islamist protest of the 1990s spread.

2. Osama Bin Laden, "Message to the American People," November 2004.

3. See Gilles Kepel, *Le Prophète et le Pharaon: les mouvements islamiques dans l'Égypte contemporaine* (Paris: La Découverte, 1984; revised ed.: Paris: Seuil, 1993); English translation: *The Prophet and Pharaoh: Muslim Extremism in Egypt*, translated by Jon Rothschild (Berkeley: University of California Press, 1985).

4. See Olivier Carré, *Mystique et politique: le Coran des islamistes, lecture du Coran par Sayyid Qutb, Frère musulman radical (1906–1966)* (Paris: Cerf, 2004).

5. Yahya Michot, a professor at the faculty of theology at Oxford University, refutes the interpretations of Ibn Taymiyya generally accepted by Islamists, notably the one popularized by 'Abd al-Salam Faraj (see Yahya Michot, *Mardin, hegira, fuite du péché et demeure de l'islam* and *Ibn Taymiyya: Mécréance et pardon* [Beirut: al-Bouraq, 2005]).

6. William E. Shepard, *Sayyid Qutb and Islamic Activism: A Translation and Critical Analysis of Social Justice in Islam* (New York/Cologne: E. J. Brill/Leiden, 1996).

7. In English in the original—Trans.

8. This text was signed on October 25, 1965, in the military prison of Cairo. It has since then been published many times in the form of a brochure (80 pages) without a date or place of publication and is currently available in Arabic on the Internet. In particular this text, probably written in response to interrogation by the security services and at their request, clearly dates Qutb's joining of the Muslim Brothers (1953), a topic debated at length by his usual interpreters. Authenticated, according to its (anonymous) preface writer, through Qutb's handwriting, this text may, however, have been shortened by several paragraphs or pages, notably the ones describing the practices used by his torturers to make him speak.

Admittedly, Olivier Carré, the most informed of Qutb's French readers, does mention its existence, but without really capitalizing on it (see Carré, *Mystique et politique*, p. 23). Also see Shepard, *Sayyid Qutb and Islamic Activism;* and Ibrahim Abu Rabi', *Intellectual Origins of Islamic Resurgence in the Modern Arab World* (New York: State University of New York Press, 1996).

9. Among the many explanations, more anecdotal than scientific, of this name, we can add one stating that Bin Laden's last wife was born in a big Yemeni market town located north of the city of Taez whose long-standing name was "al-Qaeda." The weavers of al-Qaeda were, not so long ago, still making *futas* (pieces of cloth that men wrap around their waists) decorated with the motif of planes hitting the towers of Manhattan.

10. See François Burgat, "La machine à fabriquer des poseurs de bombes," *Libération*, October 30, 1995.

11. Quoted by Oliver Carré and Gérard Michaud, *Les Frères musulmans* (Paris: Gallimard, 1983).

12. "To those young people that I thought were just being born and that I then discovered really existed, struggling on the path of God without fearing for their belongings or their life."

13. As an exception which confirms the rule, a (British) televised fiction recounted with the requisite realism the episode of the repression of the Brothers to integrate it into the process of the making of the al-Qaeda generation: Adam Curtis, *The Power of Nightmares: The Shadows in the Caves*, BBC, first broadcast January 2005.

14. "With all your knowledge, how dare you say that [the murder attempt against Nasser] was a hoax?" Salah Dessouki, one of his first interrogators, asked him. "I am not saying that it was a hoax, I am only saying that it was fabricated and that a foreign hand is involved in all this." During his stay in the prison of Tora, he tried, he explained, to learn the exact circumstances of the attack from the close relatives of its perpetrator, Mahmud Abdel Latif, who all declared that the case remained completely unexplained in their opinion.

15. The inception of the strategy of "Islamization from the top" is very generally attributed to Qutb to oppose it to the supporters of an Islamization "from below," which he seems in fact never to have completely given up.

16. "We could not answer by the same means, Islam forbidding torture or starving women and children. The state must even provide for the needs of the spouses and children of those who are condemned to capital punishment. We hence did not have any other legal means at the religious level than murder [*qatl*], first to respond to the aggression and not let the Islamic movement and its members be weakened, then to try to save . . . the greatest possible number of young committed Muslims, within a generation that is totally permissive, loose, deviant in its behavior and its attitudes."

17. Osama Bin Laden, "Statement to the Saudi Leaders," December 16, 2004.

18. Montasser al-Zayyat, *Aiman al-Zawahiri kama 'araftuhu* (Ayman al-Zawahiri as I Knew Him) (Cairo: Dar Misr al-Mahrussa, 2002); English translation:

The Road to al-Qaeda: The Story of Bin Laden's Right-Hand Man (London: Pluto Press, 2004).

19. He thus gave an appointment to one of his most faithful allies, the ex-officer 'Isam al-Qamari, on the famous square ("Kit Kat") of the working-class neighborhood of Embaba, where he knew that a trap set by Egyptian Security awaited him.

20. Reported by Laurence Wright, "The Man behind Bin Laden," *New Yorker*, September 16, 2002 (available at www.lawrencewright.com/art-zawahiri.html); quoted by Stéphane Lacroix, in *Al-Qaida dans le texte*, introduction by Gilles Kepel (Paris: PUF, 2005), p. 228; also see *Le Livre noir: la torture des musulmans sous la présidence de Hosni Mubarak*, written subsequently by Zawahiri and available on the Internet (*Al-Kitab al-asswad Qissat ta'dhib al-muslimin fi ahd Husni Mubarak*).

21. During the summer of 1971, Bin Laden took an English course at an Oxford institute and practiced one of the favorite water sports of the students. He was also described by some who were in close contact with him in Afghanistan as a volleyball enthusiast. One of his best biographies was written by Jonathan Randal, *Oussama: la fabrication d'un terroriste* (Paris: Albin Michel, 2004). His speeches and his works (including the interviews he gave to Cable News Network [CNN] and to the British journalist Robert Fisk) are quite easily available in English on the Internet. The Arab versions have quite often been destroyed. After September 11 the recordings of his statements were sold in the streets of Sanaa, until the U.S. Embassy had their public sale forbidden.

The translations of the statements should of course be cross-checked carefully. Indeed it is not inconceivable that false declarations, like certain *fatwas* ordering an attack specifically on the Shiites and attributed to Abu Mus'ab al-Zarqawi (*nom de guerre* of a militant Jordanian considered one of the leaders of the Sunni resistance in Iraq, reputed to have sworn allegiance to Bin Laden), were circulated by those in Iraq, the United States, and the Middle East who wanted to divide or discredit the Iraqi resistance. The level of excellence attained in this area by the Algerian secret services, with the aid of some of their foreign counterparts, in criminalizing their opponents should thus always be kept in mind.

22. One of the most enlightening texts on this subject is probably the "Letter to Sheikh Ibn Baz," dated December 1994. 'Abd al-Aziz ibn 'Abd Allah ibn Baz (1912–1999) was one of the great Saudi *ulamas*, a reference for the Salafis but nevertheless the author of various discourses criticizing Bin Laden and of all forms of support granted to the Saudi holders of power. The text of the letter shows that, until December 1994, Bin Laden's strategy in regard to the Saudi *ulamas* close to the regime had remained confined to courteous criticism and the demand for reforms rather than confrontation. In his statement in December 2004, moreover, Bin Laden clarified that the combat of his supporters in Arabia was limited to American interests: "The Mujahidin, in the country of the holy mosques, have not yet started the struggle against the government. If they undertake it, they will undoubtedly start with the head of disbelief, that is, the rulers of Riyad."

23. Mamoun Fandy, *Saudi Arabia and the Politics of Dissent* (London: Palgrave/Macmillan, 1999); Madawi al-Rasheed and Robert Vitalis, *Counter-Narratives: History, Contemporary Society and Politics in Saudi Arabia and Yemen* (New York: Palgrave, 2004); Madawi al-Rasheed, *A History of Saudi Arabia* (Cambridge: Cambridge University Press, 2002).

24. As Fahd, in Bin Laden's opinion, introduced in 1990 a foreign infidel king (George Bush's father) into the territory of the sacred places of Islam, Abu Rughal served as a guide to Abraha, an infidel king, when the latter led an aborted attack against Muhammad's Mecca about 670. His grave supposedly was stoned for a long time. Bin Laden often refers to this letter to King Fahd (to be distinguished from a "Statement to the Saudi Leaders" posted on December 16, 2004, by the website www.jihadunspun.com as "Statement No. 17").

25. Quran 4:61: "Mark those who profess to believe in what has been revealed to you and what was revealed before you. They seek the judgement of the devil, although they were bidden to deny him. Satan would lead them far into error" (*The Koran*, introduction and translation by N. J. Dawood [London: Penguin Classics, 1999]).

26. "Statement to the Saudi Regime," December 2004.

27. Interview with Robert Baer, *Atlantic*, May 29, 2003 (quoted by Pascal Ménoret in *The Saudi Enigma* [London: Zed Books, 2005]).

28. Jean-Michel Foulquier, *Arabie Saoudite: la Dictature protégée* (Paris: Albin Michel, 1995).

29. Interview with Robert Baer, quoted above.

30. From the fourteenth century onward, classical Islamic thought distinguished, within the religious sphere, the "rational" from the "confessional." Ibn Taymiyyah thus dissociated what he called the "three levels"—"rational, confessional, and legal"—from the religious: "By the rational [*aqli*], we mean that which the supporters of reason among the sons of Adam agree on, whether they have been endowed with a Book or not" (spiritual texts of Ibn Taymiyya, "Textes spirituels d'Ibn Taymiyyah XIV, Raison, confession, loi: une typologie musulmane du religieux," presented and translated from the Arabic by Yahya Michot, www.muslimphilosophy.com).

31. See in particular Jason Burke, *Al-Qaeda: The True Story of Radical Islam* (London/New York: I. B. Taurus, 2004); and Yosri Fouda and Nick Fielding, *Masterminds of Terror: The Truth behind the Most Devastating Attack the World Has Ever Seen* (London: Arcade Publishing, 2003).

32. With Atta, unlike Bin Laden or other members of his group, this extends as far as an obvious misogyny, which some commentators have thought to explain by repressed homosexuality.

CHAPTER EIGHT

1. The "Muslim Gaulois," of "French stock" and converted to Islam, are considered to have played only a marginal role in its representation until now.

2. See in particular François Geze and Salima Mellah, "Crimes contre l'humanité," postface to the book by Nesroulah Yous, *Qui a tué à Bentalha? Algérie, chronique d'un massacre annoncé* (Paris: La Découverte, 2000), pp. 281ff.

3. Habib Souaïdia, *La Sale Guerre* (Paris: La Découverte, 2001).

4. Mohammed Samraoui, *Chroniques des années de sang: comment les services secrets ont manipulé les groupes islamistes* (Paris: Denoël, 2003).

5. Lounis Aggoun and Jean-Baptiste Rivoire, *Françalgérie: crimes et mensonges d'États* (Paris: La Découverte, 2004).

6. Honorable exceptions: *Le Canard enchaîné, Les Inrockuptibles, Libération,* and *Politis* (see Lounis Aggoun, "Omerta sur un livre ou la presse française à la sauce bananière," *Le Croquant* 43 [October 2004]: 110–114).

7. The most complete and best-documented study to date on the manipulation of the armed Islamist groups by the Algerian secret services is the one by the journalist Salima Mellah, *Le Mouvement islamiste algérien entre autonomie et manipulation,* CJA/TPP, www.algerie-tpp.org/tpp/presentation/resume_19.htm.

8. Samraoui, *Chroniques des années de sang,* p. 94.

9. Salah-Eddine Sidhoum and Algeria-Watch, *Algérie, la machine de mort: un rapport sur la torture, les centres de détentions secrets et l'organisation de la machine de mort,* October 2003, www.algeria-watch.org.

10. A cooperation confirmed in his memoirs by the former boss of the Director-ate of Territorial Surveillance (DTS), Yves Bonnet, who mentions in the following words his meeting with Smaïn Lamari, who became from 1992 onward one of the main organizers of torture and mass assassinations: "It was in the luxurious secrecy of the Crillon that I met for the first time, in autumn 1984, with the inseparable duo formed by Colonel Lakhal Ayat and Major Smaïn Lamari. These were the first con-tacts between the Algerian and French services since independence, and we imme-diately found the words which brought us closer, in a complicity which should never be forgotten. . . . We sealed an alliance, . . . we started a friendship. . . . Never was a liaison developed with such celerity" (Yves Bonnet, *Contre-espionnage: mémoires d'un patron de la DST* [Paris: Calmann-Lévy, 2000], p. 339).

11. Pierre Bourdieu, "L'intellectuel négatif," *Liber* (Paris, January 1998).

12. See in particular Aggoun and Rivoire, *Françalgérie: crimes et mensonges d'États.* On another model of the perverted relationship between Western environ-ment and illegitimate regime, see Jean-Michel Foulquier, *Arabie saoudite: la dictat-ure protégée* (Paris: Albin Michel, 1995).

13. But also by one of the most bloodthirsty Algerian generals, General Khaled Nezzar, who declared in the daily *El-Watan:* "They have by their courage made the truth known." And he assured "these men of courage and of conviction" of "his greatest respect" and his "highest consideration" (quoted by Jean-Pierre Tuquoi, "Les succès de communication du pouvoir algérien," *Le Monde,* February 20, 1998). Bernard-Henri Lévy nevertheless commented confidently on the reissue of his sur-prising Algerian "report" in a book published in 2004 and (very lucidly) entitled *Récidives:* "There is the risk of making a mistake. There is the risk, when you re-

publish texts like these reports of 1992 [actually 1998], in Algeria, of retrospective refutation. Fine. That's the way it is. I don't take back anything today from the basic analysis that the Islamists were responsible for massacres. Even if I am inclined, in hindsight, to think that I perhaps underestimated the possible exploitation of these Islamists by the military power" (Bernard-Henry Lévy, "Vous pouvez dire la vérité à un barbare, il ne sera pas moins barbare," interview with Annette Lévy-Willard, *Libération*, April 24, 2004). On the network of media influence of B.-H. Lévy, see in particular Serge Halimi, "Cela dure depuis vingt-cinq ans," *Le Monde Diplomatique* (December 2003).

14. Edward Said, *Culture et Impérialisme* (Paris: Fayard/*Le Monde Diplomatique*, 2000).

15. Just like the remarkable work of interpretation of the French televised discourse on Islam over the last thirty years conducted (not on this specific program but on many others of the same vein) by Thomas Deltombe, *L'Islam imaginaire: la construction médiatique de l'islamophobie en France, 1975–2005* (Paris: La Découverte, 2005).

16. Plus, it must be added, an honorary doctorate which the University of Louvain-la-Neuve bestowed on her in 1998, demonstrating, if need be, the excellent communication skills of the officers of the junta or the sorry state of naïveté of certain officials of a great university institution. See in particular Abbas Aroua, *Horroris Causa: le féminisme à l'heure de la Sainte éradication* (Geneva: Hoggar, 2002). "Khalida Messaoudi, whose portrait this issue attempts to draw," writes Pierre Guillard, "has among others been the irresponsible but terrifying driving force behind the death of many men and the silencing of their women. She has made the age-old wager that the West, through its violence, would fit the world to her whim. If she does not finally fail in her designs, Algeria will be no more than a fiction."

17. *Le Monde*, May 21, 2001.

18. Abdelwahab Meddeb, *The Malady of Islam* (New York: Basic Books, 2003).

19. The title of an article in which Adam Katz brilliantly deconstructs the intellectual and political functioning of Fouad Ajami, who, in the United States, is the archetype of the "façade intellectual" and in whom he does not discover any principle other than respect for power. Ajami, a Shiite native of Lebanon, has gradually become the most fervent supporter of the foreign policy of the neo-conservatives. "Although he has produced little scholarly work of value, Ajami is a regular guest on CBS News, *Charlie Rose*, and the *NewsHour with Jim Lehrer*, and a frequent contributor to the editorial pages of the *Wall Street Journal* and the *New York Times*. His ideas are also widely recycled by acolytes like Thomas Friedman and Judith Miller of the *Times*. . . . Ajami's ethnicity is not incidental to his celebrity. It lends him an air of authority not enjoyed by non-Arab polemicists like Martin Kraemer and Daniel Pipes" (Adam Katz, "The Native Informant," *Nation*, April 28, 2003).

CHAPTER NINE

1. Michael Scheuer, *Through Our Enemies' Eyes: Osama Bin Laden, Radical Islam, and the Future of America* (Washington, D.C.: Brassey's, 2002).

2. Almost all the prisoners of Guantanamo have been detained for several years without any charge. The United States designates them as "enemy combatants" and denies them the status of prisoners of war and the guarantees linked to the Geneva Conventions. The prisoners detained in secret are rarely identified. From his transfer into the hands of the American authorities, after his arrest in March 2003 in Rawalpindi (Pakistan), Khalid Sheikh Mohammed, the purported organizer of the September 11 attacks, like many others before him, was long deprived of all legal judiciary procedures. In July 2005 two men imprisoned in a Yemeni jail told a representative of Amnesty International how they had been kept in solitary confinement by the American authorities in a secret detention center for more than a year and a half, without seeing daylight and most of the time chained and handcuffed, without the opportunity of getting in touch with their families, a lawyer, or humanitarian organizations, and even being ignorant of the country where they actually were. In May 2005 a report by the organization Human Rights Watch (HRW) listed sixty-three cases (since the middle of the 1990s) of purported Islamist militants who were transferred illegally to Egypt to be tortured there.

3. See in particular Fareed Zakaria, "Why They Hate Us," *Newsweek*, October 15, 2001.

4. There are, however, several indications of the importance the Palestinian issue holds in the political consciousness of Bin Laden, as in that of the vast majority of Muslims, particularly Arabs. One of them is the fact that very early on he consorted with Abdallah Azzam, the Palestinian in charge of the enlistment of "Arab Afghans" in the struggle against the Soviet presence in Afghanistan. This did not prevent him from at times expressing positions which could appear more narrowly "nationalist" (if not "Saudi"), by declaring, for example, that between the two shrines of Medina and Mecca and that of Jerusalem (all three restored by his father) "his heart was closer" to those which were on Saudi soil.

5. On the beginning of the inversion of North-South media flows begun by the creation of the Qatari channel al-Jazeera, see Olfa Lamloum, *Al-Jazira, miroir rebelle et ambigu du monde arabe* (Paris: La Découverte, 2004). Few observers to this day have pointed out that since the beginning of the American campaign in Iraq in spring 2003 Washington's pressures have led to an in-depth "normalization" of the "rebel" channel, which, among other areas, has made essential concessions to Washington's categories of analysis in the coverage of the Iraq conflict (but not only there).

6. The community of Muslim believers.

7. Gilles Kepel, *Fitna: guerre au coeur de l'islam* (Paris: Gallimard, 2004).

8. See my own article "Débats," *Le Monde*, April 30, 1992, addressing the Algerian situation, in the Appendix.

9. Notably *Le Destin*, awarded gold in 1997 at the Cannes Festival, a caricature and a simplistic attack on the origins of the Islamist trends and their intellectual and political purview.

CONCLUSION

1. On November 27 and 28, 1995, in Barcelona, the governments of twenty-seven countries, the Council of the European Union, and the European Commission created the Euro-Mediterranean Partnership (EMP), whose main objective was to make the Euro-Mediterranean basin an area of dialogue, exchange, and cooperation in order to safeguard peace, stability, and prosperity.

2. Better late than never: some American Democratic think-tanks have rather belatedly come round to this perspective. "The Key to Arab Reform: Moderate Islamists" is the title of an article by a researcher at the Carnegie Endowment for International Peace in July 2005 (Amr Hamzawy, "The Key to Arab Reform: Moderate Islamists," Policy Brief No. 40, July 26, 2005, www.carnegieendowment.org/publications). Before any significant reform could take place in the Arab world, this author asserted in substance, the United States and Europe must start to establish relations with moderate Islamists, an undertaking less thorny than it might appear, for these Islamists have made democratic rules their own and have shown a very real support for the rule of law. The European Commission has also organized several surveys taking into account this demand, which is, however, far from being accepted by its leaders. The essayist Alexandre Adler, for his part, is even further removed from any such perceptiveness: learning that the British prime minister, Tony Blair, had decided to associate Tariq Ramadan with the thoughts of his government on terrorism, he preferred to vent his considerable vexation on the air (France Culture, September 3, 2005).

3. Karcher is the brand name of a high-pressure hydraulic cleaning apparatus, used as a rhetorical figure by the French presidential candidate Nicholas Sarkozy, then minister of the interior (so directly responsible at the time), when speaking of the kind of action he intended to take in his policy toward the violently disaffected unemployed youth of the French city suburbs. This metaphor definitely has a "Putinesque" ring to it, albeit in a minor key—Trans.

APPENDIX

Originally published in "Débats," *Le Monde*, April 30, 1992.

INDEX

'Abd al-Khaliq, 'Abd al-Rahman, 84

'Abd al-Malik, Mansur, 26

'Abd al-Wahhab, Muhammad, 33, 35, 36, 86, 101

'Abdelhakim, Mahmud, 164n18

Abdallah, Azzam, 177n4

Abdel Latif, Mahmud, 172n14

Abderrazak, Mustapha, 34

Abduh, Muhammad, 34, 35, 73

al-'Abidin Surur, Muhammad Ibn Nayif Zayn, 84

Abou Zahab, Mariam, 158n8

Abou-Hassad, Hani, 171n5

Abu Rabi', Ibrahim, 172n8

Abu'l-A'la Mawdudi, Sayyid, 104

Addi Lahouari, 160n19

Adelkhah, Fariba, 163n42

Adler, Alexandre, 1, 171n6, 178n2

al-Afghani, Jamal al-Din, 33–35

Aflaq, Michel, 36

Ageron, Charles-Robert, 163n7

Aggoun, Lounis, 175n5

Ahmad, Leila, 162n34

al-Ahnaf, Mohamed, 165–166n5

Aït-Larbi, Meziane, 160n19

Ajaml, Fouad, 176n19

Allende, Salvador, 161n24

Amara, Mohamed, 168n10

Amin, Ahmed, 159n7

Amr, Khaled, 82

Aroua, Abbas, 160n19, 174n16

Atatürk, Kemal, 51

Atta, Mohammed, 32, 48, 101, 105, 118–120

Azzam, Abdallah, 177n4

Badr al-Din al-Huthi, Hussein, 71, 166n11

Baer, Robert, 127

al-Banna, Hassan, 32, 33, 34, 72, 73, 78, 79, 81, 114, 104, 107, 167n13

Baring, Evelyn (Lord Cromer), 49

Baubérot, Jean, 139

Baydani, 'Abd al-Rahman, 69

Bedjaoui, Youcef, 160n19

Belhassen, Souhayr, 164n11

Ben Ali, Zine al-Abidine, 46, 82

Ben Badis, Abdel Hamid, 36

Ben Ganna, Khadija, 53, 54

Benhaj, Ali, 29

Bennabi, Malek, 10, 17, 33, 36, 56

Ben Youssef, Salah, 164n11

Berlousconi, Silvio, 97

Bin Laden, Osama, 2, 18, 39, 41, 42, 47, 55, 71, 77, 87, 89, 95, 97, 98, 101–103, 111, 112–117, 119, 135, 141, 142, 173n21

al-Bishri, Tariq, 35

Blair, Tony, 87, 92, 94, 178n2

Bonnet, Yves, 175

Boumediene, Houari, 58

Bourdieu, Pierre, 131, 132, 133

Bourguiba, Habib, 38, 51, 52, 54, 56, 58, 164n11

Bouteflika, Abdelaziz, 21
Bouteldja, Houria, 50
Bugeaud, Thomas, 57
Bush, George W., 2, 18, 43, 87, 94, 117, 143

Chahine, Youssef, 147
Chalabi, Ahmed, 138
Chbeilat, Leith, 94
Chelbi, Hind, 51, 52, 54
Chenouda III, 135
Chirac, Jacques, 92, 138, 169n16
Clinton, Bill, 43, 45, 115, 145

de Chateaubriand, François, 34
De Gaulle, Charles, 50, 92
Deltombe, Thomas, 176n15
Dessouki, Salah, 172n14
al-Din, Yahya Hamid, 23
Dorlian, Samy, 168n4
Dray, Julien, 170n1
Duhamel, 170n1

Ebadi, Shirin, 53
Entelis, John, 157n4
Erbakan, Necmettin, 28
Erdogan, Recep Tayqip, 28, 77
Esposito, John, 157n4

Fadh, King, 104, 113–114, 174n24
Faisal, King, 70
Fanon, Franz, 50
Faraj, 'Abd al-Salam, 102, 171n5
Farouk, King, 80, 111
Farrere, Claude, 34
Fielding, Nick, 89, 139
Fisk, Robert, 173n21
Fouda, Yosri, 89, 139
Fuad, King, 80

al-Ghannoushi, Rashid, 37–38, 82
Gilani, 'Abd al-Qadr, 85

Girard, René, 123
Glucksman, André, 132
Guillard, Pierre, 176n16

Hamilton, Lee H., 89
Hamzawy, Amr, 178n2
Hanoune, Louisa, 28
Huntington, Samuel, 132
Hussein, Saddam, 33, 43, 71, 114, 144

Ibn al-saud, Muhammad, 35
Ibn Baz, Sheikh, 173n22
Ibn Isma'il al-Amir, Muhammad, 34
Ibn Taymiyya, Taqi al-Din, 2, 89, 168, 106, 171n5, 174n30

Katz, Adam, 176n19
al-Kawakibi, 'Abd al-Rahman, 73, 159n4, 167n15
Kawakibi, Salam, 73
Kean, Thomas H., 89
Khalidi, Rashid, 40
Khan, Walid, 15
Khomeini, Ayatollah Ruhollah, 28
Kouchner, Bernard, 92

Lamartine, Alphonse, 34
Levy, Bernard-Henri, 132, 135
Lewis, bernard, 121, 135
Loti, Pierre, 34
Lounes, Matoub, 138

al-Maghrebi, Abu Hassan, 84
Mahmud II, Sultan, 162n38
Major, John, 115
Marzouki, Moncef, 127
Massu, Jacques (General), 50, 53, 54
Meddeb, Abdelwahab, 176
Mellah, Salima, 175
Ménoret, Pascal, 7, 68, 83, 139, 165n21
Mermier, Franck, 98
Messaoudi, Khalida, 133, 134

Michot, Yahya, 171n5
Mitterrand, François, 44
Morin, Edgar, 139
Mossadegh, Mohammad Hedeyat, 43
Mubarak, Hosni, 21, 80, 81, 104, 118
Muhammad, 69
al-Munajjed, Mona, 161n30
Muqbil Ibn Hadi al-Wadi'i, 22–27, 83, 84

al-Nabhani, Taqi al-Din, 77
Naguib, Muhammad, 80
Nahnah, Mahfoud, 168n5
Naïr, Sami, 139
Nasrallah, Hassan, 77
Nasser, Gamal 'Abd al-Nasser, 10, 24, 26,
    32, 38, 67, 69, 75, 80, 101, 105, 107, 108
Netanyahu, Benjamin, 45, 46
Nezzar, Khaled (General), 175n13

Ouertani, Manoubia, 49

Pahlavi, Mohammad Reza, 51
Pape, Robert A., 99, 171
Philippon, Alix, 170n24
Pinochet, Augusto, 161n24
Pipes, Daniel, 157n4, 176n19
Piscatori, James, 157n4
Putin, Vladimir, 2, 45, 46, 144

Qaddafi, Muammar, 147, 164n16
Qadri, Ajmal, 85
Qahtan, Mohamed, 65, 160n20, 167n16
al-Qaradawi, Yusuf, 168n9
Qutb, Sayyid, 2, 3, 7, 10, 32, 38, 83, 89, 95,
    97, 98, 101–110, 114, 118, 119, 120, 167,
    171–172n8, 172n15

Ramadan, Tariq, 1, 2, 159, 83, 92, 169n16,
    171n6, 178n2
Randal, Jonathan, 173n21
Reagan, Ronald, 94
Rice, Condoleezza, 157n1

Ridha, Ahmed, 34
Ridha, Rashid, 33
Rodinson, Maxime, 157n4

Sadat, Anwar, 69, 80, 110
al-Sadda, Hoda, 162n33
Said, Edward, 132, 157n4
Saleh, Ali Abdallah, 22, 26, 27, 71,
    164n16, 166–167n12
al-Sallal, 'Abd Allah, 75
Sallal, 'Abd Allah, 69
Sallenave, Danièle, 139
Saud (King), 70
al-Saud, 'Abd al-'Aziz ibn 'Abd
    al-Rahman, 67
Scheuer, Michael, 1, 112
Schwedler, Jilian, 167
Shaarawi, Hoda, 49, 53
Sharon, Ariel, 1, 18, 42, 147
al-Shawkhani, Muhammad, 34, 35, 36
Sheikh Mohammed, Khalid, 177n2
Sidhoum, Salah-Eddine, 175
Souaïdia, Habib, 175
Souiah, Sid-Ahmed, 163
Steinberg, Guido, 159
Stiftl, Luwig, 167
Stora, Benjamin, 163
Sultan Pasha, Muhammad, 49

Thatcher, Margaret, 94
Todd, Emmanuel, 39
Touchent, Ali, 130
Tozy, Mohamed, 42
Triaud, Jean-Louis, 170n22
Turabi, Hassan, 21, 28

ul-Qadri, Tahir, 85

al-Wartilâni, al-Fudayl, 167n5

Yahya (Imam; Muhammad Hamid
    ed-Din), 34, 67, 74

Yakan, Fathi, 77
Yasin, Ahmed, 27
Yeltsin, Boris, 46
Yunan, Ugharit, 170n4

al-Zarqawi, Abu Mus'ab, 2, 173n21
al-Zawahiri, Ayman, 18, 40, 47, 77, 79,

80, 101, 104, 109, 110, 111, 119, 120, 135,
161n28
al-Zayyat, Montasser, 109
Zidane, Zinedine, 124
Zindani, 'Abd al-Majid, 75, 84
Zubayri, Mahmud, 74, 165n22,
166–167n12